LEGENDS AND SOLES

LEGENDS AND SOLES

THE MEMOIR OF AN AMERICAN ORIGINAL

SONNY VACCARO

WITH ARMEN KETEYIAN

HARPERONE

An Imprint of HarperCollins*Publishers*

HarperCollins books may be purchased for educational, business, or sales promotional use. For information, please email the Special Markets Department at SPsales@harpercollins.com.

FIRST EDITION

Designed by Bonni Leon-Berman
Unless otherwise noted, photographs courtesy Sonny and Pam Vaccaro
Photograph of Peter Moore © 2025 Ina Heumann
Photograph of Rob Strasser © 2025 Roger Thompson
Photograph of Sonny and Rob Ades © 2025 Sam Ades
Photograph of Marino Parascenzo © 2025 Marina Parascenzo-Brush
Photograph of Mark H. McCormack Sport Innovators Lecture © 2025 Steve McKelvey, JD
Air image provided by Amazon Content Services LLC

Library of Congress Cataloging-in-Publication Data has been applied for.

ISBN 978-0-06-342343-5

24 25 26 27 28 LBC 5 4 3 2 1

CONTENTS

To Rob Strasser and Peter Moore, my Dream Team
partners whose belief, vision, and creativity took Nike,
and the rest of us, from an obscure running shoe maker
to the legendary culture-shaping icon it has become.

To Natale and Margaret Vaccaro, my parents,
whose unconditional love and honesty that they
instilled in me continue to guide and lift me.

To EJ and Pauline Monakee, for always believing
in me and welcoming me into their lives with
love—because of them I found . . .

Pam, my wife, a life partner I could have only dreamed
of, who's been by my side through every single step
of this perpetually meandering adventure.

And to those thousands and thousands of amazingly
gifted young athletes whose hopes, dedication, and
aspirations have kept me young forever.

My undying gratitude to Mary Jo Monakee, the book's guardian angel, a gifted writer who for years urged me to get this all down on paper and who relentlessly organized, encouraged, cajoled, edited, and drove the writing forward through every aspect of this project, keeping all of us focused on the vision and the dream, even as she valiantly fought the cancer that took her from us before she could be here to share the joy of this moment. She blessed every life she touched, beginning with Pam and me.

You have enemies? Good. That means you stood
up for something, sometime in your life.
—VICTOR HUGO

I'm kinda amazed I wasn't more amazed.
—KRIS KRISTOFFERSON

PROLOGUE

On a breezy June afternoon in 1994, Paris was alive with its usual early-summer buzz surrounding the French Open. Pam, my wife of ten years, and I were in the City of Light to catch the Open after a short but wonderful side trip to Calabria in southern Italy to bring my eighty-three-year-old father back to his hometown of Falerna. It would be his last opportunity to visit his birthplace and reconnect with the eighty-nine-year-old sister who helped raise him after his mother passed away when he was an infant.

Martina Navratilova, Steffi Graf, Pete Sampras, Stefan Edberg, and Boris Becker were the marquee names in world tennis at the time, Graf back to defend her title from the year before. Steffi was synonymous with greatness in tennis and was Adidas's (my then employer's) top female athlete.

Earlier that day at Roland-Garros we'd watched Arantxa Sánchez Vicario beat Anke Huber 6–3, 6–2 to advance to the quarterfinals. After the match, we headed back to the venerable Hôtel de Crillon, built in 1758, a half block off the Place de la Concorde.

Around 6:15 that night we summoned the elevator to the fifth floor on our way to join ESPN broadcaster Dick Vitale and his wife, Lorraine, for dinner at a chic little brasserie a block or so from the hotel. We were headed down to the lobby when the elevator bell dinged to announce a stop.

The doors parted and an apparition appeared before our very eyes.

Phil Knight. My ex-boss, sporting the usual Nike cap, no shades, longish blond curls hanging over the collar of his Swoosh-embroidered Nike shirt.

Without acknowledgment, Knight stepped into the cramped lift.

When his eyes met mine, I simply said, "Good evening, Mr. Knight."

I greeted him as if he wasn't the *force factor* behind my sudden, shocking firing three years earlier. As if he hadn't influenced the FBI and a Portland grand jury to investigate me for alleged "corporate espionage." As if it hadn't been barely seven months since he failed to attend marketing genius Rob Strasser's funeral in November. Standing beside me, Pam's eyes widened as she sensed the palpable tension that had altered the air in our confined space.

A person I had worked for, for fourteen of the most innovative, groundbreaking, productive years either of us has ever had, couldn't muster even a grudging "Hello" or "Good evening" in reply.

Instead, Knight, as if we weren't even there, turned and faced the front of the car. No gesture, no nod, not a hint of goodwill. I knew he was known to hold grudges; it's just somehow more affecting when you confront that sobering vibe eighteen inches from your face.

Message received, sir, loud and clear.

The rest of that silent descent was so awkward, weird, and unseemly that even thirty years later I can't actually find the words to frame the moment. Stunned? Astonished? Both? Ninety surreal seconds that I can still *feel* now.

"What was that?" was the thrust of our conversation as Pam and I walked the Rue Royale toward the brasserie and dinner with the Vitales.

Later, back at the hotel, I remember feeling unsettled, unable to fall asleep for a couple of hours. I could feel my heart pounding in my chest from time to time, a sort of nervous intensity coursing through my mind—undoubtedly a reaction to the graceless affront hours earlier in the elevator.

Sometime around 3:00 a.m., I got out of bed.

I didn't realize it at the time, but a medical episode was *in progress*. I was fifty-four years old and had no idea what was going on, but I was experiencing something that to this day I've never talked about publicly and have no recollection of. I'll leave it to Pam to recount what she witnessed:

In the middle of the night, I opened my eyes and there was Sonny standing at the end of the bed. Even in the low lamplight, there was a vacant, puzzled look in his eyes that told me he did not recognize me. He had gone blank.

I asked him a couple of "Are you okay?" questions, but clearly he was not.

I immediately called the front desk to summon an ambulance. In the frantic twenty minutes that followed, I had to overcome my panic to maintain the illusion of calm and control. The ambulance crew spoke no English and I spoke no French. They began treating Sonny for a suspected heart attack. I was sure it was a stroke, but I couldn't communicate "stroke" to them. After arriving at the first hospital, a doctor wearing a white smock over a bare chest explained, while smoking a cigarette, his recommended testing protocol. Even in shock, I knew I had to get Sonny out of this place. Our friend Owen, who had arrived to help, quickly made a call to the residence of Robert Louis-Dreyfus, the chairman and CEO of Adidas who had invited us to the Open. The Madame, Robert's mother, answered the phone and, after hearing Owen's frantic explanation, advised us to get Sonny to the American Hospital of Paris immediately. Robert made a couple of calls on our behalf, and Sonny arrived at that hospital just before dawn—and remained there for three full days as his memory slowly but steadily edged its way back.

Within a week, my faculties had somehow restored themselves to normal and I felt like my old self. Pam had already arranged for appointments with specialists back home at UCLA before we departed on our twelve-hour flight from France.

The diagnosis: *TGA*, short for *transient global amnesia*.

As I would learn, TGA is a rare, sudden-onset temporary episode of complete memory loss—which, I can assure you, leaves nothing in its wake but empty space.

The only lingering question is whether that brief encounter with Mr. Knight after our bitter falling-out is what set off some chain of events that might have caused my TGA episode. Did the shock of the moment trigger it? Was it a coincidence or *the cause*? I honestly don't know.

What I *do know* with absolute certainty is it's the *only* episode on these pages I cannot recall in full detail and sharp relief.

. . .

IF ONE HAD TO PREDICT the chances of a middle-class kid from a single-stoplight steel town in Western Pennsylvania going on to play what others have generously described as a seminal role in modern sports shoe marketing, record-setting endorsement deals, and a landmark legal decision, the odds would probably be somewhere near . . . zero.

I had always known (or maybe just hoped) my life would revolve around sports, but I had no idea it would morph into the career it became. Then again, as you shall see, the course of my life has been chartered by what I like to call the Theory of *Improbability*, with improbability as my constant and mercurial companion.

Whether destined or otherwise, strange twists of fate routinely put me at the center of events that changed the world of sports in ways that still resonate today. I was the iconoclast *ESPN The Magazine* once described as "the man responsible for the most points, rebounds, assists and highlight plays in NBA history" and *Sports Illustrated* called a "ubiquitous power broker"—achieving a level of recognition and national media renown far beyond anything I could have ever imagined back in Trafford, Pennsylvania, when my greatest ambition was to be a professional baseball player.

To that end, there is no lack of anecdotal information in the zeitgeist referencing my name. A legion of critics and supporters—from *60 Minutes* to campus newspapers—have quoted and referenced me and my influence in every medium imaginable. But despite nearly fifty thousand Google links and thousands more quotes, articles, and accolades, including a hit movie (*Air*) and a documentary (*Sole Man*), there remains so much more none of them could have known.

Until now.

. . .

AT VARIOUS TIMES I'VE BEEN an athlete, teacher, coach, shoe marketer, lecturer, advocate, broadcaster, sports celebrity, gambler, rock promoter, inventor, and the originator of what were regarded as the premier events in summer basketball. One writer's lofty description ordained me "the Godfather of Summer Basketball."

From provocateur to prophet, hero to antihero, my narrative has been framed by others in a patchwork of conflicting themes. I've been lauded and vilified, praised and discredited. Anointed "the destroyer and corruptor" of amateur basketball.

As a young man, I spent one weekend after another in stifling gymnasiums coaching grassroots teams and evaluating players. Grassroots is where the seeds are planted, where you get your first glimpse of the athletes to come, where the stars begin to separate themselves. Spending countless days and nights watching waves of talented young athletes putting their skills and competitive fire to the test was the catalyst that led to the first national high school basketball all-star game, which led to Nike, then Nike to Michael Jordan, then Nike to world dominance. Before it was all over, things occurred that changed the entire trajectory of sports and sports marketing. New star-driven creative strategies—"Just Do It"—intensified the behind-the-scenes battles for generational talents like Jordan, Kobe Bryant, and LeBron James, who would leave their imprint on the game and alter the landscape of sponsorships and endorsements. Being in the middle of a good number of those tumultuous battles offered me several careers worth of high-stakes drama, exhilaration, triumphs . . . and occasionally heartbreaking tragedies I still bear the scars of.

Self-aggrandizing prose, however, was not in any way the purpose of writing this book. Rather, my goal was to simply allow the stories and situations to unfold as they occurred—the characters, the risks, the stakes, the Hall of Fame coaches and athletes, inflection points, and the landmark *O'Bannon* lawsuit—in hopes of capturing the game-changing, life-altering moments in time, direct from the front lines and fierce battles in the Shoe Wars. None of this is revisionist history. None of this is about "settling scores."

I've carefully attempted not to overstate my contributions—nor to understate them, either.

This book is a catharsis and lifelong goal.

It's finally down on paper.

Only this time, there's a difference.

This time, it's told by me. The one person capable of connecting all the dots. And for more than fifty years I've been collecting the facts and documents to back up every last word.

That said, this endeavor would be hollow, indeed, if I had failed to acknowledge the thousands of hopeful, tireless, courageous athletes who had the innate talent and grit to believe in themselves and their God-given potential. The most profoundly affecting influence in my life was watching them put themselves on the line in front of their peers and the critical eyes of the biggest coaches in the game in their quest to reach for the golden ring of true greatness.

It was they who had to take advantage of the opportunity, they who had to live up to the performance expectations in that highly judgmental, potentially life-altering spotlight.

My journey from the beginning has been a collaboration in one way or another. Not just with the giant shoe companies of the world, but with those young athletes. They have been the *constant* throughout the narrative of my working life.

In truth, my story has always been *their* story, a parallel universe of sorts.

Through all the glorious highs, deflating lows, triumphs, and disappointments, I hope you find the journey as captivating, surprising, improbable—and utterly unimaginable—as I have.

1

Backstory: Steel Town Kid

On the clear, crisp Saturday morning of September 23, 1939, a bleary-eyed Natale Vaccaro stood in the middle of First Street in Trafford, Pennsylvania, and raised the barrel of a .32-caliber Colt pistol over his head and fired it three times toward the heavens—*blap! blap! blap!* He was surrounded by family and friends, many recent immigrants like himself, who cheered and clapped before shepherding him safely back inside, lest one of the small town's three police officers showed up to cite him for malicious mischief.

Joyous and tearful, twenty-nine-year-old Natale was celebrating the birth of his first child. He and his wife, Margaret, had had a difficult time conceiving. Though it had taken three years, through the grace of God she was finally able to grant her husband his most treasured wish—a son.

John Paul Vincent Vaccaro.

Sonny.

Me.

My father had left Italy at age nineteen in 1929 to join his father, Giovanni, who'd immigrated to America a decade earlier and was working at a steel mill in Gary, Indiana, south of Chicago. Though Natale spoke little English, his father found piecemeal work for him around the mill—sweeping up, knocking scales off hot ingots with a sledgehammer, unloading railcars, and other odd jobs. But at seventy cents an hour, it was less than a living.

Within a few years, Giovanni began making inquiries to match-makers back in Italy regarding his son. Through a series of handwritten notes that took months to crisscross the Atlantic, he received a formal letter of introduction to Angelo and Josephine Mastroianni, who lived 475 miles southeast in Trafford with their six beautiful daughters. Margaret, who had recently turned twenty-one, was suggested as the most suitable match.

A chaperoned meeting was arranged for the families to introduce Natale and Margaret two weeks later. A nervous Natale, along with his hopeful father, arrived by train to meet the Mastroiannis. Over the course of two days, several meals, and a number of polite encounters, the parents assessed the possibilities. The consensus was that the couple seemed quite compatible, and even infatuated with one another.

The wedding took place in Trafford on June 18, 1936. Seventy-five guests filled the pews at Saint Regis Catholic Church and joined the families for a festive reception in the backyard of the Mastroiannis' home. Wine flowed, with pan after pan of homemade ravioli, lasagna, sausage and peppers, eggplant parmigiana, cannoli, and other traditional fare all vying for space on the tables. The crowd hugged and laughed as envelopes of cash were discreetly passed to the newlyweds while couples danced the tarantella through the night.

After a honeymoon in Niagara Falls, the newlyweds returned to Trafford, packed up Margaret's belongings in two trunks, and headed west to begin a new life in Gary, Indiana.

Now a young married man, Natale began to mingle with some of the other émigrés who gathered daily around the factories in search of work to help their families. Someone knew somebody, and he was soon introduced to a lucrative branch of the delivery profession: bootlegged bourbon and gin.

At first Natale began by loading up trucks at night. Later, he rode shotgun on runs. After learning to drive a stick shift, he started making deliveries on his own through the silent, dark highways and dusty back roads of Illinois and Indiana. On one of those night runs, the cops pulled my father over and hauled him off to jail. When they interrogated him, he had nothing to say, because at the time, he really didn't know who he worked for.

Frustrated by both his broken English and his repetition of *"No lo so"* ("I don't know"), the cops finally relented, realizing they'd get nothing from him. Besides, they weren't after the drivers; they wanted the bosses.

Early the next morning, a local judge slapped Natale with a fine and he was released. Margaret was distraught, and Giovanni was getting concerned that his son might be risking deportation if he got in too deep with local elements on the wrong side of the law. The notion was raised, to the delight of his homesick wife, that they move back to Trafford.

The following day, a gentleman in a finely tailored suit and expensive polished shoes showed up at their—let's charitably say—"modest" apartment in Gary. He expressed his appreciation that Natale had shown discretion, praised him as a "stand-up guy," and handed over a basket of food. The gentleman then shook Natale's hand and disappeared as quickly as he had arrived. Tucked inside the basket was an envelope with $150 in cash.

That money financed their move back home to Pennsylvania. Arrangements were made for my parents to reside in a small apartment, where another family member had previously lived and where yours truly was ultimately conceived. My mother was ecstatic to return to her family and friends, and relieved to put my father's foray into the "delivery" business behind them. By all accounts, it appears he may have worked for the guys who took over Al Capone's territory after the infamous mob boss went to prison in 1931. But who could say for sure?

And so ended Natale's entanglements with the wrong side of the law. Well, except for gambling, which he indulged in with great skill and even greater pleasure throughout his life.

. . .

TRAFFORD, PENNSYLVANIA, IN THE FORTIES and fifties was the kind of town you might see depicted in a Norman Rockwell painting or portrayed in a Frank Capra film starring Jimmy Stewart. The buildings lining its streets had the feel of a movie set come to life. Here was the post office, down the block was the hotel. A water tower, the train station, the school, the mills farther down the road, mom-and-pop stores, an enormous factory, a gas station at the main intersection, and a church—several churches, in fact. Up the hill, there was a sprawling park with a bright-green, neatly trimmed lawn, swings and seesaws in constant motion. Mothers and grandmothers leaned out windows calling their children and grandchildren to dinner; men laughed loudly in the streets, some still in filthy coveralls from the toil of a long shift at the mill. Trafford: the quintessential Currier and Ives image of small-town America.

My world unfolded predominantly in a three-square-mile area. There were eight streets going in one direction and six avenues intersecting them. Cavitt Avenue and Brinton Avenue were the two main arteries. A few blocks away sat the old railroad bridge, next to which were the 120 steep concrete steps leading down to the huge Westinghouse Foundry, which employed hundreds of our neighbors, including a fair number of my relatives.

Two hills dominated the landscape, with beautiful tree-lined streets running up to the top and down the other side of the largest. Falling leaves or spring blossoms defined the change of seasons. In winter, Trafford symbolized a picture postcard sprung to life. When snow fell, we'd slog up Short Street and fly downhill over ice and snow on a sled, cardboard box, or garbage can lid.

An ethnically diverse town, Trafford was populated by Italians, Poles, Czechs, Serbs, African Americans, and the Irish, a melting pot of nationalities and ethnicities who flocked to the Alleghenies to pour their energy into the grinding daily routine, drawn to solid and secure factory jobs, anxious to build their futures on the promise of the American Dream.

The workforce, hardy and full of resolve, were the living, breathing round-the-clock engines of America's transition into an industrial power. My father and uncles were pistons in that engine. With World War II raging on two fronts, our steel mills, coal mines, and the Westinghouse Foundry were in full swing to support the war effort. The railroad ran throughout the day, transporting workers and raw materials back and forth from Pittsburgh, seventeen miles away.

In my earliest years, six of my uncles were away at war. Foremost in everyone's mind was my uncle Jimmy Mastroianni, who had been captured around 1944 and was a prisoner of war. The family kept him in their thoughts and prayers, hoping we hadn't seen him for the last time, and thank God, at the end of the war he returned home to the great relief, hugs, and endless tears of his mother and nine siblings. "*Grazie a Dio*" they repeated over and over again. "Thank God."

My father's entire working life was spent at the Duquesne and Homestead mills on the Monongahela River near McKeesport, twenty miles south of Trafford. He sat at the controls of one of the rotating monster cranes that, day after day, twenty-four hours a day, pivoted side to side, swinging huge cauldrons of red-orange molten steel into position to pour it into forming molds, one ton at a time. His job was considered so critical to the war effort that it earned him a deferment from the military. At various times during his forty-three years in the mills, my father worked one of three shifts: 7:00 a.m. to 3:00 p.m., 3:00 p.m. to 11:00 p.m., or 11:00 p.m. to 7:00 a.m. The ten-second howl of a huge steam whistle that could be heard all over town rang out three times a day to signal each shift change.

Then there was Margaret. Everyone loved my mother, *the* kindest, most giving person I and many others have ever known. Always she fed, fed, fed, and gave, gave, gave—to my friends, to the neighbors, to relatives, and to visitors. She opened her home and her heart to make everyone feel welcome, regardless of who you were or where you came from.

My mother was a housewife until my younger brother Jimmy reached junior high in 1958, which is when she entered the work-force. She started as a saleswoman at the Pink and Blue women's and children's shop on Cavitt Avenue, before moving up to assistant manager. Later, she became a buyer and manager at Gimbels in Pitts-burgh, making her one of the top female employees at the store. She'd ride the bus twenty or so miles each way to Sixth Avenue downtown five days a week. With two incomes, our family built a comfortable, sustainable middle-class life, and I never wanted for anything, except perhaps my own car.

As far as jobs, I was industrious enough to scrape together a buck or two here and there, doing the kind of odd jobs often left to kids. I'd sell evening newspapers after school at the bottom of the steps by the Westinghouse plant. Sometimes I would help my friend Pat DiCesare and his father peddle fresh fruit off the back of their farm truck. In the fall, I'd rake leaves to earn a shiny "Walking Liberty" fifty-cent piece.

In 1947, when I was eight, we moved next door to the DiCesares on Fourth Street. My best friends then were Pat, who was my age, and Joey Schopp, a year older. Pat and I were like brothers, and his older brothers and sisters were like aunts and uncles to me.

I always thought of Joey, with his Steve McQueen swagger and cool James Dean hair, as a real rebel. When we were teenagers, he had a Triumph motorcycle, which we'd tear down the streets on, the muffler torqued up to be heard blocks away. Joey was supremely con-fident and utterly irresistible to girls. Whenever we'd go to the local clubs—the Peppermint Lounge or the Burke Glen Ballroom—Joey always got the prettiest girl and I'd usually end up dancing with one of her friends.

As kids, our main hangout was Weyandt's, a classic forties or fifties *Happy Days* drugstore. The soda fountain was set in chrome with stainless-steel dispensers, highlighted by a line of nickel-a-tune jukeboxes spaced out along the counter, end to end. Booths, upholstered in red vinyl, were in a single row opposite the stools. We crowded the long counter and spun on the stools, drinking cherry or lime Cokes or malts, or splitting fudge sundaes with each other. They sold a chocolate-covered ice-cream bar on a stick called "Lightning Jims" that were a mandatory treat several times a week.

. . .

LONG BEFORE I TOSSED MY first nickel against a curb, gambling was a social ritual for most of the immigrant families—and not limited to just men. Women enjoyed the diversion and camaraderie as much as men did. The fact that it was illegal deterred no one. Almost everyone gambled. The police couldn't arrest and charge virtually an entire town.

Entrepreneurs in those days were more than happy to provide thousands of steel and railroad workers with the requisite diversions. In the center of town, within a three- or four-block radius, there must have been at least ten or twelve bars, beer gardens, pool halls, and poker joints with names like Louie's, Pinocle's, Grande Beer Garden, Mixie's, and Dom & Apie's.

All over Trafford, there were poker games, gin games, and pinochle played in living rooms and ethnic social clubs—Italian, Polish, Serbian—or behind fake walls in the basements of bars and homes. At Sunday picnics in the town park, card games happened every weekend from late spring through summer.

From the time I began shooting marbles with my buddies, trying to win their purple swirlies or cat's-eye shooters, I was drawn to almost any game of chance. I found gambling to be every bit as competitive as sports—exhilarating, mentally challenging, a pipeline to a network of great friends—and, later, a secondary income stream.

My dad would tow me along with him to card games at the homes of relatives or friends, usually within walking distance from our apartment. A little fireball of energy, my aunts would often chide me to "go sit" when I became too obtrusive and my running around interrupted their poker games. They would exile me to the couch to color with crayons or read children's books or watch black-and-white television with my cousins. This was about the time TVs—Philco, Westinghouse, Admiral, RCA, Motorola—started showing up in living rooms across America, replacing the old radio consoles and Victrolas of the day. Watching *Arthur Godfrey*, *Milton Berle*, *Gunsmoke*, and *Bonanza* kept me occupied while the grown-ups ate lasagna, sipped homemade wine, and played poker long into the night under a bright crystal and gold chandelier at the dining room table.

By the time I was twelve or thirteen, my dad began to let me watch the games over his shoulder. Arms folded, leaning on the back of his chair, watching the cards he was dealt, watching the faces around the table. Unbeknownst to me then, those gatherings served as an invaluable informal education that years later proved pivotal in sizing people up in matters far more weighty than a neighborhood poker game.

I remember one evening in my early teens, my mom sent me to the smoke shop to summon my dad away from a poker game to come home for dinner. When I walked in, he was in the middle of a game with some local regulars. One of the players—a man named Buitti— was widely known around town as a cheat. On our way back home, I asked my dad, "Why do you allow Buitti in the game? Everyone knows he cheats." My father's answer remains with me to this day: "It's because *I know he cheats* that I can play with him. He can't fool me." Those words would resonate with me throughout my life. Simply put, if I know who's in the game—their character, their ethos, their integrity—the better I can play the game.

Even though mob guys ran many of the gambling enterprises throughout the state, it wasn't thought of as some nefarious, shameful occupation. Gambling and gaming were as commonplace as going to work or church—an intrinsic part of the social fabric of blue-collar working families all through the East. Most towns had a "numbers guy," who took your quarters or loose-change bets to win based on the last three numbers of the stock market close or the finishing order of the horses at a track in New York. The game itself was called "the numbers," the "daily number," or the "Italian lottery." A runner would take the betting slips to the local bars, which were home base for the game. The odds were long—around a thousand to one—but the payoff was 600 to 1, still a handsome payday for the winner. Every morning, people religiously checked the stock market or sports page to see whether or not they had that winning three- or four-digit combination.

Marbles was perhaps my first habitual dabbling in gambling. At the schoolyard, we'd draw a circle in the dirt with a twig, remove the rocks and pebbles, toss five or ten target marbles in the circle, and begin. You had a favorite "shooter" marble that you'd use to knock the opponent's marbles outside the circle. You'd keep shooting until you failed to knock the other guy's marble outside the perimeter. Then it was the next guy's turn. You kept the marbles you knocked outside the ring. A dead-eye aim, a strong thumb, and a big shooter were the top three prerequisites.

Somewhere along the way, marbles gave way to "pitching pennies" or nickels against curbs or the side of a building—my first recollection of actual money entering the picture. Winning depended on whose coin landed closest to the curb or wall. If you could land your coin on top of the closest coin, then you would win, even if the other guy's coin was technically closer to the curb.

Next to my participation in baseball, football, and basketball, gambling—poker in particular—was one of the great educational pursuits of my life.

. . .

IN A PREVIEW OF THINGS to come, I was a hyperkinetic dynamo of spring-loaded energy, always bouncing from one activity to another. Whether in sports, playing marbles, or running down to the market for my aunts, I just naturally revved at higher RPMs. That excess energy found the perfect outlet in sports—nothing less than the North Star in my childhood.

I'd spend hours tossing a ball against the wall on the side of my nana's house, fielding the rebounds, pretending to turn a double play or throw someone out at the plate. Sometimes I'd make it career off the bricks, sending it over my head so I could turn and make a spectacular catch, à la Willie Mays. On other days, I'd throw footballs up in a high arc and scamper to make the winning touchdown catch in an imaginary Notre Dame game.

Around the neighborhood, we played one game or another anywhere and everywhere we could—in vacant lots, on the street, or sidestepping cow patties in one of the nearby pastures. Stickball, baseball, football, dodgeball, you name it, our group against your group. Seventh Street versus Fifth Street. A victory against one of the other blocks offered a swagger bonus and bragging rights.

Though neither of my parents was athletically inclined, I was somehow born with gifts that most above-average athletes share: quickness, energy, competitiveness, and a feel for the game. I parlayed those skills to excel in both baseball and football.

I was easily among the fastest pure runners in Trafford. One year I ran a one-hundred-yard dash against a kid named Red Mack, who went on to become a great football player at Notre Dame, finishing his short pro career with the Steelers and Eagles. Red was the only kid who ever beat me in a race during my high school days.

My dad was a big fan of my athletic exploits, but more as a spectator than a participant. Uncle Jimmy took on the surrogate role as my sports mentor. He and Uncle Vic were the ones who stoked, encouraged, and supported my interest in sports. When I was a kid, they took me to watch the Pittsburgh Pirates at Forbes Field. I loved those breezy summer afternoons in the stands, eating peanuts and watching my Major League heroes like Roberto Clemente, Dick Groat, Elroy Face, and Bill Mazeroski.

Uncle Jimmy ran a coal delivery business and later became Trafford's police chief. He was a terrific baseball player as well and served as a player-coach for a local team. From the time I was nine or ten, I would tag along when they played sandlot teams from around the area. I'd be the batboy and shag balls at practice. Observing how I loved swinging a bat when I wasn't much taller than the bat itself, Uncle Jimmy began coaching me, taking time to teach me the game. After games and practices, he'd stick around and hit one grounder after another and have me throw strikes across the diamond to first base. He taught me how to hit, turn a double play, round bases, steal bases, and slide.

"Hey, kiddo, bend your knees a little more," he'd say. "Lower your elbow. Keep the bat like this. Be patient, you don't have to swing at every pitch."

By the time I was eleven, he would pitch to me like I was an adult. It was frustrating at first, but once I started making contact, I was hitting as well as kids much older than me. I'd come home from these coaching sessions, my pants and jersey practically caked in dirt. I can't tell you how many times my mom said, "Tell Uncle Jimmy to stop making you slide, you're tracking up the house! Take those off now!"

My childhood dream was to make a living in a sport I loved. I wanted to take my place among the great Italian baseball icons of that era: the DiMaggios (Joe and Dom), Phil Rizzuto, Yogi Berra, Bobby Del Greco, and the Lombardis.

Playing sports was a year-round pursuit. Baseball was my best sport, football a close second. I played shortstop and second base during both the ten-game high school season and the summer prep league schedule. I was a halfback on the midget and high school football teams. At fourteen, in a Midget League football game, I suffered my first serious injury. Rushing in to block a punt, I missed the ball and got kicked in the head, full force. I was knocked out cold. Diagnosis: a serious concussion.

Uncle Jimmy and the doctor kept me on the sidelines the following two seasons. I wasn't allowed to play football until my junior year in high school. Then I was appointed team captain—a role I was honored to accept.

. . .

LIFE WASN'T ALL ATHLETICS, of course, but in my mind schoolwork seemed somehow a meddlesome intrusion. Compared to the fun and competitiveness of sports, high school classes bored and stifled me. I enjoyed the camaraderie of my friends, but the curriculum itself proved a burden. Having to sit quietly, confined to a desk for six periods a day, paled next to the kinetic energy of sports.

The term *ADHD* didn't exist then, but I certainly had some of the symptoms. I bristled at the confines of school and, looking back, was never academically inclined. I took mandatory algebra, geography, and Latin. Anything else was just to get me through school, like woodshop, physical education, and music. I never challenged myself mentally and couldn't conceive of any life-altering consequences that could come from not mastering Latin. The results were predictable. My grades languished at the wrong end of the bell curve and I graduated third from the bottom of my class.

In general, I don't believe teachers are particularly amenable to students like me: a motormouthed extrovert and disruptor who managed to underachieve academically. Whichever gene pairing produces hyperverbosity was operational in me from the moment my language skills emerged. I liked cracking jokes while teachers were trying to teach. This didn't exactly endear me to the staff.

The lone exception was a guidance counselor by the name of Mrs. Alice Giglio ("Gee-lee-oh"), a kindhearted woman who ended up having a profound impact on my life.

Few people are as perfectly matched to their occupations as Mrs. Giglio, whose office was on the second floor of Trafford High. Compassionate and approachable, she had a way of asking questions that helped you understand and deal with whatever the issue of the moment was, including your plans for the future.

Though I don't use the word often, Mrs. Giglio was *fastidious*. She would dress for school with the same deliberation as one might to go out to a nice restaurant or church. Her perfect makeup and bouffant hairdo weren't to show off, but were rather a natural reflection of her assured, quiet elegance. In her dignified way she recognized something in me that I hadn't thought of as exceptional. She made me aware *there was a path to success that wasn't dependent on my athletic ability alone*.

As the captain of the football team (and because of my outsize personality), I was the go-to guy to deliver the "rah-rah" school spirit speeches on Friday afternoons in front of the students, cheerleaders, faculty, and band. I had none of the adolescent self-consciousness or timidity that many kids have when they get before an audience or group. While I've never considered being a politician, I'd have made a helluva campaigner.

In addition to those speeches, there was a long-standing tradition whereby the captain of each school's football team would speak at the opposing school's pep rally. The final week in our football season, the captain of the Pitcairn Railroaders football team up the road came to speak at our pep rally, and I went to speak at our archrival's gym.

I can't remember the topic from six decades ago, but my sense is I probably spoke to the effort both teams would make, our long-standing rivalry, and the indomitable spirit of both student bodies.

Whatever I said, I got my first standing O.

The next afternoon, on a typical crisp Saturday in November, the Trafford Tomahawks ended up in a 6–6 tie with Pitcairn.

Spirits were still high at our weekly post-football dance in the gym that evening. The hundred or so students were still feeling the excitement of our reasonably successful football season. One of the coaches took the microphone to cap the year. He ended his brief speech by talking about how proud he was of the team's efforts. Then, he brought me up on the stage. "Now our team captain will give us *a few words*. That would be a first, wouldn't it?" he joked. "Sonny, come on up."

Before the "last dance" began, I spoke on behalf of the senior athletes who ended their high school football careers that day. It was also the end of my high school football days and, though I choked up once or twice, the climax was rousing, a worthy appreciation of the football team's noble efforts in our last season together.

Which circles us back to Mrs. Giglio.

As one of the chaperones at the festivities, she was positioned stage right. As the dance continued, she called me over. She called me Sonny. Most of the teachers called me John.

Though I always admired her as one of the best people in the Trafford High hierarchy, I might have spoken to her only once or twice a semester. Elvis Presley's "Jailhouse Rock" was playing through speakers, and kids were dancing when Mrs. Giglio leaned down to speak.

"That was quite a moving speech, young man," she began. "I have to tell you that I've heard you speak a few times this year and your ability is really quite remarkable. You have a gift. You should really think about going to college."

Given my academic deficiencies, that stopped me in my tracks.

"No one in my family has ever been to college . . ."

"That doesn't mean you can't be the first. I want you to consider it. Seriously. I'll write a letter to whichever school you're interested in."

For the first time in my young life, Sonny Vaccaro was at a loss for words. This wasn't a coach telling me "good job" after a thirty-yard first-down run. This was someone who thought I could succeed in college on factors other than my athletic ability.

Speaking over the blaring music, I said to Mrs. Giglio, "First, thank you for the compliment, but I don't know if college is a good fit. I don't think my study habits are going to improve much by next year . . . and I've got a chance at a Minor League contract with the Pirates to play baseball."

(In both 1956 and '57 I had caught the attention of a Pittsburgh Pirates scout named Lenny Levy, who invited me to the Pirates' try-outs. At one of these I worked out under the watchful eye of manager Danny Murtaugh and Hall of Fame third baseman Pie Traynor. Mr. Levy offered me a Minor League contract that was quite generous in those days: $3,000 to play with the Bristol Twins in the Class D Appalachian League over in Virginia.)

"Sonny, that's wonderful! I didn't know. Congratulations!" Mrs. Giglio said. "It's still many months till graduation. You've got time to think about it. You let me know how that works out. If you change your mind, I'll still be here.

"Enjoy the dance," she added, then returned to her chaperoning duties.

I wanted to hug her but managed to suppress the instinct. Mrs. Giglio's compliment—and the confidence she'd shown in me— was one of the most inspiring moments of my young life. She had confirmed, to me at least, that I had potential that might take me places far beyond a diamond, the gridiron—or a steel mill job.

. . .

ON A FREEZING NOVEMBER FRIDAY afternoon in 1956, I remember running down the block over an icy sidewalk to Jack Praisner's newsstand to get the local paper. I'd been singled out in the sports section a couple of times that season, but after a painful back injury sustained in the Sewickley Township game—two chipped vertebrae—I gutted out the remaining five games plagued by pain. I wanted to see if the excruciating effort was worth it—whether I'd made the All-WPIAL (Western Pennsylvania Interscholastic Athletic League) team.

Paper in hand, I ran back home, then quickly turned to the inside spread of the sports pages and ran my finger down a column of tiny print under a small headline, "WPIAL All-Stars Announced." My mom could hear my joyous "Whoopee!" all the way in the kitchen. There it was, emblazoned in a list for all eternity (along with the other WPIAL All-Stars): John Vaccaro—halfback—Trafford HS. That single line of six-point type was the proudest moment of my life to that point. Despite us not making the playoffs, the colleges had still noticed me.

That mention in the paper secured me a scholarship offer from head coach Blanton Collier at the University of Kentucky, a few hundred miles southwest of Trafford in Lexington. Collier was famous for leading a program that had risen to prominence in the early fifties on the arm of Babe Parilli, an Italian quarterback from Pennsylvania who was one of my idols. Collier later went on to coach the Cleveland Browns. That Parilli connection made Kentucky my first choice, and I passed on the other scholarship offers from West Virginia University and Youngstown University.

Having offers to play Minor League baseball or accept a football scholarship put me in an enviable position as a senior with his whole life in front of him. But it also placed the weight of a life-altering decision on my shoulders: I could either be the first in the Vaccaro-Mastroianni universe to go to college or take the lucrative signing bonus and play Minor League baseball.

I agonized for over a month with my dad and Uncle Jimmy, as well as my friends Pat and Joey. In the end, the University of Kentucky won the day. I was headed to a four-year college on a full scholarship.

Or so I thought.

2

Ticket Out of Trafford

One of the traits that would later define me emerged between my freshman and sophomore years at college. Nothing roiled me more than hypocritical phonies, false prophets, and entrenched power structures that lacked accountability and often displayed a certain disdain for opposing viewpoints, fairness, and equality. That's not quite how I would have put it back then, but those sentiments are the triggers that have always incited me to *say something*.

Even as a kid, I could never seem to turn the other cheek. By temperament and conviction, I came to abhor injustice and abuse under the color of authority. My contempt for gross miscarriages of justice may simply be a natural facet of my personality, but it was certainly reinforced by an incident that occurred when I was between semesters in college and working a summer job with the city of Trafford running summer events and overseeing sports activities at the town park and central playground adjoining Trafford High.

The town was preparing to hold its annual picnic, and I needed some benches and chairs for seating. Knowing that Saint Regis had a large inventory, I went there with a kid named Bobby, who happened to be "not of the faith," to see whether we'd be able to borrow a few for the day. Father Gillen flatly denied my request. Taken aback at both the "No" and the tone, I asked why, probably with a miffed look on my face. Nodding toward my Protestant sidekick, he said, "Your friend here doesn't go to our church. The benches are for our Catholic parishioners, John. We can't make them available to everyone."

"But I thought the church was here to help people. Isn't helping people what the church is all about?"

"Yes, John, it is. We do that every day," he responded with an edge of annoyance in his voice.

"Well, these benches are for the whole town," I pleaded. "I only need them for the day. We'll clean 'em up and bring 'em back after the picnic."

"I'm sorry, John."

At that point the venerable priest and I got into a rather—how should I put it?—*spirited* back-and-forth, and I told him that his decision was, if nothing else, uncharitable.

"That's just wrong" burst out of my mouth. "Let's get outta here, Bobby."

By the time I got home that night, word of our confrontation had spread across town. My entire family was devoutly religious, and they revered Father Gillen. Even so, my dad wanted to hear my side of the story. I explained exactly what happened and how I felt about it. Wasn't the church supposed to help folks? I wasn't being mean or an idiot, but I had talked back to the priest. My defiance grew from a sense of injustice, which always seemed to trigger a surge of rebellion in me.

"You believe he's wrong, son?"

"He *is* wrong, Dad."

"I believe you."

This wouldn't be the last time I witnessed supposedly respected authority figures behaving in a manner contrary to their *principles, mission, and vows*. And it helped immensely to get my father's validation.

That said, I never did get the church benches or seats. And Father Gillen never changed his mind.

. . .

MY COLLEGIATE FOOTBALL CAREER BEGAN in 1957—not as I had anticipated at the University of Kentucky, but rather at Reedley

College, a two-year community college twenty-five miles southeast of
Fresno in California's heat-soaked San Joaquin Valley. In the middle
of "America's breadbasket," surrounded by miles and miles of peach
and lemon orchards, lettuce fields, and broccoli farms, my school col-
ors became orange and black, my jersey number 27. I was the starting
halfback for the Reedley Tigers.

Coach Collier had "farmed me out"—literally—to Reedley because
of my sketchy transcripts; I needed to make better grades in junior
college to be eligible to play at UK. Together with Jimmy Culliver and
Joey Drakulic, two other Trafford High football players, I boarded an
airplane for the first time in my life and flew to San Francisco, then
hopped on a Greyhound bus headed south on Highway 99 to Fresno.

At the Greyhound station we were picked up by an assistant coach
and taken to a small apartment in Reedley. It was the first time I
had the realization I was a minority athlete. The Reedley Tigers football roster was made up of mostly Hispanic and Japanese players. The
quarterback was Danny Villanueva, a talented Mexican American
who went on to become a kicker with the Dallas Cowboys and Los
Angeles Rams.

Our team was excellent, led by Villanueva and Larry Iwasaki, a
running back and our best player.

That season, I won Player of the Week recognition one time, then
in the eighth or ninth game, I reinjured my back. My last carry as a
junior college football player took place in Reedley's end-of-season
bowl game in 1958.

This time, there would be no comeback. Reedley head coach Jack
Morris called from the West Coast to inform Coach Collier back in
Lexington that I was beyond repair. In response, Kentucky rescinded
my scholarship.

I was 2,500 miles from home, hobbled by injury, and out of a scholarship. Damaged goods. A nineteen-year-old facing a very uncertain
future.

In desperation, I reached out to a guardian angel. I asked Mrs. Giglio if she would mind if we revisited her promise to provide that letter of recommendation—a last-ditch effort to reactivate a football scholarship I'd previously been offered at Youngstown University (soon to be Youngstown State University) in nearby Ohio. She said she'd be delighted to.

I'll never forget the way her letter began: "John 'Sonny' Vaccaro lives on a tree-lined street in a small Western Pennsylvania town called Trafford, where most of the people work either at Westinghouse, in the coal mines, or the steel mills. Sonny has the ability to reach people and communicate to them as well as any student I've ever had in Trafford High School."

And with that recommendation, the next chapter in my life began.

"Yeah, John Vaccaro, I remember you," longtime head coach Dike Beede told me. "I'll put in the paperwork. I can always use a quick halfback."

That golden opportunity soon disappeared. At football practice one humid August morning I pushed my ailing back one play too far. I was barely a shadow of the player I'd been a year and a half earlier. My quickness was gone, my speed a distant memory. I never played a down of varsity football. Again, in the midst of another setback, an improbable break came my way—a lifeline.

Dom Rosselli, an assistant football coach at Youngstown who also served as the head basketball and baseball coach, was somehow amused by my personality and enthusiasm. *There's something about you that's contagious,*" I remember him saying.

"You think you can help me get some players, Vaccaro?"

He always called me Vaccaro.

"Football, baseball, or basketball?" I asked.

"Basketball, from your area in Pennsylvania, Pittsburgh."

"Hell, yes, Coach."

That's when Coach Rosselli offered to keep me on scholarship. In *basketball recruiting.* Holding on to that scholarship felt like my life had been saved. I knew I'd be able to finish college.

So with that miraculous stroke of luck, I went from the ranks of the recruited to helping sign recruits—as a traveling recruiting assistant for Western Pennsylvania and parts of Ohio. Getting players for Coach Rosselli was my introduction to the world of young basketball talent and their parents. Beginning in '59, during spring break and all summer long, when the high school season had ended, I'd assemble a team—something of a local all-star team of skinny, athletic young kids in their Converse or Pro-Keds, most meeting for the first time. With tall kids who barely fit in the back seat and an assistant coach tagging along, we'd drive to tournaments in towns like Steubenville and Youngstown in Ohio, or Braddock, Sharon, and Oakland in Pennsylvania. To help defray travel costs, I picked up some sponsorship money from Mr. Minto, the local milkman, and formed the Trafford Mintos in his honor. These tournaments were played in sweltering gyms: a local high school or Salvation Army or Jewish center outposts. No air-conditioning, unbearable humidity, but those creaky bleachers were still jam-packed with fans.

Every summer, talented teams would roll in from New York, Chicago, DC, or Philly, allowing me to get to know quite a few coaches from those cities—and players like Bob Lanier and Connie Hawkins, who went on to become NBA superstars.

The high point of my Mintos summer tournament days: One of my teams won the Hoyle Tournament in Sharon. It was such a joy to see those kids celebrate—how much it meant to them to prove to themselves that, at least for that weekend, they were the undisputed best. That was the essence of the kids' experiences I later witnessed at hundreds of other tournaments—the chance and desire to show your peers just how good you were.

As I expanded my world of recruiting throughout Ohio, Kentucky, Pennsylvania, and West Virginia, another revelation struck me. Right from the start I seemed to have the ability to connect and communicate with young athletes, and coach them with a good bit of success. In the process, I'd do my damnedest to get them to put Youngstown on their college short list and make an on-campus visit where I could introduce them and their parents to Coach Dom. I was all of twenty years old.

I took recruiting damn seriously. I'd travel to the high school games in Pittsburgh and McKeesport and Turtle Creek. I'd scour the Pittsburgh papers, learning who the budding stars were at the high schools. I knew the top local coaches. I'd go visit kids' homes and convince six to eight a season to play for my tournament teams. Before long I came to realize I had a gift for finding and attracting players. I related very well to the kids and could speak to their parents with assurance and authority, though I was barely older than their sons.

For Coach Rosselli, I managed to come through with some terrific players like Jim Himmelwright, Fred "Red" Jones, and David Culliver, who became one of the top scorers in Youngstown history, and others who made Youngstown one of the perennial national powers in its division. Jones and Culliver went on to be inducted into the Youngstown State Athletics Hall of Fame.

. . .

MY IMMERSION IN THE GAMBLING arts continued throughout college, almost exclusively on the top floor of the Dana School of Music at Youngstown. We called this makeshift version of an athletic dorm the Cave.

A repurposed version of old music school classrooms, the Cave was an elongated thirty-by-sixty-foot space divided into four areas, three of which had bunk beds arranged in fours. Another larger space in the "Jock Dorm" was one large room with five bunk beds on each wall. I rate the accommodations roughly on par with your basic

Army barracks: drab and utilitarian, the pervasive smell of sweats hanging off bedposts a near constant. There was one staircase going up to the Cave from the lower floor. Outside, there was a rusted fire escape we used when the weather turned warm. Down a flight of stairs were toilets and washbasins where we'd get ready for classes each weekday. Most of us showered over at the gym. You learned to sleep through the constant thunder of footsteps going up and down those stairs. I slept on a top bunk.

There was a recreation area with a Ping-Pong table in the middle. At the far end, there was a community closet resembling a coatroom, where we hung up our jackets, scarves, caps, and assorted sweats, tees, and workout gear. Most of us propped a trunk or large suitcase from home at the foot of our bed to keep our clothes in. I carried my suitcase back and forth to Trafford on the weekends for my mom to wash and repack my clothes for the coming week.

At any given time perhaps fifteen to twenty of us called the Cave home—a far cry from the upscale athletic dorms of today—and I don't recall thinking the place was subpar because in 1958 no one expected anything more. Besides, it was free, like our tuition and books. After practice or studying elsewhere, the sound of cards shuffling went deep into the night—mainly hearts or poker.

Everyone went home on the weekends—except during the season. The Cave wasn't a place where anyone did extended stays—90 percent of the kids were locals from nearby Canfield, Boardman, Poland, or Struthers. I was probably one of the few players from any distance; Trafford was eighty miles away.

Along with the sound of cards shuffling and the crack of Ping-Pong balls on wood, the music students provided a constant, irregular soundtrack. Saxophones or drums, violins or an opera student voicing scales: Everyone was either practicing for recitals or preparing for the next football game.

As the players drifted in after practice at the end of the school day, they'd wait to get in on a game of poker or hearts. At folding card tables surrounded by dinged-up metal chairs, the games ran around the clock, with a break occurring from morning until early afternoon. The stakes were a nickel or dime a hand, never more than a quarter. Sometimes two tables ran at once. Since I wasn't on a team, my only responsibility (besides class) was being an assistant and "gofer" for Coach Rosselli at practice during basketball season. With light responsibilities, I was up for a card game 24–7. Cards were my main extracurricular source of amusement and income. (If I'd devoted the time I spent playing cards to studying, I'd likely have earned a PhD.)

For three years, along with Tommy Richards, Butch Morelli, Frank Ganare (a graduate assistant coach in basketball), Jim Rich, Larry Gelsig, my buddy Mike, and a rotating cast of my compatriots, we shuffled and dealt our way through college.

Tommy Richards had more than athletic skills, however: I'd rate him a semiprofessional gambler whose card playing ability far exceeded my own. Just as musicians recognize how their playing is insufficient when compared to a piano virtuoso or Jimi Hendrix or Pink Floyd's David Gilmour on guitar, Tommy was at another level.

Mike was the other semipro in the dorm. He had some of us betting on pro football games. From Canton, Ohio, Mike was the guy who carried the weekly "spot sheets," with the betting lines and matchups we'd bet on during the NFL season. We'd place our bets on Thursday, Friday, or Saturday, and Mike would lay off our wagers with the bookies in Cleveland.

Every Sunday, in the early sixties and seventies, a Philadelphia radio station, KYW, updated the sports scores once every half hour. Late during one football season, Mike simply disappeared on a Monday, never to return to Youngstown. It seems he'd taken the action himself on a big West Coast Packers–Rams game that didn't beat the spread. That Monday everyone who won was asking, "Where's

Mike?" Mike skipped out on his debts—and the rest of college. (I ran into Mike a few years later in Las Vegas, where he worked. We shared a rueful laugh at his absconding with our winnings years earlier, and our friendship picked up right where we'd left off.)

In the spring of 1962, at the tender age of twenty-two, I graduated from Youngstown with a bachelor of science and education degree (aka, physical education) and, honestly, a co-major in gambling. The first-ever Vaccaro-Mastroianni degree in hand, I turned my attention to getting a real job.

That's when another door in the basketball world suddenly opened.

3

The Roundball Classic:
My Professional Birthplace

Following my graduation from Youngstown State in May of 1962, I got a call from one of America's premier collegiate coaches: the great Ralph Miller at Wichita State, four states west in Kansas. He'd heard about me from one of his players, Tony Morocco, who was a family friend from Trafford. One of Miller's assistant coaches, Lanny Van Eman, from nearby McKeesport, had been a terrific two-sport athlete at Wichita. We weren't friends, but Lanny told Coach Miller about my involvement in the high school tournament scene, the precursor to the AAU summer league circuit that developed a few years later.

That year, Wichita State had finished 18–8, which was for them a rather mediocre season. The Shockers had long proved they could play with almost anybody and had just signed a future All-American and NBA star in Dave Stallworth. But WSU wanted to expand its recruiting footprint. That's where my name came up.

By this time Coach Miller was already a legend—he ended up with the most wins in Wichita State history and was later inducted into the National Collegiate Basketball Hall of Fame. I was honored when he offered me a scholarship as a graduate assistant in charge of the intramural sports program and a spot on his roster as an unofficial assistant coach. As if that wasn't enough, he and his wonderful wife, Jean, a warm, openhearted mother figure for university athletes, offered to let me stay in the guest bungalow over their garage and got me enrolled in a postgraduate program at Wichita. Thus, the kid who'd barely had the grades to graduate high school was now on his way to a master's degree in educational psychology.

At Wichita in the fall of 1962 I went to practices and sat behind the bench during games and watched Coach Miller as he made key adjustments and substitutions, switched assignments, and sent in plays, seeing a beautiful game in an entirely new light. In my then twenty-three years I'd never attended a big-time college basketball game, and here I was sitting with a behind-the-bench vantage point, watching Ralph Miller's every move as frenzied fans cheered on their fifth-ranked Shockers. Who wouldn't want to spend a life around this kind of excitement?

And as fate would have it, I flew home for Easter break in 1963, anticipating the joyful festivities surrounding a big family gathering and the requisite church appearance. Holiday or not, I still had Wichita State recruiting duties to attend to. One particular prospect in my sights was a promising 6′5″ forward from Turtle Creek, a small town up the road from Trafford. That gray late April morning, I jumped in my dad's car for the short five-mile drive to see Walt Ayers play in person, five miles that foreshadowed the creation of the Dapper Dan Roundball Classic not long afterward.

Heading north on Mosside Boulevard toward Turtle Creek, I drove over a glassy patch of late-spring ice on a downhill curve and lost control of the car. In an instant, I swerved, careened into another driver, and ended up backward in a snowy roadside ditch. The guy I hit was Ronny Crookston, a former classmate who'd graduated a year ahead of me in high school. There were no airbags in those days. My knees smashed into the lower dashboard, breaking my right leg. I could feel a gash above my knee soaking my jeans with blood, and I was barely able to breathe from the pain of being crushed against the steering wheel. I sat there in shock, a single thought echoing in my head: *My dad's gonna kill me for wrecking his car.*

Thank God, Ronny was only shaken up but not injured. He slid down the embankment to my wrecked Ford to check on my condition, then yelled for a woman watching from a nearby house to call an ambulance.

After a two-week stay in Braddock General Hospital, I was released, still adjusting to crutches and the cumbersome ankle-to-hip cast on my right leg. For the next three months I found myself going stir-crazy in my old room, hobbling around on crutches, growing more anxious by the day and impatient with my forced confinement. You can only read so much on a given day.

I phoned Coach Miller and told him about the sudden turn of events and informed him I would not be returning to school. In turn, he informed me that he had accepted the head coaching position at Iowa. He'd been at Wichita for thirteen years. I'd been there for seven months, and now neither of us was going back.

In the weeks it took to get myself walking again, an incandescent flash of inspiration had struck me, a whim really: As soon as the doctor sawed that damn cast off, I promised myself a getaway. Las Vegas came to me. Why not test my mettle in the mecca of gambling? If I could play poker on par with Tommy Richards in Youngstown, who was damn good, why not gauge my skills against the *real-deal* gambling pros in Vegas?

I had often pondered what the next level of poker might be like. The back and leg injuries had effectively—and permanently—ended my athletic aspirations. Perhaps Vegas was a test run for plan B. Did I have the guts and skill set to cut it as a professional gambler?

The whole plan was probably harebrained, but what was the worst that could happen? The loss of a few hundred bucks and maybe a harsh, embarrassing reality check? If nothing else, I'd end up with a scenic, glitzy, sleep-deprived vacation and a passel of priceless stories to regale my friends with back in Trafford. I bounced the idea off Pat DiCesare.

"Pat, what d'ya think about a trip to Vegas?"

"Vegas, like two-thousand-miles-west-in-the-desert Vegas?"

"Yeah, let's go check it out," I said. "Let's gamble against some real gamblers, the big shots. Maybe we could use your dad's car, split the gas, take turns driving. What do you think? We can make it in two or three days. Let's see what Johnnie thinks when he gets here."

When our cohort Johnnie Mikan walked into Louie's Pool Room, we waved him over to our table. "Hey, Johnnie, you up for a trip to Vegas?"

No surprise, he was. After hastily packing our suitcases and duffel bags on a Sunday summer evening, just after dark, in 1963, three amigos, all in our early twenties, said goodbye to girlfriends and parents, loaded up Mr. DiCesare's 1963 light-blue four-door Ford Falcon with no air-conditioning, and took off up Brinton Avenue, headed for the mythical green felt tables 2,200 miles away. To a trio of small-town Pennsylvania kids, Vegas was Nirvana—a pilgrimage of discovery—no limits, no faking it. If you could play there, you could play anywhere. Credibility was calculated by the size of the chip stack in front of you.

I was electrified with excitement and anticipation, undiluted adrenaline flowing. I couldn't sleep. Our first glimpse of America's Great Plains began to emerge as dawn lit up our first day on the road. That long cool night gave way to dense summer humidity for the next leg across Illinois and into Iowa. Windows down at seventy miles an hour, the roar of warm air, and visions of an adventure mere hours away elevated our spirits. The guy riding shotgun was in charge of calibrating the radio dial to find a station—any station out in the middle of nowhere—in search of Big Joe Turner, Bobby Darin, or Ray Charles, staticky or not.

We were making good time traveling past wheat and cornfields, cattle ranches, countless windmills, single-stoplight towns, fruit stands, and country stores. We took turns catnapping on the clammy fake leather back seat. Just past noon on the third day, I could swear I heard a chorus of angels as we came over a desert rise, and forty or fifty miles in the distance, Las Vegas appeared on the horizon, a shimmering mirage in the midday heat. The fatigue of the marathon drive receded as the sight of that gleaming casino wonderland drew ever closer.

This wasn't only fulfilling a fantasy: I knew this trip was the beginning of an entirely new phase of my life. My brain synapses were lighting up like the neon signs up and down the Strip. I was about to make a connection with a city that would define my persona for the next five decades in ways I could not have anticipated.

Walking into the lobby of the Dunes, I thought, *God! We're here!* "Euphoric" is the word I'd use to describe that moment. I'd always regarded myself as more worldly than one might expect of a small-town kid. I'd been to Pittsburgh for Pirates and Steelers games and spent a year in California at a junior college. But Vegas proved light-years different and more dazzling, an eye-popping new dimension in sight and sound and action. I was literally like a kid with a lifetime pass to Disneyland. A pervasive sense that we were, momentarily, free of all the rules and restrictions of the parochial, regimented Midwest lives we'd temporarily escaped. The buffets, seemingly a city block long, piled high with irresistible seafood, rare beef, salads, breads, delicacies, and desserts to induce unreserved gluttony—costing maybe four or five bucks. Gambling and gluttony seemed the perfect match.

We were *all in* before we'd laid down our first bet.

After we'd checked in and dropped our bags in the room, I was too excited to crash. Turning out of the elevator into the din of slot machine bells and cheers and groans from the dice tables, I walked past a double row of blackjack tables, craps tables, then a bank of roulette tables neatly stacked with rows of red and black chips. Over to the left were parallel rows of garishly lit slot machines, wheels constantly clicking to the accompaniment of bells and whistles. I loved *everything* about the place—the *bing-bing-bings*, the *thrurrr* of cards shuffling, the screams of over-amped gamblers erupting around the room, the allure of big-name entertainers displayed on posters in the side lounge and showroom. I was on the same harmonic wavelength of this city. We were mesmerized—hopelessly in thrall to the "let your hair down" Vegas vibe. A universe away from Louie's Pool Room on Cavitt Avenue. The affinity was as strong as anything I'd ever felt outside of my love of sports.

And then *the moment* had finally arrived: my initiation, my first rite of passage into the celebrated Dunes poker room. It had maybe twenty round tables arranged in two long rows. Over the next five days, I'd spend a minimum of eight hours a day in a haze of cigarette smoke, honing my skills in draw and stud poker, sitting down to play against "the big boys"—my first taste of cards against *real casino* gamblers. In the days that followed, I played against a cast of characters, from marks and chumps to brilliant tacticians and high rollers with mad skills. I was transfixed, reveling in a graduate-level gambling academy, part math class, part sociological study, part master class, sizing up people with the same vigilance as the cards in my hands (several hundred hands, in fact).

In between, Pat, Johnnie, and I walked the Strip in sweltering August heat as prototypical wide-eyed tourists, visiting all the showplace casinos—the notorious Flamingo, Sands, Stardust, Frontier, Caesars, and the Thunderbird. Back then, there were no sports books in the casinos themselves. Churchill Downs was the only place that took action on sports and the ponies—an enormously popular betting joint in constant motion updating race and game results populated by a cast of characters straight out of *Casino*. We made our way downtown to see the famous Golden Nugget and Benny Binion's Horseshoe casino, two cascades of flashing neon facing each other across Fremont Street.

By the second day in the Dunes' cardroom I concluded with a fair degree of assurance that the kid from Trafford could hold his own at tables that could teach expensive lessons to amateurs. I considered it a monumental success that my original $500 stake survived the week and I was going home with money in my pocket and expenses paid. My "Las Vegas Baptism" complete, an unshakable realization coalesced in my mind: There was a much bigger world beyond the confines of Western Pennsylvania, and one day, sure as I was sitting there, I was going to be part of it.

· · ·

IN THE MID-SIXTIES MY DREAM of somehow breaking away banged headlong into the cold, hard realities of blue-collar steel town life. I moved back home, bounced between teaching jobs—special ed, health, and phys ed, as well as assistant football, baseball, and basketball coach—the seeds of an idea germinating in my head.

I started thinking more and more about the springs and summers I'd spent in small steamy gyms, coaching my makeshift all-star teams. I'd seen how kids from Pittsburgh and around Western Pennsylvania and Ohio had stacked up against teams from Chicago, Cleveland, Philadelphia, and New York. Our area was nationally famous in football, producing star quarterbacks like Joe Namath, Johnny Lujack, and Babe Parilli. But the fact that the area had equally talented basketball players had gone unnoticed. After four or five summers with my traveling teams, I'd witnessed the drawing power and fan interest surrounding tournaments in Sharon, Farrell, Braddock, and other hotbeds of high school ball. The fans were rabid, the tournaments packed. I'd seen firsthand a phenomenon few would have considered noteworthy. In my mind there was a hidden *fervor* for emerging high school talent. But no one had realized it.

Suddenly, it dawned on me: We should show the world just *how damn good* our Keystone State basketball talent was. We could play with anyone. Why not put on a showcase to prove it?

As expected, Pat DiCesare came by a few days after my latest epiphany. "Pat, I got an idea . . ."

He shot an "Oh, no, not another one" look my way.

"We should do a game," I said. "I've seen the talent all over this area. Let's put our kids up against the best players from the rest of the country. Pennsylvania versus the USA."

Pat was a dreamer too. Within a year he would be working with a very successful music impresario named Tim Tormey, who later became an executive with Dick Clark Productions in New York. Tim and Pat were eventually part of the team that brought the Beatles to the Pittsburgh Civic Arena in the fall of '64. Together they would go on to promote major stadium concerts with acts like the Rolling Stones, Beach Boys, Janis Joplin, and Sly and the Family Stone. Through his event promotion, Pat knew Charlie Strong, the general manager at the Arena.

"You can get good players?" Pat asked.

"I can get the players and line up the coaches," I told him. "Can you figure out a way to finance the game?"

Pat had been to several high school tournaments with me during his time at Youngstown and remembered the talented teams and the jammed local gyms.

I added, "You think we can cover the costs? You got travel, hotels, meals. . . . Pennsylvania versus the USA. I think it's got legs."

Pat thought for a beat, then said, "Okay, let's give it a shot."

I reached out and pulled him into a big back-and-forth hug. "Yes! We can do this!"

. . .

I'VE OFTEN PONDERED WHAT ONE might call *a person whom you met just once in your life*—thirty short minutes at most—who led you to avenues and adventures you never envisioned embarking on.

A momentary mentor? A role model? A gift?

Arthur Morse was all those things—though it's hard to imagine someone making that kind of impression based on a single brief conversation. Yet in our one encounter, Mr. Morse planted a lasting vision in my mind that expanded my understanding of how events with inherent fan appeal could be created—put together, packaged, and promoted—both live and on broadcast television. For a young graduate assistant with no particular plan for the future, my entire perception of possibility was changed by this singular man. He led me to take that first tentative step into the world of producing and promoting high-profile highly entertaining sports events.

I first met Arthur in graduate school at Wichita State in February 1963 in a hospitality suite at Henry Levitt Arena, in a pregame gaggle of school officials, boosters, media people, coaching staff, and others. Coach Miller made the introduction.

"Sonny, this is Arthur Morse," he said. "Arthur, here's the kid I told you about."

Morse was well known in sports circles around town and quite the character. Peering from behind black horn-rimmed glasses, impeccably dressed in a suit and tie, he was short, bald, and constantly twirling an unlit cigar stub between his forefinger, middle finger, and thumb. Morse was widely admired as an influential, successful, and popular event promoter. A Chicago lawyer by trade, he had an eclectic range of professional interests, most notably as a player agent who represented the likes of Dick Butkus and Gale Sayers in professional football and—closer to his heart—the athletic program at Loyola, the Catholic university in the North End of Chicago on the edge of Lake Michigan.

In the early sixties, Arthur held the title of assistant to the director of athletics at Loyola. He was the school's top booster and promoter, who came up with an ingenious plan to build the university's reputation by putting its basketball team on television. Beginning in the early sixties, he staged made-for-TV doubleheader events featuring top-ranked teams at the old eighteen-thousand-seat Chicago Stadium—long before ESPN dominated ranked-powerhouse TV matchups. Morse's games always included Loyola along with the University of Illinois to stoke regional interest. He then added premier teams from other parts of the country—usually plucked from the previous year's Final Four.

By the time I met Arthur, others were already copying his events across America. His beloved Loyola Ramblers had recently won the national championship, beating Cincinnati in an overtime thriller 60–58.

By sheer coincidence, Mr. Morse was in town to catch the Wichita State–Cincinnati game, one of the premier matchups of the season, in February 1963. Cincinnati, riding Oscar Robertson's heroics to Final Four fame, was enjoying a thirty-seven-game winning streak, and Arthur fully intended for the Bearcats to be part of his next doubleheader.

A man of Morse's stature had more important things to do than spend even a minute or two talking to a twentysomething graduate assistant, yet here we were. It seemed to me at the time that Morse and I had at least one thing in common: an unusually elevated energy level. I wasn't just impressed with him; I was spellbound. This was a businessman, a rainmaker who *made things happen*. He was gracious, generous with his time, and had the uncanny ability to make you feel valued, to show interest in your aspirations.

"Very nice meeting you, Sonny," he said. "If you need advice or have any questions, my door is always open."

On that afternoon, in an arena in the middle of Kansas, I thought to myself, "My God, that's who I want to be someday."

That Arthur Morse moment had repercussions far beyond anything a twenty-minute chat might suggest.

Regrettably, I never had a chance to thank him for the pivotal impression our chat made on me that day. He had fortified my resolve, focused my energy, provided a template. My decision to take the

Roundball Classic idea from a notion in my head to an actual real-life event was activated by that moment.

How would Arthur Morse handle it? was a question I asked myself on any number of future ventures later in life, and it has never lost its resonance.

• • •

MY FIRST OFFICIAL PHONE CALL prior to the realization of the Roundball Classic was to Marino Parascenzo in early fall of 1964. Marino covered high school sports for the *Pittsburgh Post-Gazette*. I read the *Post-Gazette* sports pages *every day*, even away at college. Some strange telepathic thunderbolt told me I needed to start with him. I flipped through the Pittsburgh phone book and found Mr. Parascenzo's home number. I called around dinnertime, the phone ringing and ringing before he finally answered.

"Mr. Parascenzo, you don't know me, but . . ."

He sounded a bit miffed, annoyed that some stranger had called him at home, but to my relief, he listened, perhaps thinking I was just another reader calling to complain about something he had written in the paper.

In researching this book, I contacted him decades later. His recollection of our conversation went like this:

Your idea was to hold a high school all-star basketball game, best from Pennsylvania versus best from the US. Funny thing is, my first reaction wasn't whether it was a great idea or a goofy idea. It was, How can this guy possibly pick the best players from all over the country? Then I thought, wow, what a great idea. And finally you said you would hold it at McKeesport High School and asked what I thought of the idea. McKeesport had about a 3,500-seat gym. And I said I liked the idea, except forget McKeesport. You should hold it at the Civic Arena. You said, "How the heck could that happen?" That's when I thought of the Dapper Dan Club. If the game was a Dapper Dan event, the paper would promote it, and the club would get a cut for its charities. And I said, "Come in and talk to Al Abrams."

When I hung up the phone, I thought, *Wow, my pie-in-the-sky idea had just been validated by a professional sportswriter.* Even better, Parascenzo had enlarged the scope of my dream. Hold the game at the Civic Arena instead of a high school gym? Why not? As a bonus, we'd have the enormous reach and publicity power of the *Post-Gazette*'s coverage behind the game. And with Pat's new connection to the people over at the Arena, I dared to think things were coming together rather nicely.

I followed up on the call about a week later, after Marino had had time to bounce the idea off his sports editor. Al Abrams was skeptical to say the least, given his beats were baseball, boxing, and horse racing. He had little or no interest in basketball, much less high school basketball. Still, Abrams was the president of Dapper Dan Charities, one of the most prominent and influential in the city. As such, there was a potential charitable angle to the game, which I believe finally nudged him to meet with us.

Pat and I were both on edge as we rode the elevator up to the fourth floor at the old Press building at 34 Boulevard of the Allies, in Uptown Pittsburgh, a block north of the Monongahela River. We made our way to the sports department and a secretary led us to Mr. Abrams's office, which resembled something out of the movie *The Front Page:* Stacks of books and papers populated the shelves; one of the walls was lined with photos of Abrams with several of Pittsburgh's greatest sports figures—Roberto Clemente, Pie Traynor, Bill Mazeroski, Willie Stargell—all hung neatly in black frames.

Dressed in a vest and bow tie, his hair slicked back, the man who could make or break our dream stood up to shake hands.

"So you got an idea for an all-star game," Abrams said. "Marino told me about it. Lemme hear what you have in mind."

Given that I was the more loquacious half of our partnership, Pat let me take the lead. The pitch poured out in a rush. I laid out the plan to the city's top sports editor, painting pictures of the frenzied crowds at the summer tournaments, talking up and naming the top high school players locally and nationally and my connection to their coaches, who I was ready to recruit for the game.

Abrams raised his hand and stopped me cold.

"Slow down, Mr. Vaccaro," he said. "You're going a mile a minute."

I caught my breath and slowed down but proceeded with no less enthusiasm. He seemed convinced we were on to something here and began laying out his terms: A fair portion of the proceeds would go to Dapper Dan and the charity was to be featured in the game's name and prominently displayed in all of the promotion and branding.

"Of course, of course," I assured him.

"Alright," Abrams said. "We've got a deal. You two start putting the thing together and keep me updated. I need names, dates, details. You good with that?"

"Absolutely." I smiled, practically jumping out of my chair to hug him.

Naturally, being a reporter at heart, Abrams had one last question.

"If nobody shows up, who's going to cover the arena and pay the bills?"

"I will," Pat volunteered.

"And how will you do that?" Abrams asked.

"I'm Pat DiCesare. I work with Tim Tormey and we are part of the team that just brought the Beatles to the arena." That single sentence immediately validated Pat's credentials and tempered any of Abrams's misgivings.

"Alright, good. Now get outta here, boys. I've got a deadline to meet."

We shook hands and Abrams settled back into his swivel chair, turning to tap away on the Underwood typewriter behind him.

Earlier, I had noticed the rat-a-tat-tat of a wire service Teletype machine spitting out a white paper tape as it printed out up-to-the-minute sports news in a little cubbyhole to the side. I stuck my head back in the doorway.

"Excuse me, Mr. Abrams . . ."

"Back already?"

"Would it be okay if I dropped by every once in a while to use the *Gazette*'s phone and get stories on players off the Teletype?"

"Yeah, help yourself, kid . . . but don't make a nuisance of yourself."

"Great, thank you very much, sir. I won't."

In the brief span of a few weeks, the nation's first high school all-star game, the Dapper Dan Roundball Classic, was born. Now all Pat and I had to do was pull it all together.

The following months I was fully consumed with a never-ending list of details. Pat worked on issues with the Civic Arena, handling the deposit and locking in the date: March 26, 1965. With less than six months to showtime, I started compiling player names for the Pennsylvania and US teams. I needed ten players for each team, and I needed stars. Fortunately, the Pittsburgh basketball scene in 1964–65 was graced with a couple of exceptional teams. Midland High, featuring Norm Van Lier, Simmie Hill, and Ron Brown, breezed to a 29–0 state championship–winning season. South Hills Catholic, led by 6′3″ Hank South, who averaged over twenty points a game, won the Catholic state championship, going 28–1. It was a banner year for local teams, and they formed the nucleus of my Pennsylvania roster. Larry Cannon, a 6′5″ guard out of Lincoln High in Philadelphia who later went in the first round of the NBA draft to the Chicago Bulls, was another key player I recruited. Coaching duties were left in the very capable hands of Hank Kuzma of Midland and Jerry Conboy of South Hills, both state champions. Before long I had a Pennsylvania team in place that wasn't just talented but stacked with stars. These kids could play.

For the national team, I dug into Street & Smith's high school basketball publication and pored over newspapers from all over the country. I drove with Lanny Van Eman to watch the Power Memorial team from New York play DeMatha Catholic in a titanic high school basketball battle. I wheedled my way into a meeting with Power Memorial's coach, Jack Donohue, to invite him and the nation's number one player, Lew Alcindor, soon to be known as Kareem Abdul-Jabbar, to the game.

"What's the Roundball Classic?" Donohue inquired.

"The nation's first high school all-star game," I replied. "You've got the best player in the country right now, and we'd like to make him the centerpiece of the game."

"Where did you say it was being played?" Donohue asked.

"Pittsburgh, in March."

He acted like there was no need for Alcindor, headed to John Wooden and UCLA, to play in any all-star game.

"Lemme think about it," he said, noncommittal. Thirty years later, when Kareem came to the Roundball to speak, he told me that Donohue had never even so much as mentioned the Roundball to him.

In the end, we did succeed in getting DeMatha's coach, the legendary Morgan Wootten, to coach the United States team, bringing with him two great players, Bob Whitmore and Bernie Williams. The rest of the United States team I recruited from the phone at the *Post-Gazette*.

To help promote the game we decided to open practices to the public, free of charge, so local fans could glimpse the future of college basketball. We had practices at the Community College of Allegheny County in Pittsburgh's North Shore location on Thursday night and Friday morning.

The main event featured two games: an "undercard" with Western

Pennsylvania All-Stars against the City Catholic All-Stars that tipped off at 7:00 p.m., leading up to the main event at 9:00 p.m. with Pennsylvania versus the United States.

Every year (with the exception of two) I held the Roundball on a Friday night to take advantage of the businesspeople who worked downtown. They could have dinner and then walk over to the Civic Arena for the game. Most of the early arena photos of the Roundball showed the majority of the crowd in suits—ties removed. Businessmen staying in the city after a long day at the office.

Things were falling into place nicely—and surprisingly quickly. But I knew there would never be a second Roundball Classic if I couldn't generate a groundswell of interest all across the East. I worked my way onto any radio show I could find.

I appeared regularly on Myron Cope's radio program at WTAE. He was the voice of the Pittsburgh Steelers and originated the yellow Steeler "Terrible Towels," seen at every game to this day. I used the *Post-Gazette* phone to call college coaches all over the region to invite them to see the best high school players in the country compete. I worked with the advertising department to run ads in the paper. I *out–P. T. Barnum'd* P. T. Barnum for ten or twelve weeks straight.

My spirits soared as I got confirmation from more and more players and coaches. Every media appearance left me exhilarated. Word was getting out.

Pat fronted the money to cover transportation and hotel accommodations at the Hotel Webster Hall on Fifth Avenue, not far from Carnegie Mellon University. I secured the gym for the practices.

I enlisted the help of local family, friends, ex-athletes, and people Pat and I knew from Pittsburgh to spread the word, and had them "circle the date" to be at the Roundball themselves. "Bring the family, bring the kids. It's going to be a great party," I told everyone.

I spoke to the executive committee and important local business executives connected to the Dapper Dan around Pittsburgh.

Finally, after weeks of anxiety, a million details, endless meetings, a thousand phone conversations, tirelessly cajoling commitments, and trips all across the East, on March 22, 1965, the players and coaches arrived by plane, train, car, and bus. We were as ready as we'd ever be. Ticket sales were brisk. *My God, could we pull off a sellout?!*

I'm proud to say four days later, America's first national high school all-star event came off without a hitch. It was as if the moment had been preordained, some part of my destiny fulfilled.

The Civic Arena was filled to capacity. I'll never forget the attendance: 10,336. Sold it out! Dozens of head coaches and assistants from across the country attended the game, many of whom became close friends.

As the Civic Arena finally emptied out that first night, I could barely contain my emotions, tears filling my eyes. I was twenty-five years old. Unquestionably, I would have had a completely different life had it not been for basketball and the exquisitely gifted young people who made the Roundball Classic one of the springtime rituals on every coach's calendar.

Almost overnight, I became a local hero of sorts. Suddenly, the motormouthed kid from tiny Trafford found himself thrust into the media spotlight, basketball's early version of LinkedIn, the conduit to a nationwide network of talent scouts, coaching contacts, and street-level eyes and ears. The "ultimate insider," as one reporter wrote.

Over the course of the next five decades, many of the game's great players made names for themselves at the Roundball—and I'm proud that I went on to form long-lasting relationships with many of them. We sold out virtually every game, generating hundreds of scholarship offers for young athletes at both major and mid-level collegiate programs.

I don't believe it's an overstatement to say the Roundball became the nation's premier prep showcase where legions of fans were treated to sneak previews of Moses Malone, LeBron James, Kevin Garnett,

Kevin Love, Kobe Bryant, Patrick Ewing, Shaun Livingston, Paul Pierce, Greg Oden, Felipe López, Mike Conley, O. J. Mayo, Adrian Dantley, Dominique Wilkins, Jermaine O'Neal, and Shaquille O'Neal. Fans who returned year after year proudly cheered local stars like Kenny Durrett, Brad Davis, Dick DeVenzio, Billy Knight, and Maurice Lucas, who lit up the leagues around Western Pennsylvania.

In 1986, I decided to reformat the game, mixing Pennsylvania players with the national all-stars, and we went to a Western All-Stars versus Eastern All-Stars format. Fan interest only seemed to grow.

As time wore on, the Roundball Classic eventually gave birth to a deluge of copycat successors, from the McDonald's All American Game to Jordan/Nike games and many others. Since we were "the original," my Big Mac adversary had to keep on their toes to recruit against me. Even when the NCAA limited participation to only two all-star events, we took on all-comers, maintaining the quality and stature of the game to the end.

Each year, we presented the players and coaches with a memento of the game: a signature big white equipment bag. It became a coveted status symbol sought after by players across the country. Mark Jula, out of Ambridge High northwest of Pittsburgh, who missed out on being selected in the seventies, was invited to coach the game in 1988. After accepting the invitation on the spot, he paused to ask if he'd get a bag. He did.

After Nike and I parted ways, the Roundball remained in Pittsburgh for just one more year. Then the game traveled to suburban Detroit, where it became known as Magic's Roundball Classic when I invited Earvin "Magic" Johnson to become the face of the event. Our final years played out at the United Center in Chicago, where we set our all-time attendance record of 19,678 in the 2003 game that featured LeBron.

In the end, the Roundball Classic had a stellar—in every sense of the word—forty-three-year run. When I went from Nike to Adidas to

Reebok, the Roundball went with me and remained perennially in the top-two all-star games annually. The run finally ended in 2007, leaving behind more than a lifetime full of fond memories, unforgettable moments, and treasured friendships.

Whatever direction my life might have taken after the Roundball, one fact remains indisputable: There would never have been a connection of any kind to Nike without the Roundball Classic. It established my place in the game and introduced me to a legion of Hall of Fame coaches, future stars, and members of the media elite. In the basketball and sports marketing side of Sonny Vaccaro, it was, without question, my birthplace.

4

The Other Big Ten

Two years after the Dapper Dan Roundball Classic soared to success, the idea for the second Sonny Vaccaro basketball venture began to take shape in my mind: a summer basketball camp.

Back in the spring of '68 I was still teaching special ed and coaching football and basketball at Trafford High, surviving on a schoolteacher's salary. But if I could do it right, a Sonny Vaccaro–branded summer basketball camp might prove to be a reasonably decent source of outside income. I had summers off, so why not?

Admittedly, this idea lacked the originality of the Roundball, but it offered an opportunity to fill some otherwise quiet months. Now that I had acquired a modicum of celebrity, I could capitalize on the credibility I'd gained with players, coaches, and my Pittsburgh fan base. Another basketball-related event seemed a logical expansion.

In sports-crazed Pennsylvania, school-age athletes customarily attended one summer camp or another in football or basketball, usually run by college or high school coaches. So I approached a friend and lawyer from Trafford who I knew through his brother. His name was Jimmy Morocco. Handsome and already successful at age thirty, he seemed the ideal person to share my camp concept with. Jimmy was the son of Tony Morocco Sr., the patriarch of one of Trafford's most prominent families; they owned the state-of-the-art Blue Dell Drive-In Theatre and public pool (on a property four times the size of a football field), and when I was growing up, they had admired my athletic exploits. Jimmy's younger brother, Tony Jr., was a talented basketball player and we were all Trafford High alums.

"Jimmy, I got an idea I want to bounce off you."

"Yeah, Son?"

"It's a basketball camp. I want you to partner with me. We'll do it during the summer, when all the kids are off school. I know coaches all over the state—the kids on their teams attend at least one camp every summer. I know I can get 'em."

"A camp?" He paused. "Do they make any money?"

"Not if we do a one-off, but I'm thinkin' we run a camp a week over the entire summer. I'll be there to run it. I think it'll more than pay for itself."

"Okay. You got a plan?"

"We find a good location. I get the coaches to bring their kids. I can put together a great curriculum, get some coaches to drop by and speak. We can run 'em for eight or ten weeks. A hundred kids per camp, say, ninety-five bucks each. I've worked the numbers; the money wouldn't be bad. We can split the profits 50–50. You put in half, I go half."

Jimmy rubbed his chin in thought.

"You know," he finally said, "I know a ski resort about forty miles from here. My law firm has done some work for them. . . . Seven Springs, up in the mountains near a town called Champion. Nice family named Dupre owns it. They basically shut down over the summer. . . ."

"Yeah, I know Seven Springs," I said. "Let's take a drive up there."

"Okay. Lemme make a call and see if he's interested. I think he'd at least consider the idea."

As it turned out, Mr. Dupre wasn't available. Instead, we met with his son-in-law, a guy named James McClure, who was the operations manager at Seven Springs. And he was interested.

The following weekend, I picked up Jimmy and Tony Jr. and we headed east on the Pennsylvania Turnpike into the Allegheny Mountains. As we climbed into the hills and highlands through stands of spruce, pine, hemlock, and cedar, the air turned cooler—a pleasant escape from the stultifying humidity in the valley down below. Beautiful country that filled me with that sense of anticipation, adventure, and rejuvenation you have on vacation. I knew the kids and coaches would love coming up here.

We talked details on the forty-minute drive. The facilities we'd need, a snack bar, dorm rooms, staffing, what to charge, getting the word out. With Jimmy on board, he would handle those kinds of details; I would promote the camp and invite the staff. Running a local camp seemed child's play compared to the logistics and planning involved with the Roundball.

Pulling up to the main lodge, I got out to survey the surroundings. About five hundred yards up an incline, there appeared to be a large dormitory building. Probably where the employees were housed during ski season. Perfect. Down the hill in the other direction, I saw a couple of acres of flat meadow surrounded by trees. Before we went inside, I'd already decided where the basketball courts could be built.

We stretched our legs and headed toward a pair of rustic pine-slab doors to meet the son-in-law. After a few moments a jovial young man came out of a hallway and greeted us. James McClure looked like a sports enthusiast, probably a great skier. We shook hands and he offered us soft drinks before we began our tour.

"If you're going to have a camp, I think you should see the employee dorm first," McClure suggested.

He led us up the hill a quarter mile or so from the main lodge.

Adjacent to one of the now-barren ski slopes, there was a barracks-style wooden dorm facility. We marched up three steps and across a covered outdoor porch toward the door. He unlocked the double door and began the tour of the ski-season crew housing. It was a sturdy wooden structure, nothing fancy, but serviceable—low ceilings, walls

clad in simulated mahogany paneling, bluish-white fluorescent lighting flickering to life above. In the bunk area, the corridor was divided into communal rooms that probably slept sixteen, with eight
bunk beds per room, a total capacity of around 120. The bathroom
and shower area was at one end, kitchen facilities and a mess hall at
the other. There was a large social room with a covered porch area
outdoors. The accommodations were made to order. I could already
envision it crowded with staff and campers.

"Where are you going to play basketball?" McClure asked. "We
don't have a basketball court."

"We'll build the courts," I said.

"You'll pay for them?" he inquired.

I pointed down the hill to the flat ground I saw when we arrived.

"You provide the land, and we'll pay for construction," I said. "That
spot down there would work."

Before the afternoon was over, the plan for Sonny Vaccaro's Big
Ten Basketball Camp was in motion. The name had a bit of cachet
from the Big Ten Conference but actually referred to the ten-week
camp schedule I had initially planned on. We never ran for more than
five weeks during our four summers there, but what the heck, the
name was catchy.

Jimmy, being a lawyer, worked out all the contract details and
numbers with the owner. We reserved a block of weeks. with a three-
summer commitment. Each camp would be five days, with check-in
Sunday afternoon and campers out the door on Friday by noon.

I borrowed $3,500 from my uncle Jimmy Mastroianni, pulled in
a $1,000 loan from another friend, and kicked in some of my own
money.

Back down the mountain was my hometown full of steelwork-
ers, railroad people, coal miners, and construction workers. Finding
a contractor to build concrete basketball courts was a piece of cake.
Concrete would be cooler in the summer heat than a cheaper asphalt

court. With Jimmy handling the contractors, we ended up building two parallel concrete slabs about thirty-five feet apart that would accommodate the ninety-four-by-fifty-foot courts. Naturally, we had a regulation hoop set up at each end, with fresh nets, lines, and a clean jump circle in the middle.

During court construction, I put the word out to my cadre of coaches. Right from the start, commitments—and deposit checks—began rolling in. I made every coach aware that this was going to be a *Sonny Vaccaro event*; my involvement added assurance it would be done the right way. Coaches jumped on board immediately to sign up their teams—at ninety-five dollars per camper per week. Even after construction expenses, we turned a profit right from the start.

For each camp session, I needed ten coaches, one for each ten-man team. I recruited some of their assistants as camp counselors. You needed energetic guys looking to climb the coaching ladder, teachers who could organize a drill and keep the hundred or so teenage campers on plan.

Sunday afternoons, after check-in and a trip to the dorm, the kids, coaches, and counselors gathered for the orientation, where we introduced the staff, outlined the daily schedule, and fielded questions. Then everyone gathered in the dining area for a meal. The first night, kids would be introduced to one another, and daily schedules and team assignments were finalized and posted on a bulletin board.

Monday mornings began with drills and skills. Monday afternoon, the first games took place. Assistants would keep score and tabulate fouls. In those days there were no outdoor scoreboards.

The routine remained the same all through the week, with occasional variations. Periodically, we had notable coaches from Pennsylvania come up to do clinics or give inspirational talks to the kids. Inside the dorm building, we set up a little concession stand, selling sandwiches, hot dogs, chips, candy bars, soft drinks, and T-shirts.

As anyone who's run a camp can attest, managing a sizable

cluster of active kids requires a high degree of vigilance and time management—especially in a competitive environment. Fortunately, the kids dissipated most of their energy during the drills and game competition all week.

But after a few years I realized I had made a serious miscalculation that ran contrary to my restive nature: Two repetitious months turned out to be an eternity. The routine and responsibility of an ongoing summer commitment became tedious, and I found my original enthusiasm flagging.

What began as a summer side business started to feel less like a lark and more like a job.

By 1970, after a three-year run, a couple of coaches who ran football camps approached me at just the right moment. They wanted to expand their schedule to include basketball camps. I made a deal. We sold our name and contacts to the new group. The Big Ten Camp remained a success into the eighties, long after my involvement was a distant memory.

• • •

TEACHING (NOBLE AS IT MAY BE) had lost its attraction by then, and I was certain I wouldn't be retiring from that profession any more than from the steel mill.

So if something sounded interesting, I was open to new avenues and freelance opportunities. In 1969, I started working with a couple of agents signing players for the NBA rival American Basketball Association (ABA); in the fall of '71 I promoted some rock concerts, one by the rhythm-and-blues musician Edgar Winter, another by the rock group Grand Funk Railroad at the Coliseum in Columbia, South Carolina, thanks to my relationship with Frank McGuire, USC's legendary basketball coach; in '73 I represented sharpshooting guard George Gervin when he signed a three-year $150,000-a-year contract (plus a car of his choice) with the Virginia Squires of the ABA, out-lining his deal on the back of a napkin; I promoted an all-star wrestling show at the Civic Arena and met with officials at McDonald's headquarters in Northbrook, Illinois, regarding sponsorship of the Roundball, only to have them start a competing All-American game a year later, right off my blueprints.

Reflecting back on those years, I originally thought the Big Ten Camp was just another source of income. But, in retrospect, it had a lasting impact in two critical ways. First, it inspired me to take chances on ideas I believed in. Watching the hundreds of high school players compete during those summers in Seven Springs reaffirmed the growing confidence I had in myself. My Arthur Morse mode had convinced me that the impresario in me, the showman, the promoter, was destined to play out somewhere other than Western Pennsylvania.

Second, and far more consequential, was a moment of pure happenstance, the result of one fleeting encounter during the third and final year I ran the camp. The morning slate of games had just ended, and a swarm of noisy, sweaty campers were huffing and puffing up the hill to the mess hall for lunch when a tall, athletic fifteen- or sixteen-year-old kid I'll call "Charley" caught up with me.

"Mr. Vaccaro! Mr. Vaccaro! Could I ask you a question?"

"What's on your mind, young man?"

"It's about tennis shoes, Mr. Vaccaro."

"Tennis shoes?" I repeated, glancing down at his canvas Converse high-tops months past their prime, the rubber heels worn down to an angled slant on each sole and the canvas frayed to the point his little toes threatened to poke through at any moment.

"See, I've only got this one pair of shoes. . . ."

I picked up a note of embarrassment in his voice. "Thing is," Charley said, "I gotta wear 'em everywhere . . . school, church, not just for basketball. I was just wonderin' why nobody makes tennis shoes that are cool enough to wear anywhere? Look at these . . . they're really too raggedy for anything but hoops."

I could empathize. In school, I was one of those kids who wore tennis shoes everywhere.

I'd been around ten thousand kids and never once considered sneakers as anything more than standard, utilitarian footwear. My mind flashed on things I'd seen kids do on playground courts and gyms and sidewalks. Some had mashed down the back heel and wore them like sandals. Some laced them in odd or creative ways, skipping rows of eyelets. Some walked around with the laces untied.

"I can't tell you why nobody makes cool sneakers . . . but I think you're on to something," I said.

At that moment of insight, the realization hit me: Kids *were* probably hungry for shoes with some distinctive design, a way to express their individuality.

As fleeting and insignificant as it might have seemed at the time, that moment and that off-the-cuff conversation would one day alter the course of my life.

Another kid came bounding up and poked Charley on the shoulder. "C'mon, I don't want to end up at the back of the line. Hustle!"

Charley turned to thank me with a thumbs-up and yelled, "Cooler shoes, Mr. Vaccaro. *Please!*"

I never had the opportunity to see Charley again. I remember he was tall and athletic. I imagine he went on to play high school and possibly college basketball. Several years passed, and the unfathomable, serendipitous workings of the universe finally revealed the intended destiny of that less-than-two-minute encounter with Charley.

It was the catalyst that would lead me to Nike.

Soon, a burlap bag in hand, I would be on a flight to Oregon.

5

A Bagful of Shoe Ideas

I can't pinpoint the exact moment the notion hit me or the reason the idea suddenly bubbled up from my subconscious, but at some point my mind reconnected with that question raised by the aforementioned Charley several years earlier at my Big Ten camp: *Why can't someone make cool basketball shoes that you could wear for things besides basketball?*

I recall I was in Trafford visiting my parents in the spring of 1977 when I noticed the stitching on one of my favorite loafers had worn out and a flap at the tip had separated from the sole.

That required a visit to my friend Bobby DiRinaldo, master shoe virtuoso on Cavitt Avenue, a short walk from my parents' home. For generations, DiRinaldo's was the only place people went for repairs. Bobby's father, Rinaldo DiRinaldo, was a fourth-generation master shoemaker from Italy, the consummate craftsman and a magician with leather and soles.

Bobby had apprenticed with his father from the time he was eight or nine, and ran the shop as a very young kid when his father was occasionally out sick.

A little bell jingled as I pushed open the glass-paneled door. I'd always loved walking into the shop, the uniquely musky aromas of shoe polish, leather, and glue flooding your senses. Bobby yelled from the back workbench behind a wooden partition, "I'll be right with you."

"Bobby, *paisan*, it's Sonny," I yelled back.

A minute later he came around the counter and we hugged.

"I got a pair of loafers I want to leave with you, Bobby." I pulled the shoes out of my bag and showed him the damage.

"That's an easy fix. I'll do it while you're here," he said.

"There's something else I want to talk to you about."

"Okay, shoot."

"Listen, I've got an idea. It's about basketball shoes, you know, tennis shoes. I want to do something that's never been done before." I briefly related the story of Charley and the epiphany it had sparked.

"Yeah, I could do sneakers. What're you thinkin'?"

I explained a few of the concepts I'd come up with, reading from the notes I'd made on the back of a white envelope. Some of the ideas were crazy by conventional basketball standards but each had at least one innovation. The smartest thing I did that day was ask Bobby if he could come up with any ideas.

He bought in immediately. He asked if I could give him a few days to work on some sketches.

Elated that I had a real prodigy on board, I said, "Fantastic! I'll see you next week."

When he returned fifteen minutes later, he handed me a pair of beautifully polished loafers with new half soles.

"What do I owe you?" I asked.

"Nothin', Son. We'll settle up next week."

When I returned to his shop the following week, Bobby pulled a spiral notebook from under the cash register and flipped it open. The first sketch was a rendition of my sports sandal idea. His version had a rubberized strap around the back, explaining to me the construction and engineering necessary to make it work.

"Nice," I said. "You can make that?"

"No problem. Wait here a second."

He stepped to the back and returned with a fuzzy little square of fiber and pressed it together with another small square patch. He squeezed the two together, then pulled them apart with a ripping sound and repeated the process.

The patches stuck together, almost like magic.

"What in God's name is that?"

"Velcro. It's a helluva product. Brand new."

It's the first time I'd seen this Velcro thing in action. "This stuff's amazing," I said, sticking and unsticking the two squares myself. Bobby showed me how we could use the Velcro on straps to make a shoe that closed securely without laces.

Oh my God, I thought. That's a big idea. I'd never seen anything like it.

"I got something else I want you to check out," he said, disappearing once more.

He returned with a sample of soft, supple white leather.

"What d'ya think about this? It's light, thin, and flexible. I can punch vents into it. It would make a nice-looking shoe."

This was years before I saw the same kind of soft white leather used in Reebok's wildly popular aerobic shoes that became the rage in the early eighties.

Bobby looked down at his notebook and showed me sketches of other designs—nine or ten in all. We agreed he should proceed with six.

The opportunity to design athletic shoes from the ground up animated the usually reserved Bobby. His brainstorming had resulted in some sensational ideas for "tennis" shoes.

"I'll see you in a couple of weeks," he said. "These are gonna be like nothin' anyone's ever seen."

When I returned to the shop, Bobby had the samples ready. Imagine: Totally new shoe ideas custom-made with an Italian craftsman's touch. Shoes different from anything anywhere.

Design by design, he went through the lineup. One pair had multicolored glittery sparkles; Bobby described them as "disco" sneakers. Another pair featured a soft white leather design. Still another had an open-toed design and triangular air vents running atop the soles.

"These'll let the air flow through, keep their feet cool," Bobby said.

I told him I was going to get a shoe company to produce our new inventions and we'd be partners. I couldn't wait to get these prototypes in front of a shoe company executive. My intuition and familiarity with basketball kids told me they'd respond positively to at least a couple of these inventive and unexpected designs.

Bobby neatly packed the samples into spare shoeboxes wrapped in brown packing paper, two to a box.

"What do I owe you, my friend?"

"We're partners, Son. You find someone to make 'em and we'll settle up later."

I carried our prototypes outside and carefully arranged them on the back seat of my car. I told him I'd keep him in the loop on the shoe company search and headed back to my apartment with a good feeling about this new endeavor. I've always had an otherworldly prescience when I know an idea is going to succeed, and my instincts were throwing off sparks on this one.

My first calls were to industry leaders Converse and Pro-Keds, hoping for a meeting. I knew people at both, but my calls were never returned.

Then I tried a different approach: working through one of the agents doing athlete endorsement deals with shoe companies. Those agents turned out to be Jerry Davis and Lewis Schaffel with All-Pro Reps, Inc., one of the top sports agencies in America. They had more player marketing deals with the NBA and ABA than anyone else at the time. I knew them through the Roundball Classic, where they returned each year to scout future prospects.

I went to New York and told Jerry Davis about the shoe ideas and the samples we were building back in Trafford.

"You designing shoes now, Sonny?" Davis inquired, gently mocking me.

"I've got some ideas. Maybe it sounds crazy, but I want to talk to someone to see whether there's anything to this."

I prevailed upon Davis to put me in contact with a shoe company.

"Look, there's this company out in Oregon. They mainly make track shoes, but they're trying to get into basketball," Davis said. "I'll see what I can do."

Turns out, one of Davis's clients, star NBA guard Phil Chenier, had signed an early endorsement deal with that company in Oregon, formerly known as Blue Ribbon Sports and now renamed Nike after the goddess of victory—although, early on, I kept pronouncing it "Nick-ee."

Jerry wrote a very flattering letter of introduction and sent it to one of the cofounders, a Mr. Phil Knight. Davis spoke of my knowledge of the luminaries in the basketball world, how "Mr. John Vaccaro" had some new shoe ideas Knight might find interesting.

Apparently, Knight never responded. Nike also failed to respond to a follow-up phone call. Being ignored didn't sit well with highly respected agents like Lewis Schaffel and Jerry Davis. They had little idea of the chaotic operational craziness that typified Blue Ribbon Sports in those days, a company that was still processing invoices by hand.

Jerry fired off a second letter to Knight that barely concealed his displeasure.

This time Knight apologized and responded immediately, in July 1977. Davis notified me that Knight had agreed to meet at my earliest convenience. Jerry's secretary arranged an initial meeting in the hinterlands of Oregon.

In August, at thirty-seven years old, I took a flight on my dime from Pittsburgh to Portland. For some odd reason I recall it cost $130.25. I threw the prototype sneakers into a burlap bag that still had the "Idaho Russet Potatoes" label attached, packed an overnight bag, and headed to the Greater Pittsburgh Airport in hopes of selling our quirky atypical shoe ideas to a complete stranger.

Full of nervous apprehension and hope, it was wheels up on my 2,150-mile trip to a company I'd never heard of in a place I'd never been before. Tigard? Where the hell is that?

6

On Board with Nike

I landed in Portland, hailed a cab, and headed west across town, then south on Interstate 5 to a suburb called Tigard. Oregon was like a foreign country to me.

In Tigard, the modest rented offices somehow seemed appropriate. I grabbed the burlap sack, jumped out of the cab, and found my way to the door with the engraved plastic "Blue Ribbon Sports" placard next to it. Inside their offices, another BRS logo hung prominently on the wall behind the reception desk. On another wall, there was a shoe display unit with a selection of running shoes and a Nike Swoosh above. I announced myself to the receptionist. "Sonny Vaccaro here to see Mr. Knight or Mr. Strasser."

"Please have a seat, and I'll tell them you're here."

At the time Nike was a $28-million-a-year running shoe company that wanted a broader customer base than the sport of track and field could deliver. In 1972, Nike had produced its first basketball shoes and began signing NBA athletes in an attempt to dislodge the category leaders, Converse, Pro-Keds, and Adidas. Their forte was Adidas-quality knockoffs made more cheaply in Asian factories with a Swoosh sewn on models boasting names like Blazer and Bruin.

Outside of track and field, they were getting little traction. I think the University of Oregon was the only college wearing Nike basketball shoes at the time, and it took CEO Phil Knight a couple of years to make that happen—even though the Ducks' legendary former

track coach, Bill Bowerman, was a Blue Ribbon cofounder. What had
worked so powerfully and effectively in their running shoe strategy
was flatlining in other sports; basketball sales were barely breaking
seven million a year. I had the feeling they gave away almost as many
as they sold.

A few minutes after I arrived, a hulking 6'3" guy entered the
lobby, a mountain of a man who immediately brought the TV character Grizzly Adams to mind. "Sonny Vaccaro from Pittsburgh!" he
boomed in a jovial voice through a strawberry-blond beard. He thrust
his right arm toward me and we shook. "Good to meet you. Come
on in."

Rob Strasser was Nike's new marketing director. As I would soon
learn, he'd been hired as Nike's chief counsel in 1974 after Knight lured
him away from his cousin's law firm in Portland. At that firm, Strasser
had been instrumental in helping Blue Ribbon fend off a takeover attempt by its Japanese shoe supplier, Onitsuka. The Japanese company
had demanded that Knight sell them a controlling interest in Blue
Ribbon or they were going to discontinue their distribution rights in
the United States—which would have effectively put Blue Ribbon out
of business. In a do-or-die lawsuit that went to federal court in 1974,
Blue Ribbon / Nike walked away with a $400,000 settlement.

As a journeyman lawyer fresh out of Berkeley, Strasser had done a
majority of the legal heavy lifting and strategic planning on the Onitsuka case as a junior member of the law firm. Over the months and
months of preparation for the legal battle, Knight was impressed with
Strasser's unwavering confidence, his tireless double-shift work ethic,
and his lighthearted bravado. With the momentous lawsuit behind
them, Knight realized what a tremendous asset Strasser could be at
Nike, and hired him shortly thereafter. As the world would soon find
out, it was one of the smartest decisions Phil Knight made to this
very day.

As I soon discovered, Rob hated practicing law. He shuddered at the thought of spending the rest of his career in a suit and tie confined to the constraints and formality of the legal profession. He loved the free-spirited informality he'd experienced when he interacted with Knight and Nike, and jumped ship the second Knight offered him a job. Of course, he still handled some legal work at Nike, but now he could do it in a Hawaiian shirt and flip-flops. With Phil's offer, he was free to jettison the drab, methodical monotony of a lawyer's life and have some fun in a far more gratifying specialty: sports marketing.

. . .

STRASSER SHOWED ME DOWN THE hall to the corner office and introduced me to a slight, athletically thin gentleman with a shock of longish blond hair and large pensive eyes.

"Phil, this is the guy Jerry Davis sent our way. Sonny Vaccaro."

Gesturing toward the burlap sack, Phil Knight joked, "I see you brought along an actual bag of tricks." We shook hands.

We landed in a modest conference room with a long wood table under fluorescent lighting. Knight and Strasser called in a couple of other members of the original Blue Ribbon marketing team: Jeff Johnson, the first guy hired at Blue Ribbon, and Bob Woodell, an intense, wiry young man with hippie long hair who got around comfortably in a wheelchair. My impression was that Woodell seemed like the only adult in the room, more serious, more reserved. Del Hayes, another executive with a gray-flecked beard and a big fella like Strasser, settled into another chair. Hayes had been Knight's boss when Knight worked as an accountant at Price Waterhouse in Portland following grad school.

The group was loose, informal, and spontaneous. A good sign. After the usual introductions, Knight opened the meeting.

"So I understand you have some shoe designs for us to look at. You know we don't do outside designs, but let's see what you brought."

"That's fine. I'd just like to get your impressions, see if there's anything you see potential in."

I began the presentation by telling them my "Charley" story. "That's the reason we came up with these," I explained. I could see their curiosity growing, wondering what secrets remained hidden in my burlap bag.

"So let's see 'em already," Strasser said, cutting off my preamble.

As I would soon learn, Strasser liked to get to the point.

Instead of an orderly, one-by-one reveal of the shoes, I turned the potato sack over, letting all six samples fall on the table in a pile. That alone brought a round of guffaws as they collectively began to survey the newfangled designs. They began grabbing them to examine each more closely. The chatter started immediately.

Strasser appraised a sandal-like design first. The open-toe prototype evoked a chorus of laughter and complaint.

"What happened to this one—you ran out of leather?"

"Who's gonna get their toes stomped in these?" someone else remarked.

Knight grabbed the "disco shoe," the one Bobby had designed with colorful clear acrylic jewels embossed into the soft leather, featuring red and blue panels at the toe and heel. Knight assessed it, turning it around in his hands. He smirked, said nothing, then passed it on to Hayes. Another shoe with Velcro straps seemed to draw a couple of "hmmms," as did a shoe with triangular air holes running just above the contour of the sole for better air circulation to fend off sneaker smell. Next, the attention turned to a design made of soft, white calf-skin leather. Rob took notice of the sole that had a quarter-inch-deep inset running across the sole, side to side.

"What's this for?" he inquired.

"That's the bicycle shoe," I said. "That groove fits over the pedals so the foot won't slip off."

Despite the levity and ridicule, I knew this peculiar assortment of footwear had struck a chord. I could see the shoes had piqued their curiosity, and they may have recognized three or four features that deserved further exploration. Maybe the Velcro strap idea—which indeed would be featured in Nike models not long after.

Hayes asked if they could borrow the samples and examine them further. I later found out they sent them to the lab guys and designers back at Nike's factory in Exeter, New Hampshire.

"Yeah, you can hold on to 'em, but I'd like 'em back," I said, before looking over to Knight and Strasser. "And, of course, if you want to develop any of these ideas, I'm sure we can work something out."

They gathered the samples, put them back in the burlap sack, and carried it down the hall. I never saw a single one of Bobby's samples again.

The Blue Ribbon / Nike group seemed both bemused and perplexed by the little Italian who'd shown up at their doorstep. Oregon was a northwest outpost, overwhelmingly white, outdoorsy, and insular. Reading between the lines, I had a sense that they had typecast me as a character right out of *The Godfather*, the movie that had captivated the country a few years earlier. Strasser told me later that Knight had actually suggested a background check on me.

Rob took over. I was waiting for a spirited discussion about next steps with my shoe samples.

No such luck.

Strasser announced it was already past lunchtime. He struck me as a guy that didn't skip lunches. We adjourned and walked down to a family-run Chinese place a couple of blocks from Nike's offices.

In the darkish, kitschy room, we pushed two square tables together. The decor was just as you'd expect: Chinese art, dragons, bamboo, chopsticks in paper wrappers on the tables, and red, black, and gold-leaf everything. The Blue Ribbon guys ordered a Chinese beer called Tsingtao. I'd never seen a Chinese beer before. I ordered a root beer, no ice.

The owner's wife returned to take the order, slowly repeating the individual selections out loud as each guy named a dish. The order seemed to fill up four pages in her notepad. Over spring rolls, mu shu pork, shrimp fried rice, and perhaps eight bowls and plates of other Chinese dishes, the conversation took an improbable turn.

To my dismay, there was no more attention directed at my shoe designs. The trajectory had veered into familiar territory: the Dapper Dan and my basketball connections. I could tell everyone there was trying to get a handle on this ebullient, talkative guy who'd arrived from "somewhere near Pittsburgh" on that bright Northwest morning.

I thought I'd landed in Oregon to pitch a new line of shoes. Turns out the universe had something else in the offing: a wonderful, fortuitous twist on my original intent. I sensed Strasser might have other plans in mind for me.

Strasser proceeded with theatrical brio. He was speaking to a half dozen faces, but the real audience was Phil Knight.

"Lemme tell you who this guy really is."

Strasser explained what he had learned from Jerry Davis in New York. "Sonny runs the biggest event in high school basketball, the original high school all-star game. You guys know about the Dapper Dan in Pittsburgh?"

Drawing blank stares, Strasser explained the level of talent the Roundball attracted. How hundreds of coaches from everywhere went there to scout future stars, how it's circled in red on every coach's calendar across the country. How Sonny knows everyone in the game.

That got the interplay rolling on a freewheeling hour-and-a-half Q & A session. People wanted to hear about how the Dapper Dan started. I told them about the great players who'd come through. I told stories about Maurice Lucas, Moses Malone, Adrian Dantley, and Calvin Murphy, and how Lew Alcindor's coach never informed him he was invited; how one great coach after another had kick-started their careers at the Dapper Dan.

Heads nodded. Knight took it all in, barely saying a word.

Nike had endorsement deals in place with forty or so assorted NBA players at the time, some of them very well regarded. Converse and Adidas had the top-tier stars, Julius "Dr. J" Erving and Lew Alcindor, now Kareem Abdul-Jabbar, under contract.

I felt an immediate affinity for Strasser. Rob was far and away the biggest personality in the room. He asked the most cogent questions, particularly about the college game. Strasser was different from the others—genuine, unguarded, and intellectually curious. He seemed to "get" me from the get-go.

The lunch ended. The shoe samples disappeared—but not my connection with Strasser. He and I agreed to follow up by phone in a few days. I invited him to come to the next Roundball to witness how much excitement surrounded the event and the players. He said he'd make a point of it.

I had a strong sense that something important was going to come out of this meeting. Some new opportunity that wasn't part of the agenda before I arrived.

Strasser was an obsessive truth-teller, whip-smart, and quick-witted. It struck me immediately that he could process information in seconds. He seemed someone open to opportunity and possibilities—this was a man I could do business with.

Leaving Portland the following day, my sense was that this sojourn wasn't an ending but something bigger. I felt the same nervous excitement I had the night before the first Roundball a decade earlier.

Three months later, my premonition proved true.

...

AT MY NEXT NIKE MEETING in late October—this time Nike bought my ticket—the meeting was reduced to three, just Strasser, Knight, and me. Rob had probably convinced Knight that the fast-talking

Italian wasn't exaggerating about his engagement and influence in high school and collegiate basketball. They knew I could connect Nike to top collegiate talent, current and future.

The shoe development deal I had originally contacted them about never came up again. They'd done their homework since the last time I was there, and evidently, I had passed muster.

At that meeting, they confided more about Nike, describing their game plan with NBA players. I barely knew them at that point, and what came out of my mouth next may have been a little out of bounds.

"What are we missing?" asked Strasser. I suspected he sensed they had a blind spot in their strategy.

"It's all wrong, the NBA thing. You're upside down," I responded. "Your approach is top down, instead of local heroes up. You've got players the kids don't know or care about."

I told them they were wasting their money on NBA players who weren't going to move the needle for them (despite the fact they had recently invested a few hundred thousand in pro endorsements). At that time, the NBA had nowhere near the global reach and gravitas it has today. It was tainted by a series of drug scandals. Even the championship game was broadcast on tape delay. Most important, I explained to them that basketball influencers were local, found in the school gyms and on gritty urban concrete courts with no nets on the hoops. *Up close.*

"The NBA strategy is a waste of money," I said. The way to kids' hearts and minds was at street level—their heroes were the stars at the local high schools and playgrounds and the nearby colleges. The connection was more direct. Back East, the whole world revolved around districts, high school kids, the local hype, and inner-city playgrounds. I asked if they'd ever heard of Rucker Park on 155th at Eighth Avenue in Harlem, or "The Cage" on West Fourth in New York City, or Saint Cecilia's in Detroit? What about the Ozanam in Pittsburgh?

"The intensity is like nothing you can even imagine."

I told stories about all the stars that had made their bones on inner-city playgrounds, the hardscrabble courts where Wilt and Dr. J and Connie Hawkins and dozens of other icons had built their fearsome reputations. I told them about Herman "Helicopter" Knowings and an incredible player named Earl "The Goat" Manigault, whom Kareem Abdul-Jabbar once said was the greatest player he'd ever played against. I regaled them with the story of how Helicopter used to grab quarters off the top of backboards. In one game against some NBA players, he'd swatted away three shots on a single possession.

"You've got to get these kids," I said. "You want to be involved in this game, you've got to get your shoes on these kids. Let me get them on the feet of kids in Pittsburgh, Philadelphia, New York City, Detroit, LA. You gotta get the local legends in all those cities."

"High school kids . . ." Strasser said, pondering a concept they hadn't considered.

I'd given them my best pitch and they were still unsure.

Practically yelling, I said, "These kids' feet are the greatest billboards known to mankind! Get your shoes on them and you'll sell product!"

At that point I felt there was only one way to close the deal.

"Look," I said, "you guys are way out here in Oregon. Come to Pittsburgh. The Roundball is where you'll see the game at its roots. You see it one time and you'll understand. You should come."

That, in fact, was the main purpose of that second trip—to get Strasser to the Roundball in March. But I also had a secondary motive: I wanted Nike to put some sponsorship money into the game. Converse or Pro-Keds had been giving us shoes at the time, but no money. I wanted Nike to kick in ten or fifteen thousand. I mentioned the money to Strasser before I left and knew that after he got a first-hand look at the hysteria, excitement, and fan enthusiasm, he'd want to be part of it.

"You want to feel the pulse of basketball, the Roundball is it," I said. "You've gotta see it—feel it. You think every coach in the country shows up to see *me*?"

The meeting ended and I was thrilled to have a handshake deal to supply shoes, T-shirts, and sweat suits for the Roundball. Sponsorship money would follow. Adios, Converse and Pro-Keds. Hello, Nike.

. . .

STRASSER CALLED A COUPLE OF weeks later and said he'd be there. He arrived on Thursday, March 30, the day before the game. I gave him the grand tour, introduced him to dozens of coaches, and invited him to the final practices. But none of that impressed him more than the experience the next night wandering around an upgraded Civic Arena jam-packed to the rafters with over seventeen thousand people—fans, media, players, coaches, concessionaires, and staff. Strasser was caught up in the fan fever like the rest of us. He knew I hadn't been exaggerating. He now *believed*.

Amid all the hoopla, we'd talked only briefly. "I know these are *high school kids*, but this is crazy. Who knew fans would pack an arena for high school kids?" Back then, the word *amazing* wasn't as widely used as it is today, but that's how he described it.

He caught the first flight out the next morning, so we never got around to talking about a future sponsorship deal for the Roundball. Two weeks later, they invited me back out to Oregon for a big meeting.

Strasser said that Nike was ready to pull the trigger on the sponsorship money. He said they wanted to give me $10,000 and all the shoes and gear for the event. I was elated that, for the first time, I had a major sponsor providing cash, not just shoes. We were no longer dependent on ticket sales alone to cover expenses and turn a profit.

This time Strasser's agenda had an expanded vision: "What else can we do to get into basketball?"

At the time, Converse and Adidas were providing shoes for schools like North Carolina, UCLA, Duke, and others, along with some monogrammed sweat suits for the coaching staff. Most coaches were making maybe $25,000 or $30,000 a year.

I got to the point.

"We pay the coaches," I said.

"*Whoa!* Is that legal?" Knight asked. "The NCAA allows that?"

They were nervous. They always got nervous in Oregon.

"There's no NCAA rule against it," I said. "We pay the coaches, maybe they run a coaching clinic in the summer. We have them under contract, supply the team with shoes, and the players wear Nike. It wouldn't be mandatory, but if Nike shoes are free, the players will wear Nike. Other companies are paying the coaches in different ways."

They were looking for an entrée into college basketball, and they were vetting me—looking for assurance that I was the way forward.

"You think you can get that done?" Knight asked, a subtle challenge implied in his tone.

Without blinking I shot back, "I *will* get it done. I know most of the coaches personally. I can make it happen."

Knight's apprehension was still evident in the subtext.

"Look, they come to the Dapper Dan every year. I was on the UNLV team bus with Jerry Tarkanian heading over to the Omni in Atlanta at the Final Four last year."

I waited for that point to sink in. Then turned directly to Knight to wrap up my summation in a single sentence.

"You commit the money and shoes, I'll get the coaches."

I never doubted for a second that my Rolodex and the Roundball were Nike's way in.

"Okay. See what you can do," he said, forcing a wan smile. We shook hands and he left the conference room.

That's when Strasser and I began sketching out the college basketball battle plan. Primarily, how they'd fund our new partnership and the general structure of my more or less freelance/consultant employment contract.

There was, however, one rather peculiar aspect of our nascent working arrangement: Perhaps fearing I'd abscond with their money, they declined to lock up the collegiate coaching deals with *any up-front funding*—literally, I had no "operating" budget.

"Tell you what we'll do," Strasser said. "You make the deals. You write the checks. When they sign the deal, you call us and we'll wire the money into your account."

Imagine that.

Here's me, a guy who'd never had a full-time job up to that point, fronting the money for Nike's coaching contracts. Nike didn't open a $50,000 checking account to roll out the program. I wrote the checks out of my personal bank account.

They agreed to cover airfare and other expenses like hotel, rental cars, and food. It was 1978 and Sonny Vaccaro was now a $500 a month "consultant" with the putative title *head of college basketball*.

Nike and I were off to an iffy start, with an uncertain future, the only certainty being my own, the *absolute certainty* I could get the coaches and teams to make it all work.

"Let's see what happens and go from there," Strasser said as he wrapped our visit up. As much as I liked Rob, I had no guarantee I'd ever see him or Knight again.

I had a job—based on a handshake agreement—and my marching orders.

I'd gone to a suburb of Portland about the size of Trafford with a burlap bag full of samples in hopes of getting some shoes made. I ended up in a momentous relationship with Nike that would last fourteen years. The fuse suddenly lit on a revolution that was about to change the entire financial dynamics of collegiate sports, a collaboration destined to take Nike from ground zero in college basketball to the most powerful force in the world of sports marketing and sponsorship.

But before we head to Vegas to explore my first ever coach's signing, I want to make sure I place credit for everything that followed with Nike where it is due—with the giant who made daring things possible.

7

The Inimitable, Irreplaceable
Field General

Who else to lead a worldwide takeover but Strasser, Nike's grand field marshal and dealmaker extraordinaire?

When you've lived as long as I have, some people just stand out in a special or more affecting way. They're the ones with whom you bond at an almost unfathomable level—with your own psyche, your own mind, your own soul. They make an impact on your life you never forget.

Rob Strasser was that once-in-a-lifetime person for me.

They called him Rolling Thunder, a big, imposing hulk of a man whose spirit and bold "man among men" presence lived up to that nickname. At the core of this ebullient giant was a code: a commitment to truth, integrity, and principle. In negotiations with agents, he wanted the terms to be win-win, equitable, nobody loses. His sense of justice and fairness was inseparable from his identity. Though he could out-party every last one of his peers, he had a moral center that couldn't be compromised. Strasser was a force of nature, kinetic and commanding—*momentum* personified.

At the office he was rarely attired in anything beyond his trademark Hawaiian shirts, shorts, and sneakers with no socks, unless he had to be in court or meet a group of investors.

My recollections of Rob come to mind in a blizzard of alliterative

B's: bearded, brilliant, brazen, boisterous, bold. Rob didn't just enter a room—he engulfed it. As a businessman, he displayed the kind of qualities and leadership you might see once or twice in a generation. His engaging, infectious, and lighthearted personality masked the dead-serious business acumen beneath.

So joyful, animated, and uplifting, he made doing business a party. Whatever else you expected at any gathering, with Strasser around, you knew it was going to be fun. Endlessly inquisitive and impish, with a mischievous streak, he loved to argue, debate, and jolt you out of your comfort zone.

The joviality ended when it came to competitors. Converse and Adidas were afforded no such grace. In that respect, he was as driven as Knight. He had a competitive fire, a compulsion to win—an innate aggression that demanded nothing less than subjugation of the enemy.

The furthest thing from an athlete, Strasser nevertheless had the soul of a sports fanatic. He loved the San Francisco 49ers, going back to the days of quarterbacks Y. A. Tittle and John Brodie. He could recite statistics, individual plays, all the great players and wins. He also loved the Oregon Ducks. He loved the Dodgers, but hated just about everything else about LA.

. . .

BEYOND POSSESSING A FERTILE IMAGINATION and a lawyer's attention to detail, Strasser was a natural when it came to selling an idea, formulating plans, and motivating the troops. I can't count the times I watched him deliver rousing Knute Rockne–level pep talks extemporaneously. I knew many coaches and personalities at the time, and saw few who were more confident, charismatic, or engaging than Rob.

Perhaps nothing captures the essence of Strasser's approach better than his famous "Principles" memo, conceived sometime in the late seventies. In it, he outlined what became almost our manifesto:

1. Our business is change.
2. We're on offense. All the time.
3. Perfect results count—not a perfect process.
   Break the rules: fight the law.
4. This is as much about battle as about business.
5. Assume nothing.
   Make sure people keep their promises.
   Push yourselves push others.
   Stretch the possible.
6. Live off the land.
7. Your job isn't done until *the* job is done.
8. *Dangers*
   Bureaucracy
   Personal ambition
   Energy takers vs. energy givers
   Knowing our weaknesses
   Don't get too many things on the platter
9. It won't be pretty.
10. If we do the right things we'll make money damn near automatic.

Ironically, a portly, heavyset man who was the antithesis of the elite athlete (or even a weekend jock) proved perfectly brilliant at articulating the *"Mind of Nike"*—that innate self-confidence, self-awareness, and aura the Swoosh bestowed upon individuals in each of its disparate market segments.

Strasser and Peter Moore were the architects of Nike's brand image and design sensibility. As a team, they were unquestionably the duo most influential on Nike's meteoric growth and public perception.

Their understanding of the *psychographic profile* of the Nike customer motivated millions to embrace all things Swoosh.

It went beyond just the athletic gear you wore and merged into a state of mind. That may be my own biased assessment, but Strasser and Moore's creative campaigns and distinctive brand iconography positioned Nike not as mere logo-branded merchandise, but as a lifestyle choice. They were the brains that guided Nike's surge to the pinnacle of cultural relevance. That bedrock brand identity and target customer profile hasn't changed appreciably since they defined it several decades ago.

Yes, Phil Knight was the Boss, the Whole Boss, and Nothing but the Boss, as you'd logically assume—no one questioned his genius, his mind, or his authority. That, however, wasn't sufficient to change the widely understood belief within the industry that Strasser was the guy driving Nike's success.

. . .

BEYOND BEING GIFTED WITH A formidable intellect, Strasser had a photographic memory. His passion for sports was exceeded only by his love of history, a subject in which his knowledge rose to an academic level. While you and I might know of Patton and Eisenhower, Strasser was well-versed on generals from Alexander the Great to Napoleon. He was captivated by Winston Churchill, able to quote him verbatim. That grasp of history informed Strasser's strategic approach and the tactics we applied to lay out our battle plans against competitors.

Though he could dominate a meeting, a party, or a presentation, Rob nonetheless shunned publicity and media attention. I think he was more than happy to see me doing the sports shows and interviews.

Having Rob's belief and faith in you infused your being with a sense of invincibility. Once you made the cut with Rob, you recalibrated what you believed you were capable of accomplishing. He uplifted your spirits and confidence, and stirred you to take chances, implode paradigms, rewrite rules, and push boundaries.

Rob was endlessly curious as well. He sought to extract the maximum information from every encounter or situation in life, and filed it for later application. No factoid was too esoteric or insignificant for him to file away.

In that vein, my Italian background held a certain fascination for him. He had a kind of perverse preoccupation with the mob and always cajoled me about whether I had "any ties"—whether I was connected to the guys who ran the Las Vegas casinos. He was captivated by the fact that my brother Jimmy was one of the top oddsmakers in Vegas; Rob was completely taken with the city's dark undertones and mafia history. He knew the backstories of the Flamingo, the Stardust, and the Riviera.

When we gathered our roster of a dozen or so elite coaches to present a Nike stock offering in the early eighties, we didn't meet in Beaverton or at the Final Four; at Strasser's request, we gathered everyone at the Barbary Coast. He loved meeting and interacting with my colorful circle of Vegas friends.

From the time I was hired and first hit the road, we never went more than a day or two without touching base. I spent more time on the phone with him than anyone else in my life, including my family. Though we spent more than eleven months a year in different cities, I still thought of us as inseparable.

Over the ten years we were together at Nike, it was never strictly about business. We talked about everything. He knew as much about me as anyone in the world outside of Pam.

Though other factors were always in play, the Sonny Vaccaro of Nike fame would never have emerged had Strasser not been involved. Working with Rob was one of the greatest blessings anyone could hope for professionally or personally. His support and faith in me propelled not just my own accomplishments, but Nike's. As a result of those efforts, Knight was to become the king of an empire exponentially larger than the niche West Coast running shoe company he had initially presided over.

The offensive into basketball was the strategic pivot point that reversed the fortunes of the entire brand. To minimize the depth and breadth of Rob Strasser's contributions to Nike's emergence as the biggest sports brand the world has ever known would be an unconscionable omission.

. . .

FOR THOSE OF US WHO were there when Nike emerged as a global colossus, Rob Strasser's contribution will remain vivid and indelible. With swagger and decisiveness, he was our Field General, confronting Nike's challenges and challengers with brilliance, boldness, meticulous planning, and precision.

He was not just my most cherished friend, but one of the deepest, most compassionate, and brilliant men I have ever met. God rest his soul and keep his memory alive with the joy and respect he is due.

Our Field General.

A Giant.

A Brother.

Forever.

8

The Banzai Blitz of '78

It was now time for me to live up to the brash promise I'd made to Strasser and Knight. Naturally, I already had the first coach I was going to sign in mind.

Back in Vegas, where I had taken up partial residence, I drove over to the UNLV athletic building on campus off South Maryland Parkway not far from the Strip. Head coach Jerry "Tark the Shark" Tarkanian, one of my best friends, was still in the afterglow of a 29–3 season and the school's first trip to the Final Four, the Runnin' Rebels scoring more than 3,400 points—a single-season NCAA record.

I'd called earlier to make sure he'd be in the office that afternoon.

"Jerry."

"Yeah, Son."

"Look, I wanna talk some business with you. I got a deal you're gonna love. There's this shoe company named Nike . . . they're trying to ramp up their basketball business. They want some exposure."

"So what's the deal?" Tark replied.

"I'll tell you when I get over there."

Minutes later I strolled into Tark's office and we hugged hello. In his unusual gait, he shuffled back around a desk cluttered with papers, newspapers, and framed family photos and settled into his swivel chair.

"The deal is this," I said. "I give you $10,000, and a lot of Nike merchandise—shoes, T-shirts, sweat suits, bags—and you do your part: Suggest to the kids that they wear Nikes. Practices, games, tournaments. That's it."

"That's it? And all I gotta do is suggest that the kids wear free brand-new basketball shoes?"

"That's it."

"Shhhittttt . . ." he responded, rubbing his bald head, probably thinking there's got to be a catch.

No catch. If coaches agreed, I'd call Strasser's assistant, Rose, back in Oregon and start the paperwork. The home office had no idea where I was headed next or who I had on my "hit" list. I set the payment amounts, outlined a merchandise package, and got approval from each school for gym banner signage.

I slid a single, hand-scribbled sheet of paper across Tarkanian's desk and spun it so he could read it.

As Tark studied it, I continued, "Good deal for the university, good for the kids, good for Nike, good for you."

"And not illegal? The NCAA is biting at my ankles full time right now."

"Nothing illegal. Call the NCAA if you wanna check."

The man, who was currently up to his ears in an NCAA investigation for various alleged recruiting "irregularities" during his time coaching at Long Beach State, tilted his head and shot me a "Yeah, right, I'll check with 'em right away" look.

"Okay, Sonny, I'll trust you on that."

"Then you're in?" I needed to hear the words.

"Of course I'm in. Who's gonna turn down this deal?"

He was right. Nobody.

"Good, you'll be hearing from a lady named Rose Gastineau. She'll type up a contract and shoot you a signed original and a copy. You add your signature, keep your copy, and have your secretary mail the original back to Beaverton."

While I was writing out the first installment of $2,500 on a personal check (from an account with less than $1,200 in it), I asked Tark to hold the check for a couple of days. He thought nothing of my request, smiled, and said sure. I wanted to be certain that Nike's wire transfer registered in time to cover the cost of my first endorsement deal.

"One more question," said Tark. "Are those shoes any good?"

"I'll have 'em send you a half dozen pairs next week," I said. "You check 'em out. They're just as good if not better than Converse. They've got new models in the pipeline."

Honestly, I had no idea what was in the pipeline. I'd never set foot inside a shoe factory at that point and haven't to this day. Plus, I wasn't exactly on the list of those getting inside information on upcoming basketball shoes.

"You got a deal, my friend," Tark said, shaking my hand more enthusiastically than usual. "When can you get the gear to me? We start practicing in a few weeks."

In less than forty-eight hours I was batting a thousand in the endorsement department.

I couldn't wait to call Strasser up in Oregon and deliver the good news.

"Hey, Sonny, what's up?"

"We got our first coach."

"Who?"

"Tarkanian, UNLV. Ten thousand dollars, plus shoes, bags, T-shirts and sweat suits."

"That's fantastic! Runnin' Rebels in Nike! Congratulations!"

Rob was over the moon. You would have thought Nike had just won a national championship.

"We're on our way," I said. "I've got some others lined up already."

"Who you seein'?"

"I don't wanna jinx myself. I'm only gonna fill you in once they're confirmed."

"Alright. I'll tell Knight. And keep on goin', my friend."

"One more thing . . ."

"Yeah."

"Make sure you get accounting to transfer $2,500 into my account *posthaste*. I just wrote Tark a rubber check and asked him to hold it for a couple of days."

"I'm on it," Rob said, and we hung up.

The Tark deal got the ball rolling. Nike, the darling of the running world, was about to turn the sport of college basketball upside down.

. . .

IN THE FIFTIES, SIXTIES, and seventies, Converse had dominated pro and college basketball. By 1978, they were selling some ten million pairs a year, earning $150 million in revenue, and controlled 70 percent of the market, mainly with their Chuck Taylor All Star shoe. Their chief rainmaker was a gentleman by the name of Joe Dean, the designated "Sneaker God" of that era. And truth be told, the guy who blew it for Converse in college ball. The category leader took a stumble that crippled the brand, signaling its decline. Fifteen years later, Nike took ownership of the company.

At the time, shoe companies like Converse were *selling* shoes to schools, generally on two-for-one deals, throwing in signature sweat suits for the head coach and his staff. Some coaches received a $500 stipend to speak at a Converse camp in the summer. Others, at the bigger Converse schools, commanded larger speaking fees.

I simply upped the ante—or rather changed the game—crossing a Rubicon Converse haughtily claimed it would *never cross*—until it was far too late.

. . .

WITH TARK ON BOARD, he put me in touch with Norm Ellenberger at New Mexico, who networked me to Joe Cipriano at Nebraska, their early acceptance of Nike funds providing cover for the coaches who followed. Within the first two months I had eight coaches signed, but the real momentum started to build with a two-week run through the East in the summer of '78 when I flew back to Pittsburgh and began what I like to call my banzai blitz.

At the airport I rented my car of choice, a T-Bird convertible, and turned the radio dial to my favorite local station, WAMO 860 AM, to listen to Porky Chedwick, the "Daddio of the Raddio." And then set out through Pennsylvania, Maryland, Massachusetts, New York, and Jersey, a headhunting escapade—later referred to as my "kamikaze run" by *Sports Illustrated* senior writer Curry Kirkpatrick—that reinvented the concept of sports marketing.

Driving from the Alleghenies through the Appalachians, I headed to East Stroudsburg in the Poconos in eastern Pennsylvania. I'd never been to the Poconos and was struggling to navigate my way down from Highway 80 to Echo Lake, where Duke coach Bill Foster ran the famous Pocono Mountain All-Star Basketball Camp. When I arrived, I was surprised to find a facility that resembled a motor lodge more than a high school or college campus. Foster, along with long-time Temple coach Harry Litwack, had been partners in that renowned camp for more than twenty-five years. Foster had just reached the 1978 NCAA championship game with a roster that included Jim Spanarkel, Mike Gminski, Kenny Dennard, and the amazing Gene Banks, an outstanding forward who had won the MVP at the '77 Dapper Dan the year before.

Foster was an exuberant personality, a great motivator, and intellectually gifted, incessantly taking notes on a pad, shifting his attention back and forth to the activity on the court. I managed to grab about twenty-five minutes of his time courtside. I had phoned him a couple of days earlier to set up the appointment. When we met, he was wearing the latest Converse sneakers, a pair of suede low-tops, with a single star sewn on the side and a black line running along the sole. I hoped he and his team would be in different shoes by the time the season began back in Durham.

"Bill, I want to talk to you about a sneaker deal."

Like most of the coaches that first year, Foster was leery of the legal ramifications. The NCAA was a constant nemesis, even back then.

I gave him the same pitch I'd given Tark. In less than half an hour, we had a deal. Foster, the man who'd led Duke's resurgence, was suddenly a Nike coach—for $8,000 a year.

By the time I was back on Highway 80 headed to New York, I was thrumming my finger on the steering wheel listening to Sly and the Family Stone's "Dance to the Music." Which was pretty much what I was doing when I called Strasser with the latest news.

From New York I headed to College Park, Maryland, just outside DC, to sign Maryland's Lefty Driesell. Then came a deluge of future coaching greats: Jim Calhoun at Northeastern, Rick Pitino at Boston University, Jim Valvano at Iona, Jimmy Lynam at Saint Joseph's, Rollie Massimino at Villanova, Don Casey at Temple.

The Valvano pitch was a scene straight out of a Scorsese movie. We met at LaGuardia Airport, where I reached into my briefcase and put a check on the table.

"What's this for?" Jimmy asked.

I reached back into my briefcase and set a Nike sneaker on the table, allowing him to examine the shoe.

"So?"

"I want your team to wear this shoe," I said.

"How much?" V asked, thinking he would have to pay me.

"No," I said. "I give *you* the money and the shoes."

"Okay. Very dramatic, but what's the catch?"

"Foster and Tark already got deals. No catch."

With that, Jimmy picked up the check, took a long look, and said we had a deal.

By 1979, I no longer had to chase anyone; coaches were reaching out to me. I simply negotiated numbers and equipment allotments. With each coach, the deals were made on handshakes or a phone conversation taking less than twenty minutes. By this time, Strasser had approved wiring enough money (around $10,000) into my checking account so that I had an operating budget to cover the first allotment of each contract I negotiated. The typewritten contracts were kept by Rose and entered into a register by hand. I still look at copies of those registers today, amazed at how it all began.

To the next generation of elite coaches, I would assume a new persona. I was no longer just the Dapper Dan man.

I was now "the Nike Guy."

• • •

THE ONE HEAD COACH I coveted was Georgetown's John Thompson. At 6'10" and 270 pounds, John was a big man with a booming voice and imposing presence. After graduating from Providence College, he had spent two seasons (1964–66) backing up legendary Celtics' center Bill Russell in racially torn Boston. I had first met John at the Roundball in 1972 when he was the head coach at Saint Anthony High in DC and he showed up with his All-American forward Donald Washington, on his way to playing at North Carolina.

Five years later, after I had joined Nike and John was coaching at Georgetown, during one of John's frequent visits to the Aladdin in Vegas—he loved the slots—I asked if he would consider switching from Converse to the Swoosh. Unlike many of the other coaches, John was more circumspect, telling me to stop by the next time I was in DC, which I did. Not long after that, we met again for another talk at the Aladdin and I presented him with an offer more than double what I was paying other coaches. Why? The game was changing, and I saw the future in Thompson and Georgetown. And I was right. Two years later, the Hoyas won their first of six Big East tournament titles on their way to a national championship in 1984. By then, John was well on his way to being regarded by the executives at Nike as the most important coach on their roster.

. . .

THOSE FIRST FEW WEEKS ON Nike's payroll, I also began laying the groundwork for the second priority in my master plan: our headlong dive into the premier high school basketball ranks, like I'd spoken to Knight and Strasser about in Tigard. In short order, I established Nike equipment deals with ten of the top high schools in the country. I signed six-time state champion Verbum Dei High School from the tough Watts area of LA, through their head coach George McQuarn and his assistant, Rudy Washington, who would soon take over. I struck up a deal with West Philadelphia High, where Gene Banks was All-City, All-State, and All-American. Playing for Coach Joe Goldenberg, "Tinkerbell," as Banks was known, is credited with being the star who triggered the flood of great Duke recruits when, surprisingly, he signed with Coach Foster in '78, passing up offers from blue bloods UCLA, Kentucky, and many others. As a freshman, Banks led Duke to the NCAA championship finals. Next, with Coach Ken Kern, I signed the nationally ranked Fort Hamilton High team in Brooklyn, whose star Albert King I had raved about to Knight and Strasser. Now another of the country's best high school stars would be in Swoosh-branded gear.

Going into my second year, I had more than thirty coaches under contract. Obviously, word was getting out. That's when a respected reporter named Mark Asher of *The Washington Post*—writing in John Thompson's backyard—threatened to blow up the entire college program without ever talking to me.

"Driesell, Others Sign Up to Endorse Shoes" was the headline in *The Washington Post* sports section on November 11, 1978. The story was meant to incite outrage, the tone insinuating, suggesting we'd crossed a line into the impermissible, at least by NCAA standards. The gist, as described by Asher: "Nike escalated the basketball shoe war this summer with what one company official called 'an aggressive attack' at cutting into Converse's domination of basketball shoe sales."

Exactly. What else would it have been about?

We had definitely crossed a threshold, introducing a new level of commercialism into collegiate sports. Imagine the impact that story had in a little rented office building outside Portland. I got a frantic phone call from Strasser within hours of Asher's article.

"You see *The Washington Post* article that came out this morning?"

"No, what article?" I asked, waiting for my first cup of coffee to cool.

"Mark Asher. Says we're paying coaches to have their players wear Nike shoes!" Rob was literally screaming into the phone.

"Rob, for God's sake, *we are. That's exactly what we're doing.*"

"Knight's freaking out," he screamed again. "Get your butt up here on the next flight. Be here this afternoon. You better have the right answers, my friend. His hair's on fire."

The next morning, after hastily booking a flight, I found myself in Knight's office in Tigard. No small feat on a moment's notice in the seventies. Knight was on full boil, fearing a federal investigation.

"This is a disaster! They'll have us in front of a Congressional committee if this gets out of control!"

Both of them were flummoxed. Knight glared at me.

"What are we gonna do about this?"

All I could think was, *What's wrong with these two?*

"Are you guys nuts?" I replied. "*The Washington Post* wrote about us; it's the greatest thing that's ever happened to us! We just hit the trifecta. This is exactly what we want. We want coaches calling us. We want Converse in a panic. We'll get calls—we'll have coaches lining up."

As fate would have it, a divine intervention of sorts took place at that very moment—yet another improbable twist of fate—when Knight's assistant suddenly popped in.

"Mr. Knight," she began. "Sorry to interrupt, but there's a Lute Olson on the phone for Mr. Vaccaro."

Somehow, Lute Olson, the silver-haired head coach at the University of Iowa at the time, had tracked me down in Tigard. How he did it, I will never know.

In Asher's article, it had stated, mistakenly, that Jim Valvano of *Iowa* was one of the coaches Nike had signed. The paper had made a typo. They had misspelled *Iona* by one letter as *Iowa*. Turns out, Olson had called Valvano to find out how he could get a shoe contract himself.

The assistant transferred the call into Phil's office in the middle of our meeting. Knight handed me the phone.

"Lute, it's Sonny. Look, I apologize. The *Post* had a typo, it should have said *Iona*, not *Iowa*. . . ."

"That's not why I'm calling," Olson said. "I want to know how I can get one of those shoe deals."

"Are you kidding? We'd love to have you. I'll call you tomorrow. Okay, God bless. Talk to you then."

When I hung up, Knight and Strasser sat looking at one another in dumbfounded disbelief.

Like some transcendental message from heaven, God had provided a startling demonstration of exactly what lay ahead.

To this day, I'm not sure whether Knight and Strasser thought I'd set the whole thing up or not (I did not), but they never again questioned the wisdom of our strategy.

Of all the uncanny coincidences that have occurred in my life, that may have been the most *surreal*.

We signed Lute Olson less than a week later.

From the day that *Post* article broke, our numbers exploded.

From thirty coaches that day, we jumped to seventy-one a year later. When that dust finally settled, Nike owned college basketball.

9

The NCAA's Endless Tark Hunt

The NCAA had been hot on Jerry Tarkanian's trail since his days at Long Beach State, where he began winning twenty to twenty-five games a season just thirty-five miles south of UCLA down the 405 Freeway. His persecution began in the late sixties in the midst of UCLA's unprecedented championship run, when they won ten national titles from 1964 to '75. Southern California hoop fanatics desperately wanted to see a matchup of Long Beach and UCLA but Bruins' athletic director J. D. Morgan wanted no part of it. In his mind, he may have thought there was nothing to be gained. UCLA was always perceived as the gold standard and Long Beach just the opposite, a renegade program. But as history has shown, that perception was later exposed with the revelations surrounding the Bruins' close proximity to über-booster Sam Gilbert and his activities in relation to John Wooden's collegiate dynasty.

The allegations against Tark were predictable: "questionable practices" in the form of cash from boosters or special perks or benefits for players. With his hound-dog eyes, sallow face, and "Tark the Shark" nickname, the Armenian proved an inviting target. What the NCAA didn't count on was Tark's razor-sharp intellect, heavyweight circle of friends, and glib media savvy. In interviews he never passed up a chance to raise their bureaucratic hackles. Engaging with charm and wry humor, he made the NCAA look inept and outwitted.

One of the greatest quips in sports history originated when Tark observed: "The NCAA is so mad at Kentucky they gave Cleveland State two more years of probation." That hilarious punch line perfectly captured Tark's central premise: The NCAA punished lesser programs and let the power schools escape unscathed.

My friendship with Tark was the catalyst that drew me into that convoluted web of investigations and allegations, and began my own long, fractious relationship with the NCAA. My first battle in a war I had no idea existed was in 1976.

The NCAA enforcement staff had never paid much attention to me, other than to send a couple of their investigators to observe the Roundball every March or April.

Some years into the Tark investigation, I learned from his attorneys that my name had surfaced relative to a transcript of an interview David Berst, the lead investigator on the Tarkanian case, had done with Rodney Parker, a New York City street ball legend and a friend who never missed the Dapper Dan. A talent scout intimately connected to the East Coast scene, Rodney was an engaging guy with a nose for emerging talent.

Parker had been questioned by Berst about a top high school prospect named Rudy Jackson, a 6'9", 205-pound power forward out of John Bowne High in Queens, New York. Evidently, the enforcement staff considered Parker one of the nefarious hustlers who steered players to major programs—for a price. Parker had brought Jackson to the Roundball Classic in '72. Jackson didn't play in the game, but Rodney wanted to introduce him to some coaches, including Tarkanian. In Parker's deposition Berst asked whether I had provided tickets and money for Parker and Jackson to travel to Pittsburgh and implied I was recruiting him for UNLV. Both spurious accusations. Tarkanian did, in fact, meet with Jackson and Parker, as did many other coaches.

Jackson ended up playing at Wichita State before being drafted in the third round by the New York Knicks.

One player who *did* play in the Roundball became another dot that connected me to the Tarkanian investigation—a Pittsburgh player from Schenley High named Robert "Jeep" Kelley, who ended up enrolling at UNLV, recruited by Tark's assistant coach, Tony Morocco, a childhood friend of mine. Jeep Kelley was a heralded prospect many top East Coast schools, including Maryland's Lefty Driesell, were interested in. The NCAA found it curious that Kelley ended up way out west with Tark.

Up to that point, the NCAA was nothing more than background noise in my mind. Now, I was in their crosshairs and about to experience my first face-to-face encounter.

Enter Hale McMenamin, former FBI special agent.

My first recollection of McMenamin's name was a phone call one evening in April 1976. It was Morocco, now a *former* Tarkanian assistant who'd had a "misunderstanding" with Tark—a falling-out the NCAA hoped to capitalize on.

"Listen, Sonny," Tony said. "There's this guy from the NCAA who's flying in next week. His name's Hale McMenamin. He says he'd be interested in chatting with you after he interviews me. Could you do me a favor and maybe spend a little time with him while he's in town?"

A week or so later, I was on my way to a Howard Johnson's just outside Trafford to meet Tony and McMenamin for lunch. After I hugged Tony hello, he gestured toward the man he'd been talking with while awaiting my arrival.

People in the *Enforcement and Infractions Division* don't fly halfway across the country to meet because they are enamored with me. He was there for one purpose: to try to gather information on Tark. This was a holy mission in service to the NCAA's crusade.

McMenamin embodied the kind of *gravitas* the NCAA needed

to reinvigorate an investigation that seemed to take one step forward and two steps back over five vexing years. He may have captivated his NCAA bosses with a suggestion that they use a common FBI concept called a "full-field investigation," essentially a 360-degree dragnet pulling in everyone related to or associated with the target.

We made our way into a bright Howard Johnson's dining room off the main lobby. I swung into the last booth at the end. McMenamin settled in directly across from me. Tony remained standing, signaling for the waitress. "Okay," he said, "I'll leave you two to talk. I'll be over at the desk when you're through."

McMenamin was fiftyish, gray haired with a plump build. A twenty-five-year FBI veteran, he had only been with the NCAA for about a year at the time of our talk. Any semblance of cordiality dissipated by the time we opened our menus. The waitress's cheery demeanor was the last glint of friendliness for the next hour.

Scanning the menu, I pictured a wall in the NCAA's war room with a photo of my face pushpinned on a corkboard, with Tarkanian in the center and twenty or thirty other faces around him connected by lines of thin yarn. A crime family rogue's gallery of Tarkanian accomplices—all of us guilty until proven innocent.

In theatrical fashion, McMenamin opened the lapel of his sport coat and pulled out a small spiral notebook and a ballpoint pen from an inner pocket. He flipped open the cover to a blank page, making sure to convey that this conversation was on the record. His mission couldn't have been more transparent if "AGENDA" had been stamped across his forehead.

I'd been following the Tarkanian investigation closely in the papers. With the growing popularity of the Roundball, I had done hundreds of media interviews. But this was the first time I'd ever been directly questioned in regard to an NCAA investigation. I felt like I'd been subpoenaed.

"Do you need to swear me in?" I joked.

McMenamin smiled. "No, Mr. Vaccaro. I assume you'll be square with me. We know you're pretty familiar with Mr. Tarkanian and his crowd. You don't mind sharing what you know with us?"

That little dig, "his crowd," immediately rankled me.

"We're in each other's crowd," I corrected him.

I was now part of the evidence chain, one of the data points the NCAA had been amassing for years. Tidbits, factoids, hearsay, rumor, innuendo, testimony—anything that would help substantiate their foregone conclusions regarding Tarkanian. The NCAA has a predilection for foregone conclusions.

McMenamin's demeanor was straight out of the FBI playbook; he might as well have flashed a badge. His tone was purely prosecutorial with the matter-of-fact air of superiority the NCAA likes to project. The frequent emphasis on the FBI was clearly meant to intimidate and to signal the seriousness of the conversation.

"I want to know everything you know about Tark. I want to know what you hear about Tark around town in Vegas, what you've seen," he began. "You know he cheats; I know he cheats. I need you to provide me with full disclosure here, Mr. Vaccaro." He kept referring to me as "Mr. Vaccaro," even after I'd invited him to call me Sonny.

Little did he know he was in for a fight.

"Ask what you want," I said. "But you should know he's an outstanding recruiter and great coach. Gives a lot of kids a chance to play. And let me correct you, I don't *know* he cheats. First question?"

"When'd you two meet?"

"He's been coming to the Roundball Classic every year since '66 or '67. He comes there like all the other great coaches. I've known him for ten years. I visited him at Long Beach State a couple of times to scout his players for the American Basketball Association. And I see him every year when I'm in Las Vegas. I go to practice. I go to games. We have dinner. I know a lot of his players."

McMenamin paused periodically to jot things down.

"You recall a kid named Rudy Jackson?"

"I do. Rodney Parker brought him to the Roundball a few years ago. Good player."

"You paid for the plane ticket, right?" he asked, leading me.

"I only pay for the plane tickets of kids who play in the game, plus their coaches. If I paid for every kid who comes to the game, I'd be broke. The kids come to see the top players."

Possibly, to a former Fed like McMenamin, I already had four strikes against me: I gambled; I spent time in Vegas; I knew more than a few "street guys," agents, and hustlers; and I was a friend of Jerry Tarkanian. Oh, and one more strike: I was Italian, which could have, in his mind, made me the Lucky Luciano or the Tony Soprano of basketball. His contempt was palpable. Because of my heritage, the NCAA may have pegged me as some kind of "made man" in the Mafia. I certainly had friends who knew people. Hell, I grew up next to them in Trafford. The major casinos and poker rooms had a lot of characters in the seventies and eighties. Some were undoubtedly connected. But high school all-star games were nonexistent on the mob's list of priorities. I may have been the "Godfather" of high school basketball, but I was never a mob guy.

"Maybe you can get to the Roundball next year," I suggested in an attempt to break the tension. "See what high school basketball is all about."

"Maybe I will."

Like some kind of special counsel, McMenamin worked through the expected topics. I knew he was asking questions he felt he already had the answers to, trying to ferret out inconsistencies between my answers, Tony's, and the rest of Tark's acquaintances. He reeled off the names of some people in Vegas—UNLV boosters. I knew several of them. I went to Rebels games and occasional practices, and often had dinner with Jerry and his friends.

McMenamin probed the Jeep Kelley vein deeper. Did he get money or a car or a place to live? Personally, I didn't care if he did. "Jeep's a Pittsburgh kid, Tony's a Pittsburgh-area guy," I said. "He's a great recruiter. Why wouldn't Jeep go to a school where Tony coaches?"

McMenamin kept looking to land an uppercut, working one angle after another, entering more notes in his little book. I told him the truth and he refused to accept it. At some point, after the first half hour of his probe, McMenamin finally snapped. He wanted to hear his preferred version of the truth, an *alternative facts* kind of truth. He didn't want to return home empty-handed. As such, he shifted his approach to implied threats.

"I want you to know, Mr. Vaccaro, I have a lot of friends at the Bureau in Las Vegas . . . [a long pause for effect . . .]. We know everything about you. The comped suites, the show tickets, the free flights on those gambling junkets, free meals for you and your friends. Seems as if you've got Vegas pretty well wired."

It was clear he'd done his homework, who knows, maybe through the FBI. An ability to access Bureau information through his network of current and former agents would be a nice gambit to impress his new bosses at the NCAA. But he wasn't bluffing. Life during my months in Vegas after the Roundball each year were, in large part, pure, fully comped fun. I loved being paged at the Sands, walking into a poker room and hearing, "Hey, Son, how ya doin'?" It was perhaps the most carefree and happy-go-lucky time of my life. The bright lights, the big-city allure of Vegas put a spell on me. I got prime tables at great restaurants. I was never more than four rows back for the best shows. At all of my hangouts, I was one of the insiders, *Sonny the basketball guy from back East.* Half the time I was comped at restaurants or showrooms. Now McMenamin loomed as a menacing intrusion on my untethered annual trips.

The threat was no longer implicit but brazen, direct. "If you don't tell us how he cheats, your life is going to be one long agonizing migraine.

"You can help yourself out here," he added, "or we can let what we know about you run its course."

We'd reached the inevitable impasse.

"I'd only start repeating myself," I said, getting up from the table. "If you think of any other questions, you know how to find me."

I wasn't going to fabricate stories for the notoriously petty and prejudicial NCAA.

In the end, the investigation, including associated lawsuits, spanned some sixteen years, including a 1988 case before the Supreme Court. Eventually, Tark cashed a $2.5 million settlement check courtesy of the NCAA. Tortuous as it was, he got the last laugh, including a spot in the Naismith Memorial Basketball Hall of Fame. He deserved to be there not just for his on-court accomplishments but his *in-court* courage facing down an organization hell-bent on destroying him personally and professionally.

Oh, and about three or four years after our meeting at Howard Johnson's, the IRS did come calling and I'll forever believe that my encounter with McMenamin that day was the reason.

When the IRS called me in to clear up "some discrepancies" in my tax returns, they were reading right off Hale McMenamin's notes.

Full disclosure: I had been careless as hell. Ignoring the taxes on those Las Vegas comps was indeed negligent. And there was clearly value to all the freebies I enjoyed. I hired an accountant and paid the back taxes and penalties. I'd always paid my taxes in Pennsylvania but had ignored the Vegas perks in some oblivious mind space that simply didn't register them. Stupid and thoughtless on my part. Thank God I learned a lesson.

I never laid eyes on Hale McMenamin again.

He was the first one from the NCAA who framed Las Vegas and gambling as nefarious. I didn't care one whit what the NCAA thought about gambling, something I had been doing since chapter one in my life, including throughout college. If they like to insinuate that gambling in Vegas is a moral failing, I have no answer to that.

McMenamin never took me up on that invitation to the Roundball. For the next forty-plus years, the NCAA and I remained in one level of confrontation or another—they assumed the odds were stacked in their favor as they continued their yearslong media and back-channel sniping, calling out the effervescent little Italian guy from Western Pennsylvania.

We'll soon see how that worked out.

10

My Alter Ego: Vegas Sonny

Vegas Sonny" is a name Michael Jordan once called me in jest as we played gin on a flight home from Paris long ago. But it accurately captures my persona during my annual extended getaways to Vegas in the sixties and seventies.

Once the Roundball got rolling in the mid-sixties, gambling was still a presence in my life. I recall fondly many nights at the Pittsburgh gambling spot that most-closely approximated the sensibility of Vegas: the Beacon Club in the Squirrel Hill South section of Pittsburgh. I played poker and gin at the Beacon in the sixties. The Beacon was a spot where local personalities like "Bennie Tin Cups," the numbers and sports runner, held court. Other luminaries like Billy Conn, the Hall of Fame boxer who came within a whisker of beating Joe Louis in a 1941 heavyweight title fight, hung out there as well. I became good friends with personalities like "Hambone" and Joe Goldstein. There was an allure to the Beacon. No women were allowed there, period, not even female waitresses. There was a "boys will be boys" Zen to the place built around card games, gambling, and tall tales.

By the spring and summer of 1977, my life centered around two things: One was the Roundball Classic. The other was my now annual trip to Las Vegas, where I spent three to six months totally immersed in the city that never slept. After our initial road trip to Las Vegas in the summer of 1963, my fondness for neon lights and green felt had only intensified. Pittsburgh and Las Vegas became my two epicenters.

After the Roundball wrapped up each March or April (right after the NCAA basketball championships), I morphed into my gambling persona. Strictly compartmentalized from the Roundball, life took on a distinct duality. Basketball in the winter and spring, gambling over the summer into the fall. On the side, I was also acting as a talent scout of sorts, working for a couple of agents out of New York named Steve Arnold and Marty Blackman. They were acutely aware of my eye for emerging talent because of the Roundball and hired me to sign good young players to contracts for the NBA and the American Basketball Association. They paid me a $3,000 commission for every player a team signed.

In 1966, I had started going back and forth on gambling junkets run by a friend and Roundball aficionado named Eddie Caputo, who was flying gamblers in a planeload at a time under contract with various casinos.

In the Mojave Desert I found myself away from the fray, free to be the Vegas Vaccaro in the Rat Pack heyday of Frank and Dean and Sammy, switching easily into my summer persona, the effervescent, free-spirited Italian personality and gambler who showed up every day and night on the Strip or Fremont Street downtown.

Days were spent at the sportsbook, drinking coffee at Churchill Downs in the morning and catching up with sports news by the pool in the afternoon, followed by several hours of poker at the Dunes, before dinner with friends old and new at my regular haunts all across town. After dinner, more often than not, we'd catch a show—Elvis, Sinatra, Louis Prima, Shecky Greene, Wayne Newton, Dean Martin.

I was never a professional gambler, or I'd probably still be doing it. I wasn't a novice either. I played for the challenge, enjoyment, and pleasure of interacting with every personality type one could imagine. And Vegas attracted them all.

Once Jerry Tarkanian became successful as the head basketball coach at UNLV in the late seventies, my local profile rose with his. With a perennially nationally ranked team, Tark was so popular, he could easily have become the state's governor. As a good friend of his, I was known around town and rubbed shoulders with the people known back then as "movers and shakers"—hotel and restaurant owners, businessmen, boosters, entertainers, the right maître d's, and the high rollers—who frequented the casinos and night scene.

If I had to single out two local gaming legends, it would be Michael Gaughan and Jack Franzi. At the time, Michael, son of one of the original casino families, was the owner of the Barbary Coast Hotel and Casino. Franzi, known as "Pittsburgh Jack," whom I'd met through the Roundball Classic, was one of the most respected and influential oddsmakers and sports bettors in history.

At the Barbary Coast, Michael arranged for me to turn a booth in the back of the hotel coffee shop into my Las Vegas home office when I was in town.

Jack Franzi pulled my younger brother Jimmy out of Trafford and into the sports betting world. The characters I met over those years were indelible, many with the charisma of movie actors. "Crazy Louie," Bobby "Hunchy" Berent, Ray "The Spaniard" Vera, Sam "The Spinner" Brown. They were all gambling royalty in Vegas. These were gamblers as colorful as any character you'd see in a movie like *The Rounders*, *A Big Hand for the Little Lady*, or my favorite, *The Cincinnati Kid*.

As a gambler, I never made a killing like players on the World Poker Tour, but I comfortably covered my living expenses, including those occasions when I let my judgment lapse and tried chasing a series of bad hands. I never smoked or drank. Just orange juice, root beer, or Coca-Cola, no ice.

I credit poker for its notable role in my later business dealings. The intuition necessary to succeed at five-card stud or draw poker has parallels that are no less valuable in big-time sports dealmaking. Every facet of my career at Nike and beyond benefited greatly from the insights I developed across the table from extremely talented gamblers. So, to answer a recurring question that has hovered around me during my entire career: Was I ever ashamed of being a gambler? Not for a single moment in my life.

11

The Camp That Fell
Into My Lap

My West Coast "office" during the middle of my Nike years was Izzy's Deli, a redbrick institution at the corner of Fifteenth Street and Wilshire Boulevard in Santa Monica, owned by Izzy Freeman, the beloved "Deli Lama," who closed his namesake gem in May 2022 after a forty-seven-year run. For at least a decade, "The Sonny Vaccaro"—turkey, ham, Swiss cheese, and coleslaw on marble rye—was one of the Jewish deli's overstuffed celebrity sandwiches.

In 1983, the year before the Jordan era was to begin, and coming off yet another resounding Roundball success, I met Arthur "Chick" Sherrer, a Princeton graduate from Chicago, and Gennaro DiMassa, a coach from Mary Star of the Sea High School in nearby San Pedro, for lunch at Izzy's.

Sherrer, a Northwestern University English professor, had founded the AFBE Camp a year earlier, the capital letters short for Athletes For Better Education. The educational component was the thing that differentiated the camp from every other summer camp at the time. Its very location, on the bucolic campus of Princeton University, added an even greater sense of legitimacy to its educational/basketball duality.

At AFBE, the campers rose early in the morning for four hours of academic studies with accredited instructors who taught a curriculum that prepared them for the vagaries of college life: writing papers, navigating a college library, SAT and ACT test prep, verbal and math skills, sports psychology, dealing with the media, and other skills they would find rather useful as they progressed through college and the years beyond. The academic side was taken seriously. If an athlete slept through or otherwise missed a class, he didn't get playing time later that day as a reminder not to make the same mistake again.

As we enjoyed our soup and sandwiches, Chick began his pitch. "Sonny," he said, "we'd like Nike to come on board. Sponsor the camp. Maybe help us out with some shoes, uniforms, bags for the kids, money for expenses."

Chick gave me a full rundown—the history of the camp, the background of his partners and top administrators. I knew I was going to get involved. I loved the academic concept. I was delighted to extend Nike's presence even deeper into high school basketball. I viewed AFBE as the perfect pairing to the Roundball.

Right after lunch, I called Strasser up in Oregon to get an approval. Rob said he'd have to run the idea by Knight. The next day, as was often the case, Nike was the main sponsor of AFBE. 1984 was our first year.

Apparently, though, I didn't get the full story on the state of AFBE from Chick and his partner that day because a year later I got a call from the facilities manager at Princeton who coordinated events at the university.

"Mr. Vaccaro," she said. "I wonder if I can talk to you about a problem that's come up with the AFBE Camp."

In a subsequent letter, the administrator went on to explain that AFBE had failed to make their contracted payments to the university. They owed Princeton five figures in overdue rent and expenses. She wanted to know if there was any way to resolve the matter—or the camp was effectively dead.

Once again, improbable as it may seem, opportunity came knocking. I knew the event was structurally sound and wasn't about to let it go under.

I called Strasser to secure the funds and approval necessary to acquire the event and make it a Nike property. But Nike lawyers got cold feet. They were skittish about potential liability issues and lawsuits if a camper or coach got injured. When Nike declined ownership, I quickly pivoted and convinced the company to pay off the Princeton debt and put the camp under new management: *me*. I changed the name to ABCD Camp, which stood for Academic Betterment and Career Development.

With the Sonny Vaccaro association and Nike as the sponsor, the ABCD Camp immediately had the glowing aura of a winner. There was no doubt in my mind I could make ABCD the number one camp in America. Since I knew just about everybody who was anybody in high school and college basketball, staffing was a breeze. In no time we had applications flooding in to be a part of the staff each year, the camp quickly becoming one of the profession's best networking opportunities for moving up the coaching ladder.

By 1985, the transition to ABCD was complete. The excitement surrounding Nike's signing of Michael Jordan to a record-setting endorsement deal and his subsequent visit to ABCD after his sensational rookie season, along with the afterglow of winning the 1984 Olympic gold medal, put the camp on the map.

Word that Michael was going to be at ABCD had spread like wildfire. We assembled the players in the bleachers in Dillon Gymnasium at Princeton and the place lit up in a raucous welcome of cheers, yells, and applause the second I escorted Michael through the gym's double doors. The staff and I tried to calm the campers—to no avail. I introduced Michael in a sea of yelps and cheers. Every kid there had hopes of emulating him in one way or another in the not-too-distant future.

"How y'all doing?" Michael asked.

The response was instant, exuberant. He gave a short speech, his words to the campers tracking closely to themes often attributed to his success: "If you're trying to achieve, there will be roadblocks. I've had them; everybody has had them. But obstacles don't have to stop you. If you run into a wall, don't turn around and give up. Figure out how to climb it, go through it, or work around it."

As usual, Michael preferred to make his most profound impression on the court.

"Anybody here think you're ready to take me on?"

He turned, signaled one of our coaches to toss him the ball. The staff and coaches were just as excited by Michael's presence as the teenagers. Jordan casually dribbled toward the basket and threw down a thundering dunk to get the activities off to a proper start. He then coolly shot a couple of three-pointers as the kids yelled their appreciation. He walked back to the bleachers and asked no one in particular, "Who's first?"

Hands immediately shot in the air. He picked three or four kids to come onto the court, kids who had brought their own brand of local swagger to ABCD. Michael was unmoved by how young or excellent or self-assured any opponent might be: *Jordan never let up.* He treated all comers equally. His intent at all times, in any context, was domination.

Being the consummate good sport, he let each kid have the ball first. Perhaps one or two of them harbored illusions of dunking on Jordan. Not a chance. Michael *never* allowed anyone to get the upper hand. He blocked shots or stole the ball, and turned those steals into ferocious statement slams. He made short work of each camper, one by one, demonstrating the futility of their efforts. Still, the thrill of having that opportunity to go one-on-one with "His Airness" would be a treasured memory for life. Michael signed autographs, shook hands, spoke a few more words of encouragement at the end, and waved goodbye.

Over dinner before he left town, I thanked Michael for being there and his response was pure Jordanesque: "No problem, Sonny," he said.

"It was actually fun. Every one of those kids think they've got it. I just like showing them how much they've gotta improve. Hell, I'm still improving."

In short order our annual showcase became a summer fixture—a rite of passage—on the calendars of every college-bound kid and basketball program in America. In turn, ABCD evolved into a family reunion. From coaches to scouts to fans to fathers and mothers who brought their sons, if you were part of the game in any way you were in the stands watching the future of college and pro basketball. Over five straight eighteen-hour days, ABCD celebrated, evaluated, scrutinized, and marveled at players who were the future. From noon to long after dark the games went on and on and on, interspersed with drills, technique development, and offensive and defensive strategies.

Everyone who loved the game showed up in Princeton, and later at Fairleigh Dickinson University in Teaneck, New Jersey. Each year close to three hundred Division I and II programs registered at the door. A gallery of the game's greatest coaches—Jim Calhoun, John Thompson, Bill Self, Rick Pitino, John Chaney, John Calipari, Mike Krzyzewski, Jim Boeheim, Roy Williams—made the pilgrimage year after year along with their top assistants. We kept a running list posted on the gym wall of collegiate programs and pro team representatives in attendance so that players would know who was watching from up in the stands.

Previously, player rankings were determined by outsiders in magazines such as *Parade* and *Street & Smith*, based on a summary of the player's local high school performance. In actual competition, best-against-best matchups simply didn't exist—not on a grand scale—minus the rare occasion two top players happened to play in the same high school district.

The '84 ABCD Camp in Jadwin Gym was the first time where a player's performance in head-to-head competition would determine who would be anointed the number one player in America—against up to 170 of the other most highly touted players across the nation. From then on, the camp MVP was considered the consensus number one high school player of the year.

The inaugural 1984 ABCD unequivocally anointed Ben "Benji" Wilson from Simeon Vocational High School in Chicago as number one. Benji showed greatness on the court and adjusted easily to the sudden fame. He was acknowledged as an incomparable talent not only by scouts, but also by his peers.

The ultimate high of his ABCD crowning was replaced a few months later by the deepest sadness imaginable—his tragic, senseless death in a teen gun battle that had absolutely nothing to do with Benji.

The last time we talked was November 19, three days before Thanksgiving, just two days before his murder. Imagine—*knowing what you know today*—that there had never been a LeBron James. Imagine that Kobe Bryant had never played in the NBA. Or Magic Johnson. Or Steph Curry. Or Larry Bird. Or Bill Russell. That's how I look back on the senseless murder of Benji Wilson on a freezing, sunny Chicago afternoon, steps up the street from Simeon Vocational. As he lay on the sidewalk, bleeding to death minute by minute, his coach Bob Hambric rushed to his side from up the street, telling him to "hold on, hold on, we're gonna get you to the hospital, help is on the way, Benji."

Wilson was transported by ambulance to a small local hospital that was not set up to handle such a serious trauma. By the time he reached the hospital, it was approaching an hour since the two bullets had lodged in his chest and side. Without critical care staff or expertise, Benji was left on a gurney in the emergency room, awaiting a surgeon, the wounds to his aorta and liver spilling the life out of him. He fought to survive, his brain robbed of critical oxygen and blood needed to remain conscious. With a prognosis that would more than likely render him brain-dead, if he survived at all, his mom, Mary, a nurse herself, had to confront an unspeakably agonizing decision.

Benji was taken off life support and pronounced dead early the next morning—twelve hours or so before Simeon's first game of the season.

I regarded Benji Wilson—then and now—as a future great in the game. In talent, ambition, and charisma, he measured up to the greatest of the players I had witnessed in high school. A pure talent abruptly deleted from a sky's-the-limit future in a stupid, tragic, horrendous teen-on-teen street confrontation. Barring injury, he would have become an all-star and possibly a Hall of Famer; he could have changed the fortunes of a franchise.

If.

If he had gone to lunch with his teammates that day instead of walking north on Vincennes arguing with the mother of his child.

If there hadn't been a .22 pistol in the pants of a high school freshman with something to prove.

If he had been anywhere else in the world that afternoon.

This loss resonated beyond boundaries for me. I'd glimpsed the rarest of phenomena the previous summer at ABCD: a superstar on the cusp.

Maybe because of that phone call from Benji Wilson two days earlier, this tragedy hit me hard. His death remains a scar on my soul.

There's heartache and heartbreak and mindless violence in the world, but until it happens to someone you've grown to love and respect like Benji, the impact seems removed, impossible to process. Benji brought that grief full force to me.

Benji was a prodigy, a talent on his way to basketball renown. *Tragic* doesn't capture the enormity. The word "incomprehensible" was conceived for just such a moment. A life destined for extraordinary accomplishment ripped from our collective consciousness.

At the funeral in Chicago, it was estimated that nearly ten thousand mourners streamed by Benji Wilson's casket, including the Reverend Jesse Jackson, state legislators, and the entire city council. The event was covered extensively by the media. Gang arrests went up dramatically in the aftermath.

At Simeon, the top player each year wears the number 25 to honor his memory. Derrick Rose was one of those players. Simeon named the gym in Benji's honor.

There was a negligence lawsuit filed against the hospital and the city of Chicago following Benji's death.

Mary Wilson and the estate settled the lawsuit prior to a trial. One of the pivotal aspects of the suit was determining what Benji's value might logically have been had he gone to the NBA. He was surely destined for the league—more than likely as the number one pick.

In trying to assess the final settlement amount, the insurance company brought in Marty Blake, one of the NBA's greatest scouts. He later became the NBA's head of scouting. Along with him was Bob Gibbons, a high school talent evaluator who annually produced a list of national player ratings in grassroots basketball.

On Mary's recommendation, Chris Wallace and I were the expert witnesses for Benji's family. Chris Wallace was the founder and editor of *Blue Ribbon College Basketball Yearbook*, which was considered the Bible of talent assessment in the country. Chris went on to management positions with the Boston Celtics and Memphis Grizzlies.

In the pretrial depositions, Blake and Gibbons contended that there was no way you could determine what a high school player's contract value might be in the NBA—and therefore, his value was essentially next to nothing.

In my deposition, I took a stand in direct opposition to their contention, giving my best estimate for how much a player of Benji's prodigious talent could expect to earn as a player and star endorser for a company like Nike. My statement included mention of the contract we'd signed earlier with Michael Jordan. Chris and I always had the mindset that you could read talent in the game of basketball early in life. Each of our depositions were in complete alignment with that belief. There will never be a doubt in my mind of the potential Benji possessed.

Thank God, Benji's estate prevailed in the case and Mary Wilson was able to go on with her life financially secure after having to bury her seventeen-year-old son.

. . .

AS USUAL, AT ABCD, I had my hands on the wheel. If my name was attached to an event I wanted control. So every year, I took the time to curate a list of potential stars with information gleaned from a nationwide network of high school and summer league coaches. ABCD was built from the ground up to showcase *their* talents; they were the sole reason there was an event.

In celebration of that undeniable fact, we did everything we could to make sure that the campers were welcomed, acknowledged, well fed, and entertained. To support the latter, we built a players' lounge each year, outfitted with video games, foosball, air hockey, soft drinks, snacks, TVs, couches, and music. After hours, the kids could hang out, text, make phone calls, and bond with new friends. We gave them breakfast, lunch, and dinner.

For the adults, I kept a hotel suite that served as headquarters and remained busy for what seemed like twenty hours a day. The doors were always open for the staff and visiting coaches to network, entertain friends, reconnect, and catch up with parents and past players. That was the adult social hub, the place old friends wandered in and out of to see one another. There were very few moments of those five days in July that the room wasn't humming with conversation, laughter, hugs, handshakes, questions, directions, dinner recommendations, talk of a player's exploits. In a way, ABCD served as grassroots basketball's annual "Old Home Week."

Once we moved the camp to Fairleigh Dickinson, we initiated an all-star game played on the final afternoon of camp. After the last regular game was complete, the four side-by-side courts were cleared and the gym reconfigured into a single spotlight court. A small group of trusted coaches and I picked the all-stars and eventual MVP.

Top players were dressed in brand-new all-star uniforms, hand-made in Italy by Nando DiBiase, one of the most original designers of basketball apparel. The uniforms, one-off originals—never to be duplicated—became cherished keepsakes for the players. The buzzing stands filled to capacity with fans, players, coaches, scouts, parents, sisters, and brothers. Past stars of the camp such as Kobe Bryant, Stephon Marbury, and Tim Thomas invariably showed up to see and anoint the next "It" athlete. One of the biggest surprises for the players was the year Shawn Carter, better known as Jay-Z, was spotted sitting behind the bench. While I certainly knew who Jay-Z was, I had no idea what he looked like. Gary Charles, my assistant camp director, took me over to meet the superstar rapper. I introduced myself and thanked him for joining us. He said, "I know who you are, Sonny. I've been here a few times."

Made my day.

A dear friend of mine, Jimmy Bukata, along with his son, Kevin, came every year to ABCD once we moved the camp to Fairleigh Dickinson. Jimmy had an insatiable sports appetite and it fit perfectly with his professional life. As an executive with a company called IMG/TWI, Jimmy was considered a pioneer in the sports production field. He had traveled to all corners of the globe producing sports events, from marathons to the America's Cup sailing races. One night after the games, he stopped by and offered to help in any way he could. He mentioned to me that the all-star game would make for good television . . . so that's exactly how the ABCD Camp All-Star Game made it to broadcast television, coordinated by Jimmy. After the first year CSTV (College Sports Television, later purchased by CBS Sports) decided to chronicle the camp and create a documentary that explored certain players' lives and the pressures and high stakes young athletes faced during those five intense reputation-defining days.

. . .

IN THE END, IN THE world of elite-level grassroots basketball, the ABCD Camp—like the Roundball Classic—had no equal. The camp was *the* litmus test, the fire-and-brimstone cauldron for youth talent on the rise, the ultimate proving ground for fifteen-, sixteen-, and seventeen-year-old kids, a pressure-packed audition that would define their hopes and dreams. For its entire twenty-three-year run, an ABCD invitation was like a trip to the Oscars—the most coveted acknowledgment the nation's emerging stars hoped for to cap off their high school careers.

When players from all over America and later the world received that offer in the mail or in a personal phone call from me, they knew their practices would not end when the high school season was over. Instead of taking the summer off, their drills became more focused, more intense. The days leading up to ABCD were when they fine-tuned their game, stayed at the gym extra hours, got up at dawn, took five hundred shots, practiced their moves, worked on their other-hand dribble. They knew they were about to enter a world where reputations were made—or might never recover. The biggest names were always there to prove they deserved their national rankings; the young guns desperate to establish their rep. The caliber of talent was nonpareil. At home, a kid might be "The Man" on the local scene; at ABCD *every opponent* would be that man or more. Every kid could handle the ball, make plays, block shots, guard you, ultimately *test* your mind and mettle.

A quick scan of the names that emerged onto the national scene at ABCD are players who went on to impact the game. More than a few ended up—or will end up—in the Basketball Hall of Fame: Kobe, LeBron, Tracy "T-Mac" McGrady, Paul Pierce, Mike Conley, James

Harden, Derrick Rose, Kevin Love, Russell Westbrook, O. J. Mayo, DeAndre Jordan, Greg Oden, Danny Green, Eric Gordon, Stephon Marbury, Tony Parker, Chauncey Billups, Billy Owens, Carmelo Anthony, Jermaine O'Neal, Antonio McDyess, Chris Webber, Juwan Howard, Jason Kidd, Alonzo Mourning, Shawn Kemp, Jalen Rose, Joakim Noah, Chris Bosh.

The players who had higher aspirations took seriously their date with destiny over those five days in July.

I can't remember the name of the writer who once referred to ABCD as "the Portal of the Immortals," but I think that description summed it up quite nicely. The ABCD Camp set a standard that elevated the entire summer basketball scene. In my post-Nike era, it became the focal point of my player-by-player combat with the Swoosh.

But first let's revisit the genesis of Jordan.

12

The Genesis of Jordan

The Guy Who Signed Michael Jordan at Nike

That succinct description has probably been used 85 percent of the time by hosts who have introduced me to audiences, in media interviews, and at speaking engagements dating back to the mid-eighties.

While I'm proud of dozens of other things I've accomplished in my career in basketball and sports marketing, that's the caption that stuck.

The phrase isn't exactly accurate.

My signature wasn't on the contract.

I wasn't sitting at the Palmer House Hotel on Monroe Street in Chicago on the afternoon of October 26, 1984, when a then twenty-one-year-old Jordan signed what was the richest endorsement contract in NBA history before heading to Chicago Stadium to play his first-ever NBA game against the Washington Bullets that night.

Actually, the signing itself was very low-key. Two Nike guys and an agent, a deal done. It wasn't the kind of splashy staged PR / photo op with a big media presence we witness today. It was a formality. Nothing more, nothing less. All the details were settled a few weeks before.

Actually, "The Guy Who Signed Michael Jordan" should more

properly be stated "*The Guy Who Bet His Job on Getting Nike to Sign Michael Jordan.*"

. . .

GETTING A ROOMFUL OF SMART, opinionated, thoroughly unconvinced executives to risk an entire year's marketing budget on an unproven college underclassman is the feat that resulted in one of the sports world's most legendary coming-of-age stories—Nike's.

So, if you'll indulge me, let's revisit how *a committed Adidas fanatic* from the University of North Carolina, who had played most of his life in Converse high-tops, and who had never worn Nike shoes a single day in his life, somehow ended up signing with a company he knew next to nothing about.

It's a story that deserves to be told as it actually happened. And it begins with a single shot that won a national championship.

The 16-Footer Jordan Sank in My Mind

On March 29, 1982, I was sitting in the stands, mid-court at the NCAA national championship game in the cavernous Superdome in New Orleans. By this time I was heading into my fifth year with Nike. Our presence in college basketball was preeminent and still growing. The Swoosh was well-represented, with four teams in the Sweet 16, and we were elated to have Georgetown, the flagship Nike program featuring John Thompson and his star center, Patrick Ewing, in the title game.

On the other side stood Dean Smith's North Carolina team, wearing their traditional Converse, featuring James Worthy, Sam Perkins, and a relatively unknown freshman guard averaging 13.5 points per game, Michael Jordan.

That was the season Jordan made *The Shot*, the final shot of his freshman year. The basket that put the Tar Heels ahead after fifteen lead changes.

With millions of eyeballs on him besides my own, five feet inside the sideline, with North Carolina behind by one point, Jordan had called for the ball—twice. With about fifteen seconds left on the clock, point guard Jimmy Black passed it to him on the left wing. In a single motion, Jordan caught the ball, sprang skyward, and coolly launched a clean, sixteen-foot, high-arcing jumper.

The Shot that put the Tar Heels ahead 63–62.

You might be interested to know that the clearance a basketball has when passing through a standard eighteen-inch iron rim is just over two inches on either side. If there had been only a half inch on either side, that shot would still have been all net.

A defiant, calculated, confident teenager—unfazed by a moment of gigantic sports-crazed magnitude. No hesitation. *You dare me? Watch this.*

In a redline-pressure moment—*with a championship at stake*—Jordan wanted the ball.

It wasn't so much the shot itself that had impressed me—but his complete command of that moment.

Jordan captivated. *He separated himself.*

With the final shot of his first collegiate season, I unknowingly glimpsed the future of Nike. When that connection came to be two years later, Nike would never again take a back seat to any other rival in athletic gear.

That shot, now embedded in history, taken by a fearless eighteen-year-old, was the spark that ended up becoming a $5-billion-a-year business empire. Brand Jordan was born before he even knew.

Though I had no idea at the time, the frozen glimpse of that jumper would serve as the foundation of my bedrock belief in the kid at a meeting two years later in '84.

The Sagging Swoosh

That Jordan phenomenon deserves to be seen in historically accurate terms. For perspective, it's helpful to understand the reversal of fortune Nike was suffering at that time.

Beginning around 1982, the company had been utterly outplayed by Reebok and its CEO Paul Fireman. Nike was losing shelf space and market share because the company's marketing analysis mavens somehow missed the women's aerobics craze that took the fitness world by storm. Aerobic shoes were squarely in Reebok's wheelhouse and had propelled them ahead of Nike. We were now the *former number one*.

Watching Reebok storm past Nike had both Knight and Strasser unnerved.

Dismissive of Fireman and the entire Reebok brand, Knight was apoplectic that people he so fully disrespected had outflanked him. When Knight was angry, much less humiliated, the alarm level at Nike shot up to DEFCON 1.

With Nike having just suffered the worst quarterly loss in the company's history (a sixty-plus percent drop), more than three hundred employees were let go ("planked" in Nike slang) in what was called the "Saint Valentine's Day Massacre." Company stock had tumbled to less than ten dollars a share. To dump inventory, Nike held a fire sale for more than *$25 million in shoes* for a buck or two a pair. The mood was dismal, the prospects of retaking the industry lead dark. It was going to require some *reversal of fortune*—some moon shot change in strategy—to get the swagger back in the Swoosh.

With Nike hemorrhaging, and to further cut costs, Strasser had called the entire corps of agents representing Nike athletes to the company headquarters in Oregon and informed them that they were canceling dozens of NBA endorsement deals, and that they were free to pursue offers from any shoe brand they wanted.

Obviously we still had to have a pro basketball presence, but the cost-benefit equation determined that we no longer felt the need to have two or three players on every bench in the league.

After a paltry selling season, with company finances sagging, Knight and Strasser arrived at a figure of $500,000 for pro basketball signings that season—an amount down considerably from the previous year.

It was in that crisis atmosphere that Strasser invited me out to Oregon in the early spring of 1984, ahead of that year's NCAA men's basketball tournament, to weigh in on the company's high-level predraft pro-player endorsement discussion. Our cratering finances dialed-up even more pressure on the signing decisions for that year. Strasser wanted everyone's input.

That I was even invited to the meeting was an aberration. I was Nike's "grassroots and college guy"—the architect of those programs. Pro endorsements were out of my lane. Because I'd been in the game for over two decades, and with the collegiate basketball program I led dominating the category, Strasser considered me the company's resident expert on up-and-coming players at multiple levels of the game.

When Nike management types gathered to brainstorm back then, they often went "off campus." The venue for the meeting was a place I called "the Mansion," an imposing residence in an upscale Beaverton neighborhood. I don't know whether Nike owned it or if it was a fancy day rental, but it was far enough away from the frenzied energy of the offices to keep us laser-focused on the matter at hand.

Also in attendance were Howard White, who was a field representative responsible for Nike's eastern NBA clients; Jack Joyce, a former criminal attorney who now served as an executive overseeing company finances and advised Knight on legal matters; and the irascible Howard Slusher, a sports agent and salaried advisor who had become one of Knight's closest confidants in recent years.

White helped Strasser unload his ever-present easel from the back of a powder-blue Jeep Wagoneer with fake wood paneling that he'd inherited from a family member. Once inside, as Strasser set up at one end of the room, I grabbed a can of Diet Coke for him and a root beer for myself from the fridge.

After the usual pre-meeting jibber-jabber we settled into the oak-paneled great room, where it felt intentionally chilly, reminiscent of the dire situation Nike was in.

Strasser took a deep breath and called us to attention, "Okay, guys, it's no secret. We're in deep shit. Today's topic: how we're gonna dig ourselves out. I want to hear from every one of you before I get back to Phil with our collective genius."

Underneath the title "Options" written in marker at the top of the easel, he began scribbling out the names of the available players. It's astonishing now to think about all the talent in that '84 class, which included Charles Barkley, Akeem (later Hakeem) Olajuwon, Sam Bowie, John Stockton, Kevin Willis, and Sam Perkins, among others, including a junior from North Carolina by the name of Michael Jordan.

Strasser turned to Slusher first. "Howard, your thoughts?"

Considered one of the top sports agents in professional basketball and football at the time, Slusher was known for shoving negotiating terms in your face and daring you to turn him down. One of his go-to tactics was holding players out until a team relented, many times well past training camp and into the season.

For reasons few of us understood, he had become one of Phil Knight's chief advisors. It was never completely clear to any of us how Slusher had become so essential, other than Phil seemed to have a penchant for hiring lawyers in executive positions. Slusher's influence was even more mystifying because, in his capacity as an agent, his job was to get his clients the most money possible, including from Nike. Which meant Nike had to negotiate with one of its own employees to get contracts done for various elite athletes—something I'd never seen before or since.

Adding to the mystery, Knight and Slusher were polar opposites and could scarcely have been more different. For one thing, Phil hated negotiating and Slusher thrived on it. Phil was reserved, introspective; Slusher bombastic and confrontational. Phil was trim and athletic, a runner. Slusher was, to be kind, heavyset. They were so close that some folks considered him Knight's alter ego. Slusher and Strasser were constantly vying for predominant influence with Phil.

As the interloper in that meeting, I was uncharacteristically reserved for the first half hour or so, waiting for my chance to weigh in. I listened quietly as Slusher argued for signing a pool of players. He debated the issue with supreme self-assurance, outlining the benefits of signing the four to six top prospects in the draft. It was understood—without any vocal objection—that he could possibly represent some of these same Nike recruits shortly. Several of his clients were already under contract at Nike—having survived the purge—but no one at the top-tier endorsement level of a Magic or Bird on the Converse roster.

We discussed theoretical dollar figures necessary to sign the various athletes, which team they'd end up with, and who among the names on the easel had the most fan appeal. When Olajuwon's name came up, I pointed out that he would likely be the number one pick and go to Houston, a city with minimal media cachet. As great a player as he was, his fan base would likely be regional, not national.

Slusher and Strasser were enchanted by Auburn's "Round Mound of Rebound," Charles Barkley. But they wanted to spread their risk by signing Kentucky's Sam Bowie too, who was being targeted by the Portland Trail Blazers and could very well become the local Nike star.

When the time came for me to speak, I went on record in immediate and direct opposition to Slusher's "spread the risk" plan.

"So what about you, Sonny?" Strasser turned the floor over to me.

"Just tell me what we're doing here?" I began. "Are we going to get kids that are very good, or go for the one player who has already proven he's exciting enough to capture America's imagination?"

My opener didn't come out the way I'd intended, but the image of *The Shot* had never escaped my subconscious.

The indelible footnote I had internalized that night had three key components: *advanced athletic skills, killer instinct, and stone-cold determination.* I told them it would be a colossal mistake—a missed opportunity—if we lost the chance to sign Jordan, even though he was still a junior. What I didn't say was that I only had a hunch he would decide to turn pro. North Carolina had very few players ever declare early for the draft, and Dean Smith wanted Jordan to return for his senior season. If he went back for his final year, my arguments would be on ice for another year.

"Put the whole $500,000 behind Jordan," I said. "And if there's anything left over, put it in advertising. That list of players up there, they're all good. Jordan is a game-changer. And he'll be an even bigger hero when he wins a gold medal this summer."

Some of my gambler instincts were in play. I was going "all in" the way a poker player does when he looks at his hand, sensing it can't be beat.

As their timid "what-ifs" were bandied about, I dug in. The argument became animated. My insistence on *Jordan alone* was the antithesis of Slusher's plan. And the talk took on a different tone—heated, argumentative. And at that time, the highest amount any Nike athlete had ever been paid was $100,000. Most player contracts were in the $35,000 range and only two athletes, Moses Malone and Paul Westphal (a Slusher client), were at that $100,000 level.

"That's kind of a risky proposition," Slusher objected, looking straight at me. "What if the kid gets hurt? What if he's on the bench for a couple of years? We'd look pretty naive, wouldn't we? Besides, I don't know if Knight will risk it all on one athlete."

He was trying his damnedest to sow doubt, to accentuate the risk in an attempt to faze Strasser. Neither of us were giving an inch.

"Look," I responded, "the whole point is to get a player that can energize the fans, not just in one city, but the whole NBA. *This kid is that player.* A kid like this doesn't come along every year. He's going to be something special in the league. Put everything on him. Let's get it right this time. If you don't, you may never get another one like him."

I rested my case. There was nothing more to add.

The room fell silent.

I could feel the intensity as everyone stared at me.

Strasser broke the silence.

"Would you bet your job on it?"

I didn't hesitate. "You're damn right I will. *And you can hold me to it.*"

No decision was made that afternoon, but the opposing points of view were now on record. In truth, *neither side* of the argument mattered until the final decision was blessed by Mr. Knight. Strasser met with him the next day. As he recounted to me over several phone calls, everything discussed was presented.

Strasser, who trusted my instincts, remained firm on my recommendation to put the whole budget behind Jordan. Peter Moore, Nike's brilliant creative director, was in agreement as well.

"You're sure about this, Rob?" Knight asked. It was clear from his tone that Slusher's position had already made its way to him.

"Yesterday at the meeting, Sonny bet his job on Jordan. He believes the kid's *as good as the best he's ever seen.* I'm trusting him on this one."

Knight, still unconvinced, got up to signal their meeting was over. "You both better be right." Which was Knight-speak for I'm leaving the final decision to you.

Strasser went with Jordan. And Nike was in no position to be wrong.

With the decision set, now all we had to do was convince Michael Jordan that Nike was a better choice than Converse or Adidas.

To do that, I first had to meet him.

13

Sonny, Meet
Mr. Michael Jordan

My first introduction to Michael took place in Los Angeles just before the 1984 Summer Olympics during the pre-Olympic training camp. The US men's team was practicing on the West Coast at the time, and it couldn't have been more than a week or ten days from their first game against China on July 29 at the Forum in Inglewood.

I wouldn't have been able to contact Michael directly, so I asked George Raveling if he could introduce us. Raveling was one of three assistant coaches on the Olympic basketball team and the head coach at Iowa. I had known George for nearly twenty years dating back to the Roundball. We were so close he had stood as the best man at my wedding to Pam three months earlier at Caesars Palace in Las Vegas.

George had attended the Olympic tryouts and witnessed the roster cut from the initial three dozen candidates down to twenty, and then to the final sixteen. It was a team so rich in talent that future Hall of Famers Barkley and Stockton didn't make the cut.

. . .

A LUNCH WAS SET AT Tony Roma's rib place in Santa Monica. This would be the first and perhaps only opportunity I'd have to demonstrate to Michael the size and seriousness of the commitment Nike was ready to make to him. Just talk, nothing on paper. The whole thing was hush-hush because the Olympic team's head coach was Bobby Knight, known for his quick temper and low tolerance for outside distractions. Had he known Raveling was arranging for one of the players to meet with a shoe company representative, he might well have fired him on the spot.

The meeting itself would never have taken place had it been anyone else at Nike making such a request. David Falk, Jordan's agent, would never have allowed his firm's new client—who had decided to turn pro early—to meet anyone without being present, and I firmly believe he had no idea this clandestine lunch was taking place. George wouldn't have consented to bring Jordan to a meeting with anybody but me. Even at George's urging, Michael would not have gone to Santa Monica to meet just any marketing guy, regardless of the brand. Jordan knew who I was from the Roundball and college basketball, even though we had never met.

Rudy Washington, a friend from the Roundball days and an assistant coach at USC, kindly agreed to drive Jordan over from the team hotel to the restaurant where George would meet up with us.

I was already seated when Rudy led Michael past a row of booths to the table. George followed them in and, after we hugged, introduced me to Michael.

"Sonny," he said, "meet Mr. Michael Jordan."

Jordan seemed a bit reticent. Still, we shook hands and I hugged him hello too. I thanked him for making the effort and taking the time to meet with me. Washington, who had brought along a friend, excused himself to dine in another room at the restaurant.

Over a meal of baby back ribs, an onion ring loaf, and a round of soft drinks we small-talked about basketball, how George and I knew each other, and also how I *hadn't* chosen Jordan for the Roundball Classic. In truth, none of the dozens of coaches and local scouts in my nationwide network had touted Michael to me. He didn't have a Chicago / Philadelphia / LA / New York City reputation. Our major stars, Patrick Ewing and A. C. Green, were far and away better known as America's top prep players in 1981. Although Jordan had been selected for the McDonald's All American Game, he wasn't even the North Carolina Player of the Year that year; a 6'4" sharpshooting guard named Buzz Peterson, another UNC recruit from Asheville, North Carolina, had won it.

As the meal moved on, Michael's reticence subsided and we settled into an easy rapport as I began explaining the dimensions of the package he could expect.

George listened intently, but never uttered a word.

I knew Michael would take what I was about to say seriously, since I was already the face of Nike basketball and Nike's presence had grown dramatically in recent years. He understood the importance of our meeting.

Looking him straight in the eye, I laid out our vision and made our position clear: Nike *wanted* Michael. I told him that no other company his agent had spoken with would be putting more money and resources behind him. No one was going to make him the centerpiece of their brand marketing the way we would.

It certainly didn't hurt that around Los Angeles the atmosphere was crackling with Nike's "I Love LA" campaign created by Strasser, Moore, and Chiat/Day advertising. Nike was not the official shoe sponsor of the 1984 US Olympic team—Converse was—but in pure renegade style, Nike had hijacked the airwaves and mindset. Freeway billboards—even the sides of entire buildings—featuring pictures of Oakland Raiders' cornerback Lester Hayes, Olympic sprinter Carl Lewis, Dodger star Pedro Guerrero, and tennis great John McEnroe were ubiquitous in spreading Swoosh imagery everywhere. The world's Olympic moment was Nike's "I Love LA" focal point.

I made clear how you couldn't go anywhere without seeing Nike's marketing power in plain sight.

"That kind of firepower will be behind you," I told him.

We spoke of a *signature shoe* envisioned by Strasser and Moore, custom designed for him, which would be vastly different from anything else in the NBA, plus a complete line of apparel and products emblazoned with the Jordan name, and—not inconsequentially—how he would have a percentage of every shoe sold.

"Michael, you'll be a *partner* in the business," I said, sketching out a vision of the future and a package of star perks that no other company would even consider.

And I made him this solemn promise: "I will never lie to you—not about what I said today or about anything we might do in the future."

Kids who played for Dean Smith knew when they were being told the truth—Smith was a man revered for his unassailable integrity. Though I did most of the talking, I could see in Michael's face that he was filing away every last detail. Falk had probably already told him at least four companies were interested, but I'm not sure he expected the kind of deal I had laid out.

Still, this was just the opening hand; to his credit, Michael wasn't hiding any of his cards. He told me up front, "I'll listen, Mr. Vaccaro, but you should know, I'll probably sign with Adidas. I've never worn Nikes. If Adidas even comes close, I'm going with them."

I had assumed his bias would be in favor of Converse and was caught off guard by his personal preference for Adidas. But Michael was unequivocal in stating his admiration and preference for the brand's shoes and clothing. He was taken with their craftsmanship, European leather, and continental styling. He considered their product line "classy," especially after wearing Converse's old-school utilitarian gear during his entire time at Carolina and years before. More than once he repeated, "I've never been in anything Nike."

The contract highlights and Nike pitch were important, of course, but that was only half the purpose of the meeting.

What about Jordan the person? His personality? His persona?

The answers came easy: self-assured and smart. Though soft spoken, he was clear and direct with an easy laugh. His confidence and personal bearing were powerful, and I took an immediate liking to him.

Roma's was only a first-time lunch, but the young star and I had an effortless connection. I had interacted with a thousand young athletes from grassroots events and college basketball. I knew when the rapport was genuine.

The only hint of dissonance and caution in the whole conversation was Nike, the company. He wasn't "anti" per se; he just had no frame of reference. At the time Nike was a running and track shoe company to much of the world.

As we finished up, I turned to Michael and said, "Look, just keep an open mind. That's all I ask. I'll send you a couple of pairs of Nikes. Not the custom kind we'll make for you, but you give 'em a try."

I knew I had piqued his curiosity. And I'd given this soon-to-be-rookie a rock-solid package and talking points he could also use to bargain for a better deal with Adidas.

Standing out front on Santa Monica Boulevard, I hugged both Michael and George goodbye. "I'm pretty sure Adidas isn't going to come close to what Nike is putting on the table," I told him. "But if they do, it was still great meeting you, young man. God bless."

Heading back home along Lincoln Boulevard, I had a good feeling. I knew Adidas wasn't going to approve a contract bigger than Kareem Abdul-Jabbar's for a rookie who had yet to play in a single NBA game, no matter how infatuated he was with their brand. And Jordan having played most of his life in Converse gear—he'd been wearing their shoes on national TV for the last three years—it was possible they'd make a play too.

When I called Strasser to fill him in on my impressions, he was also surprised by Michael's affinity for Adidas. He could have believed it if Jordan had been a track or soccer star but basketball? I understood where the quality angle was coming from and explained it as well as I could: "This is about more than the money, Rob. Jordan doesn't know Nike from 'Schmike.' Knight *has* to approve a Jordan shoe. If we don't go all in, his shoes are gonna have three stripes on 'em in October."

And if we did get him to another meeting, Strasser and Moore would need to put on a presentation unlike anything they'd ever done before.

We hung up, with Strasser saying he had to go down the hall to share the news with Knight.

. . .

A MEETING WAS SET WITH David Falk at L'Ermitage hotel in Beverly Hills, where the Nike contingent had been staying during the Games, to officially lay out the terms of the deal.

Falk was keenly aware Strasser had moved the goalposts to construct an unequaled deal for his client. An all-encompassing package like no contract the company had ever offered an individual athlete. Eye-popping, incentivized, and guaranteed.

Since I was the only person from Nike that had actually met Michael, Strasser thought it would be a good idea to have me in the room. And I already knew Falk from negotiating John Thompson's singular Nike agreement a couple of years earlier.

Strasser was the only one presenting. The contract structure and the main terms were already handwritten in marker on his customary easel set up at the far end of the room—figures, timelines, bonuses. One by one, he reviewed each item. I'd done my share of negotiations with universities and coaches, but those were far less intricate than this five-year deal—one that would make Jordan one of the world's richest athletes at that time.

The terms: a signing bonus of $200,000; a base guarantee of $250,000 a year for five years, with a $25,000 bump each year thereafter; a twenty-cent-per-pair royalty on a Jordan line of shoes; and $1 million in year one in marketing and advertising.

The official shoe name: Air Jordan.

Check, check, check, check.

One by one the details were agreed to by the affable Strasser and the canny Falk, who knew he was sitting on a gold mine.

"Good," said Falk. "Thank you for putting together a solid offer, Mr. Strasser."

Handshakes.

"Now let me just make a quick call, and I'll be right back."

Naturally, our offer would be leveraged to his client's benefit with our competitors—especially one in particular.

Falk left the room, presumably to make a call. Less than ninety seconds later, he returned and suggested a couple of changes to the deal.

"Nothing major," he assured us.

"Whoa," Strasser commented, only half joking. "We shook hands two minutes ago, and you're changing the deal already?"

Falk requested a larger signing bonus: $250,000 instead of $200,000, with a base guarantee of $300,000 up from a quarter million. In exchange, he was willing to accept a lower royalty amount, ten cents per pair instead of twenty. Falk wanted a larger cash outlay up front, with a smaller royalty on each pair of Jordans.

Strasser, with a mind that could crunch numbers in milliseconds, jumped at the revised terms.

"We can do that."

Taking more up-front cash and lowering the royalty—"Falk's Folly," as Strasser called it—would cost Jordan millions of dollars in revenue. Obviously, Falk didn't think Nike would sell a record $125 million worth of shoes in year one. Frankly, none of us could have envisioned the record-shattering sales Air Jordan would generate for Nike.

Before we could get Michael up to Oregon, we still needed Knight's *final* final blessing. He was often known to be mercurial—it was never final until it was *final*.

If Jordan didn't turn out to be everything I'd laid my job on the line for, Knight was certain to make *me* pay up.

14

Packer Seals the Deal

As internal discussions at Nike continued into the second week of the Olympics despite my assurances and the fact that Strasser was solidly behind the strategy, Knight remained unconvinced. He had heard the logic, but logic often wasn't enough. Even with Jordan's accomplishments, including winning a gold medal, Knight just wasn't there yet. A high-risk single-player endorsement strategy of this size and scale, with so many guarantees written in, was something Nike had never done for anyone in any sport. There was still some convincing left to do.

It didn't help matters that Howard Slusher was constantly in Knight's ear pushing for the usual multiplayer pool of endorsements. We needed some new element of persuasion to get Phil across the finish line. That's when Strasser called to float an idea.

"Son, Knight's still ping-ponging on Jordan," he said. "And I'm getting a queasy feeling about it. We should bring in an independent opinion, one free of Nike's internal squabbles. You think you can get Billy Packer to drop by our Olympic party to sit down with Phil? I don't want to see this fall through."

"Absolutely, whatever we need to do. I'll see if I can get hold of Billy now."

Packer was an award-winning college basketball analyst with CBS Sports, and we had been friends for more than a decade. He had been a terrific basketball player at Wake Forest, then an assistant coach before going into broadcasting. Widely regarded as one of the most astute analysts in the business, Packer had already done nine straight Final Fours for CBS, where he would go on to do a total of thirty-four before retiring in 2008. Billy was just the fiercely independent, deeply respected voice we needed. I made a couple of calls to see where the CBS folks were staying, and reached him at his hotel.

"Billy, it's Sonny. I need a favor."

"Sure, what's on your mind?"

"I want to know if you can meet with me and Phil Knight tomorrow night and give him your take on Michael Jordan. You think you can free up some time for an early dinner at our big beach party?"

Packer checked his schedule and agreed but not before throwing up a caution flag.

"Son," he said, "I'll give him honest answers to honest questions." Making sure I understood he wasn't going to lobby for me or anyone else.

"Good. That's all I'm asking, honest answers to honest questions. Besides, it'll be one of the best post-Olympic parties in town."

To quell his apprehension, Knight needed to hear about Jordan's potential upside from one of the foremost authorities in the game, someone free of Nike's ever-present politicking.

Packer was what you'd call our "river" card in poker. He was our final play and we desperately needed a face card to win this hand.

Our pitch had come down to a single closing argument. A sit-down with Billy Packer where Knight could ask him anything he wanted. Where Knight would learn what I already knew: Packer doesn't bullshit.

...

NIKE'S POST-OLYMPICS PARTY TOOK PLACE on Monday, August 13, the night after the closing ceremonies. Never a company to approach any event halfheartedly—especially one within the worldwide glare of the Olympics—the Nike Beach Bash was an over-the-top soiree held at the Sand & Sea Club, a private venue on a wide stretch of sand, half a mile north of the Santa Monica Pier. Twelve hundred invitations went out to star athletes, Olympics luminaries, A-list studio execs, media and entertainment personalities, and guests from all over the world to a seaside celebration dressed to impress. An invite to the Beach Bash was no less coveted than an invitation to one of those exclusive "be-there-to-be-seen" after-Oscars parties during the Academy Awards.

The *Los Angeles Times* reported that more than double the twelve hundred showed up.

I don't recall whether Randy Newman (who wrote "I Love LA") was there, but a couple thousand other noteworthy industry, sports, and Hollywood types certainly were. Pam and I met Billy in the lobby of the Sand & Sea as a swarm of post-Olympic partiers began streaming into the club.

We hugged hello before Pam excused herself, then made our way to a private dining area for what turned out to be perhaps the second most important meeting of my career.

Knight arrived a short while later, casually attired in a Nike Swoosh cap, T-shirt, and as always, sunglasses, indoors or out.

I introduced him to Billy. This was the first and only time they would ever meet.

"Why don't we check out the buffet before we sit down," I said. "I promised Billy dinner. And it just so happens that Mr. Knight has graciously provided a beachside barbecue for a few thousand of his closest friends."

Laughing, the three of us headed to a food fest that seemed to go on for blocks—pan after pan of ribs, hot dogs, burgers to order, barbecue, and more. We chose beverages and a selection from the sumptuous spread, beating a crowd that was quickly beginning to surge. We returned to the private room and took our seats to dine and discuss Michael Jordan.

While most ordinary people are in awe of Phil Knight, on a national scale Billy Packer was far more renowned than Knight. He was not intimidated in the least. As anyone who knows Packer can attest, he has a bracingly forthright demeanor and refuses to pull any punches. While affable and the consummate communicator, he doesn't seek approval nor attempt to curry favor. He wasn't there as a cheerleader for my Jordan push. He was there as a personal favor to provide an honest evaluation. Unbeknownst to Billy, he would be weighing in on one of the most crucial marketing decisions Nike would ever face.

I set the stage, focusing the topic on Jordan, and then turned the floor over, allowing the conversation to take its own course.

"So, Billy," Knight began. "Our Italian friend here is pretty well convinced Jordan is the only person in the draft we should do a deal with. I know the kid's good—maybe even great. Do you share Sonny's confidence that he's *that much better* than the other top kids in this draft?"

Knight wasn't naive. He knew Jordan had gone number three in the draft to Chicago, after Olajuwon and Bowie, and had just won a gold medal three days earlier. He probably heard that Jordan had been named both the *Sporting News* and AP College Player of the Year and honored as the Naismith and Wooden College Player of the Year.

Taking a sip of his drink, Packer paused a beat.

"Look, I'm not here to tell you how to run your business, or to push you one way or the other," he said. "All I can do is answer your questions."

It certainly didn't hurt that Packer had broadcast many North Carolina games over the previous three years and knew Jordan's skill set about as well as anyone in the world. He'd watched him develop his skills, style, and basketball IQ into an All-American career. He spoke evenly and thoughtfully, with obvious insider insight. He interspersed his answers with entertaining stories and relevant observations that kept Knight's kinetic mind as engaged as I'd ever personally witnessed. I think he found Packer amusing, refreshing, and deeply informed.

Packer recounted the first time he'd ever seen Jordan play in the McDonald's All American Game in Wichita, Kansas. Still in high school, he put up thirty-plus points in that game, a record. But the MVP went to Adrian Branch, whose coach, Morgan Wootten from DeMatha Catholic High in Maryland, just happened to be one of the MVP voters, along with John Wooden.

Billy described how distraught both of Michael's parents were—they felt the MVP award should have gone to their son. Packer joined them for a cup of coffee later that night and helped settle their emotions, reassuring them that in just a few months Michael would be at North Carolina strengthening his game with one of the greatest coaches in the country, Dean Smith.

Between questions, Packer related other stories, including one about Jordan's final game in college against Indiana in the '84 East Regional semifinals. UNC was the best team in the country, and maybe the best team Dean Smith had ever coached. The opponent was a very average Indiana team by Bobby Knight standards.

The evening before the game, Coach Knight had run into Packer and asked him, "Can we beat Carolina?"

The answer was an emphatic "No."

Coach Knight proceeded to describe his plan: "No backdoor cuts and Jordan can have as many jump shots as he wants beyond eighteen feet, but we aren't going to let him get inside. I don't think he can consistently shoot the ball."

Coach Knight turned out to be quite the prophet, as well as a basketball coach. Final score: Indiana 72, Carolina 68. Jordan shot six for fourteen, scoring just thirteen points in a huge upset, the last college game he ever played.

Packer explained to Phil, "With Dean Smith's team concept and style of play, you never saw any player, including Michael, take over a game. Though you could see every aspect of his play get better defensively and offensively, you didn't get to see how his killer instinct drove him, all the hours he put in to improve his weaknesses."

That wasn't the end of the Jordan–Bobby Knight saga. Coach Knight told Billy during the Olympic trials how impressed he was with Michael's work ethic, attitude, defensive instincts, and willingness to listen. His only shortcoming was a shaky outside shot against European zone teams—but he was certainly going to make the team.

Billy went on to explain that, as part of their training, the US men's team had traveled the country to play a series of pre-Olympic exhibition games against an assortment of NBA all-stars. There was no national broadcast; however, a local Indianapolis station invited Packer to announce the games for them, starting with the second one in Greensboro, North Carolina.

Packer met with Coach Knight the day before the game, along with the legendary Hank Iba, who had coached at Oklahoma A&M (later Oklahoma State) for over three decades and had two NCAA championships to his credit. When the topic of Jordan came up, Bobby Knight confided, "I love the kid, but he still can't shoot the ball."

Packer watched Jordan play a solid all-around game that night, and the Olympians had now won twice against the NBA stars.

Next up, Indianapolis. A crowd of more than twenty thousand showed up in basketball-crazy Indiana. Packer did the play-by-play. Even with some of the NBA's top stars on the floor, including Larry Bird and Magic Johnson, the Olympians won again. Jordan put in a good performance, but didn't take over the game. He had obviously earned a spot on the team, but didn't dominate the trials. His best shooting performances were twenty-five and twenty-seven points in a couple of mid-July games. Good, but not great.

Packer said what changed his mind about who Jordan *really was* happened during the fourth exhibition game in Milwaukee. "Oscar Robertson had coached the NBA stars that night and there was a 'no-foul-out' rule put into effect. The embarrassed NBA players turned the game into a slug fest."

He recalled the exact foul that unleashed the Jordan-to-be: "Michael drove to the basket and Mike Dunleavy hit him across the face, opening a cut. Knight went crazy. I never saw him that angry. Despite assistant coaches C. M. Newton and Mickey Donoher holding him back, Knight was thrown out of the game. That set the stage for the first time I ever saw Michael Jordan out-and-out dominate. When play resumed, he took over the floor and everyone who was there got their first look at who *he really is*—including me."

Almost as if he had rehearsed the anecdote, Packer reached the finale. "I'll wrap it up with one last story," he said, leaning back in his chair and staring straight at Phil.

"I was at this dinner just before the final NBA–Olympic team game in Phoenix. Bobby Knight was one of maybe ten people there. He looked at me with that stern expression of his and said, 'Packer, let me tell you about your boy Jordan: *He's going to be the greatest player to ever play this game!*'"

I hadn't heard that story before. My heart practically leapt out of my chest.

I said nothing.

Though there was little variation in Phil Knight's facial expressions and maybe an occasional nod, he was clearly engaged. Even his closest friends (among whom I was never included) knew it was impossible to presume the inner workings of Knight's opaque and inscrutable mind.

In the end, Packer arrived at his bottom line: "You guys are gonna do what you're gonna do, but Sonny's right. You can't miss with Jordan."

There wasn't a single thing I could add, no reference point I could provide that would be more compelling than what Packer had laid out. He was my last "corroborating witness."

I couldn't help but feel that over the course of that dinner Phil came away believing a Jordan signing wouldn't end up a disaster. He had the opinion he needed and I had hoped for—from an outside expert with no bias. After that it was in God's hands.

Soon the chairman excused himself to bask in the afterglow of Nike's promotional triumph at the Games. Packer and I chatted for a few moments and I thanked him with a hug. Few favors in my life have been more appreciated, or had more major ramifications over time.

Heading outside together, we heard a shout from somewhere in the throng.

"Billy! Billy!"

"Looks like you've got a few hundred fans who want to say hello."

"Sonny, I'll catch up to you later," he said, and made his way to a group of broadcast associates.

I looked around and saw Pam and Strasser standing next to a deck rail chatting. Down the beach to the left, the giant Ferris wheel on the Santa Monica Pier pierced the pastel clouds with neon reds, blues, and greens as a mid-August sunset melted into the horizon and soon gave way to a show of stars over the Pacific.

None of us underestimated how critical this informal Packer–Knight tête-à-tête would be. As I hopped up the steps, Strasser set his glass down.

"C'mon already. Let's hear it . . . how'd it go?"

"Your idea was a stroke of genius, my friend. Billy couldn't have been any better. Phil took in every word. The only other person on earth who might have come close was Dean Smith."

I filled them in, extolling Packer's deft handling of the meeting, believing that Knight's due diligence effort was now complete.

The three of us hugged, the nervous air of the past week giving way to an almost giddy mood of relief, joy, and hope.

"You gotta take me to meet Packer," Strasser said, as the ebullient giant pulled me into his barrel chest and kissed me on top of the head. "I want to give him a hug myself. We might've pulled this off after all! Nothing Slusher can say is gonna make Phil forget a single story Packer told!"

Later that night, amid the moonlit mass of partiers, Strasser and I ran into each other again. He had already spoken to Knight about the Packer meeting and had been told, "It went pretty well."

That's nearly effusive in Knight-speak.

His final verdict came down the following week in Beaverton.

"Do what you want."

He was at no point wildly enthusiastic about Jordan, but at least he wouldn't be an impediment.

We still had work to do. NBA training camps opened at the end of September, and we wanted Jordan signed in time for the season six weeks or so later. It was time to finalize Nike's richest contract offer ever and put the final presentation together. All that was left to do was get him and his parents to Beaverton.

. . .

THE CATCH IN ALL THIS shoe drama came down to one fact: The ball was in Adidas's court. If they produced a package that approached Nike's, the other brands would be also-rans, including us.

Falk met with Adidas, who saw no particular value-add in Jordan. They assured Jordan's agent that Michael would be treated like all the other premier athletes on their roster—no worse, but no better. He would be paid in line with their current stable of basketball stars, which included Abdul-Jabbar, Dr. J, and Magic Johnson. Adidas had no intention of doing anything out of the ordinary for him. They couldn't afford to alienate future Hall of Famers on their roster by paying an untested rookie more than twice as much as their own stars.

The 1968 **Roundball Classic**
in the Pittsburgh Civic Arena—another sellout

Shaquille O'Neal

slam-dunks at the 1989 Roundball Classic.

Campers and staff at the 1968 Sonny Vaccaro's
Big Ten Basketball Camp
in Seven Springs, Pennsylvania

Marino
Parascenzo
of the *Pittsburgh Post-Gazette*, 1980

Sonny with his brother, Jimmy, and his parents, Margaret and Natale
(*left to right*)

Sonny
welcoming
Georgetown's
John
Thompson
to Nike
headquarters

Sonny
introducing
Billy
Packer
as a guest
speaker at
ABCD Camp

Howard White and Michael Jordan join Sonny and his wife, Pam
(*left to right*), for dinner in Paris, August 1990.

Sonny and Michael Jordan at a Nike party—
Michael's mother, Deloris, sits across the table

Nike Coaches' Trips

Jerry Tarkanian of UNLV, Sonny, and Jimmy Lynam of
St. Joseph's University (*left to right*)

Cotton Fitzsimmons of the Phoenix Suns, Sonny,
P. J. Carlesimo of Seton Hall University, and Phil Knight,
the CEO of Nike (*left to right*)

Dick Vitale, Leonard Hamilton, Rick Pitino, Sonny, Ralph
Willard, and Bill Raftery (*left to right*)

Sonny's *60 Minutes* interview with Lesley Stahl

Sonny (*center*) presenting the 1990 Hoops That Help donation check to *Full House* actor Dave Coulier (*left*) and Comic Relief founder Bob Zmuda (*right*)

Cotton Fitzsimmons, Michael Jordan, George Koehler, and Jimmy Valvano (*left to right*) at the filming of *A Comedy Salute to Michael Jordan*, Chicago Theatre, July 1991

Sonny *(center)* with Tracy McGrady *(left)*
and Kobe Bryant *(right)* in 1997

Rob Strasser
in the attire that perfectly
captured his style

Peter Moore in his studio
reviewing designs for his
Sonny Vaccaro Academy idea

Helping Keep Kids
in the Game.

At the podium, Dick Vitale speaking at Magic Johnson's
Roundball Classic Banquet in Detroit, 1999

Magic Johnson at the Roundball Classic
with Sonny and his wife, Pam

At the ABCD Camp, Sonny (*left*) speaking with
Mike Krzyzewski of Duke (*center*) and Roy Williams
of the University of North Carolina (*right*)
during a break between games

Sonny speaking to a roomful of campers and coaches during the 2005 ABCD Camp in Teaneck, New Jersey

Pregame photo with **LeBron James** before the 2003 Roundball Classic at the United Center in Chicago

LeBron James helps sell out the United Center
for the 2003 Roundball Classic.

2003 Roundball Classic Banquet with Gloria James,
Pam Vaccaro, and Sonny (*left to right*)

Sonny delivering the 2016 Mark H. McCormack Sport Innovators Lecture at the Isenberg School of Management, University of Massachusetts Amherst

Sonny with his friend Rob Ades in 2005

Sonny, Michael Hausfeld, and Ed O'Bannon (*left to right*) during a break in the O'Bannon trial in Oakland, California, June 2013

Matt Damon with the character he plays in the movie *Air*, June 2022

Sonny chatting with Ben Affleck, Chris Messina, and Matt Damon (*left to right*) during a break in filming on the set of the movie *Air*, June 2022

At the 2023 NBA All-Star Weekend in Salt Lake City, Sonny flanked by Ben Affleck (*left*) and NBA Commissioner Adam Silver (*right*)

Pam
and
Sonny
courtside at
the NCAA
Final Four

Checkmate.

No factor was more significant in Jordan's path to Nike than Adidas's colossal miscalculation—an unforced error by the German company that effectively shut the door in Michael's face.

To this day, it's still hard to believe the *improbability* of that particular set of dominoes falling perfectly into place: the personal affinity that grew out of my lunch meeting with Michael in Santa Monica; the marketing and financial proposal masterminded by Strasser and Moore (and their trust in my judgment on Jordan); how effectively Packer had explained Michael's rare drive and competitiveness.

If you were to factor in all the ramifications—financial, marketing impact, brand perception—that happened subsequent to that initial lunch at Tony Roma's, I would argue that it may well have been one of the top five most impactful business meetings in sports marketing history.

Still, let's put what happened in perspective: Michael Jordan didn't sign with Nike because of Sonny Vaccaro or any other person—not a lawyer, coach, friend, or even his wonderful parents. Nike can thank Adidas for sending him our way. As Michael himself has said on many occasions, "Adidas helped me make the right decision. They made it easy for me."

Nike's meteoric turnaround with the arrival of Air Jordan sparked a seven-plus-year joyride in my career. Once Michael put his signature on that contract, my role at Nike evolved from running the college and grassroots programs to also include duties with a single professional athlete on the company's roster who would go on to become the most famous athlete on earth.

I doubt you'll find a single person who would dispute the fact that Nike's eventual *$5-billion-a-year* partnership with Jordan—as an athlete, a personality, and a brand—was one of the landmark moments in sports marketing history.

I certainly never have.

15

In the Vortex of Jordan Mania

From the mid-eighties into the early nineties I found myself caught up in the blaze of Jordan glory.

Week by week, month by month, the Jordan persona exceeded anything any other athlete had approached—was more than any of us had anticipated. When Michael was in front of a crowd, he sent an electrical charge through the room or arena. Being Nike's point man in basketball, I was no stranger to media attention—but Jordan's ascent kept me in the orbit of the brightest spotlight any player had ever commanded. Magic and Dr. J were electrifying as well, but something about Jordan inspired a kind of hyperadulation reserved only for the most famous entertainers and rock stars. In forty years, I'd never seen an athlete so completely capture the popular imagination. Even beyond his on-court exploits, which themselves were unparalleled, Michael had captivated the culture—kids to seniors, men and women, Black and white—on a mythological level. It would not be an overstatement to say that he was elevated to the status of an immortal in the making. Never more so than in December 1987, when cameras rolled for the Air Jordan commercials that Spike Lee directed and starred in, like the famous "Yo, Mars Blackmon here. . . . Money, it's gotta be the shoes" campaign. All our rivals made television commercials. The only ones anyone remembered were Spike's and Mike's.

Like my relationship with Strasser, what Michael and I shared transcended business. We had what one might regard as a code, an unspoken trust that allowed us to communicate with unedited candor. My allegiance to Michael superseded even my loyalty to Nike—and he knew it. To make sure his interests were protected and that Nike's MVE (most valuable endorser) was accommodated in every possible way, Strasser had assigned both Howard White and myself to ensure a path of least possible resistance for Michael's every appearance. (Howard's bond with and loyalty to Michael evolved into a deep, lasting friendship.)

My rapport with Michael was unique in that I had no formal job description on file with human resources back in Beaverton. It existed in a free-form space known as simply "Michael and Sonny." I was his de facto sounding board regarding virtually every significant project related to the Swoosh.

When the occasion or event was pertinent to expanding the Jordan footprint, Michael and I talked. We often exchanged random ideas on things that came up in "civilian" life. (He conferred not just with me; Michael sought opinions from a relatively small group of people he felt he could trust.) Our talks were always informal, generally off the record, mostly on the phone.

Michael insisted to me he wasn't "owned by Nike." He wanted a separate group of income streams under his own control, reserving the right to invest in non-Nike opportunities.

By 1991 and the first of the Bulls' six NBA championships, every major company in America knew what *Sports Illustrated* knew. In his *SI* article, senior writer E. M. Swift wrote, "It is one thing to be admired across the racial spectrum; Jordan is idolized. On the court, he is a paradigm of grace, excellence, sportsmanship and imagination. Off the court, he exudes family values and clean living. He is more superhero than superstar to vast segments of the American public."

As a result, a river of commercial opportunities flooded Jordan's way through David Falk. The Jordan franchise, the name value, was a treasure trove of current and future riches. Knight, Strasser, and Peter

Moore chafed at the thought of having to share their megawatt media asset with a growing list of outside sponsors—but they had no choice. A gold-plated sponsor list that grew to include Hanes, Gatorade, Ball Park Franks, Wheaties, McDonald's, Rayovac batteries, Coach leather products, Oakley sunglasses, and Bijan cologne. I'm not sure anyone else has ever graced the cover of five different Wheaties' boxes.

Keep in mind Michael basically had only the summer off, especially when the Bulls charged deep into the playoffs. That three-month window before training camp opened in September was the only time Michael was available for appearances, photo shoots, commercials, and goodwill tours. To preserve Michael's mystique, Strasser and Moore limited his availability to signature events designed to generate a huge marketing or PR return for Nike, like his rare appearances at the rollout of the first Air Jordan sneaker in April 1985.

I was with Michael during the promotion at Macy's flagship store in New York City's Herald Square, between Thirty-Fourth and Thirty-Fifth Streets, a photo op that resulted in near pandemonium after Macy's ran an ad in *The New York Times* announcing the launch.

The department store aisles overflowed with fans, parents, and giddy kids packed between displays and sales counters, anxious to breathe the same rare air as Michael, fidgeting, pushing, yelling his name as they waited to meet the human highlight machine, the embodiment of a cartoon sports superhero, security doing its best to maintain a semblance of order. To his credit, Michael was there for hours, refusing to leave at the scheduled time. He kept posing for pictures and signing autographs till the end, not wanting to disappoint his adoring fans.

"It's okay, Sonny. I got this," he said, waving me off when I implored him to call it a day. Hours earlier, Macy's allocation of Air Jordans had sold out in a matter of minutes (as they continue to do to this day).

A year or so later I was sharing some recent Las Vegas stories with

Michael during the offseason. I'm not sure if he'd been to Vegas before, but he mentioned he'd like to visit. He wanted to bring his father and a couple of friends with him, play some golf. Though I had wound down the frequency of my trips to Las Vegas at the time, my younger brother Jimmy was the head of the sports betting operation at the Golden Nugget downtown, which had recently been bought by the developer and casino impresario Steve Wynn, in the midst of building the astounding three-thousand-room Mirage resort with its jaw-dropping volcano fountain on the Strip. I got Michael and his group complimentary suites at the Nugget for three or four nights, during which time they enjoyed some shows, gambling, and sumptuous meals. I introduced Michael to Steve and Elaine Wynn as he developed a love for the city and its glamour, gambling, and golf that extends to this day.

. . .

IN THE SPRING OF 1991, with the Bulls on their way to a franchise record sixty-one regular-season wins, Bob Zmuda and Caroline Thompson, two of the top people with Comic Relief, approached me with a great idea: Let's put together a TV special to honor Michael. By this time, I had already worked closely with Whoopi Goldberg, Billy Crystal, Robin Williams, and the Comic Relief crew on several "Hoops That Help" sold-out televised basketball games featuring teams like UNLV, Notre Dame, LSU, Michigan, Michigan State, and Arizona, with all the profits going to Comic Relief and other charities designated by the head coaches. But this would be a *first*—there had never been a TV special devoted to a single athlete. I loved their idea.

I asked Michael if he'd be interested in being featured in a Comic Relief special. He laughed me off.

"Sonny, you know I'm no comedian," he said. "I can't tell a joke worth a damn."

In talking Michael through the idea, I assured him he wouldn't have to tell jokes—he'd just be Michael Jordan, the basketball player. The comedians would do all the acting and comedy—he'd have a string of easy laugh lines, no big monologue, no heavy lifting. All he had to do was be himself in a series of skits. We'd shoot the special at the historic Chicago Theatre downtown.

Despite his hesitation, I persisted, proposing the idea to his wife, Juanita, who was the executive director of Michael Jordan Charities, and she lit up, excited that the proceeds would be evenly split between their charity and Comic Relief. Juanita finally convinced Michael to relent.

That's when I sprung the quid pro quo on Michael: He'd have to agree to guest-host the season-opening episode of *Saturday Night Live* in return for *SNL's* production help on the special to get it scripted and produced for prime time.

The president of NBC, Warren Littlefield, was so excited to have the Jordan special he placed it on the network's prime-time schedule to air during September Sweeps Week. We settled on the title *A Comedy Salute to Michael Jordan*.

NBC recognized the huge potential of combining charity, comedy, and by far the biggest star in sports. *SNL* and the Comic Relief people helped assemble a tremendous cast, the best comedy writers in New York, and secured Billy Crystal as the host. The show was filmed in front of a sold-out live audience in July 1991. I received an executive producer credit on the special—but waived any producer fee.

The superstar cast—all performing pro bono—included Crystal, Spike Lee, Jane Curtin, Chris Farley, Patti LaBelle, Will Smith, Siskel and Ebert, and virtually every cast member from *Saturday Night Live*. George Wendt and John Ratzenberger from *Cheers* reprised the famous "Da Bulls" skit as blue-collar Chicagoans in tandem with Michael. It meant the world to us that Jimmy and Pam Valvano and our dear friend Phoenix Suns head coach Cotton Fitzsimmons and his wife, JoAnn, showed up in support of the event.

At the end of an almost indescribable night I was surprised and flattered by Michael's shout-out after he took the stage.

"When Sonny first presented this idea to me a few weeks ago, I thought—me comedy? It could never happen. But here we are. What did you get me into, Vaccaro? Seriously, folks, thank you. I've had a great time and I'm even more happy that all the fun has been for a good cause."

After conquering his preshow jitters, he enjoyed every moment of that evening as did Pam and I, sitting in the sold-out audience, a few rows behind Michael's mom, Deloris.

The only downside of the night was the disheartening fact that only one person from the Nike family attended. A week before the broadcast Nike was the only one of Michael's many corporate sponsors not to have made a donation—in the end contributing just $25,000—far less than anyone had anticipated.

A Comedy Salute to Michael Jordan was among NBC's top-rated comedy specials in 1991 when it aired at 9:00 p.m. on Friday night, September 20, 1991. Eight days later, September 28, Michael became the first athlete to host *Saturday Night Live* on the premier of season 17, a broadcast that ranked as one of the top ten rating's hits for *SNL* for many years.

. . .

LITTLE DID I KNOW AT the time, but a year earlier I had taken what would be my final trip with Michael, a ten-day jaunt in late August 1990 through several European countries as part of a Nike promotional tour prior to the 1992 Olympics in Barcelona, Spain.

Michael and Howard White, who had flown to Europe ahead of us, had spent a few days exploring Milan, Italy, before meeting Pam and me in Frankfurt, Germany, for the first Nike-centric stop on the tour.

Because the Gulf War had started less than a month earlier, safety was of paramount concern, to the point where several Nike executives canceled plans to attend the tour. Concerned for his family's safety, Michael had Juanita and their young son stay in the States. Howard's wife and daughter also dropped out. What had begun as an entourage of fifteen or sixteen quickly dwindled down to the four of us. For security reasons, Pam, myself, Howard, and Michael flew in chartered private jets to each European destination.

In Frankfurt, an exhibition game took place at Rhein-Main Air Base, where Michael did a celebrity turn on teams comprised of soldiers and airmen. As the time for tip-off approached and warm-ups were wrapping up in the gym, Jordan suddenly disappeared. A few minutes later I found him sitting alone on a wooden bench in a makeshift locker room with a towel draped over his head. His head bowed, seemingly in deep thought.

I barely nudged his shoulder. "Michael, you good?" I asked. "The game's about to start. . . ."

It was there I witnessed Michael's pregame ritual for the first time. He said, "Sonny, gimme five or ten minutes alone. I'll be out."

Michael was in a trance, psyching himself up before playing a meaningless game against a team of rank amateurs. There could be no better reflection of his true character than that moment: No matter the competition—NBA playoffs or a group of military men— you show up and never let up. As Michael once said, "I play to win, whether during practice or a real game. And I will not let anything get in the way of me and my competitive enthusiasm to win."

He played twenty minutes with both squads, scoring twenty points for each. After the game, the crowd poured onto the floor to pat Michael on the back, shake his hand, touch the towel around his neck, and shout his name. With the help of some officers, we managed to spirit him out of the gym, still in uniform, to the waiting limo outside. Jordan mania was no longer an American exclusive; Michael was now an international sensation.

From Frankfurt, we jetted seven hundred miles south-southwest to Barcelona for the central purpose of the trip: Michael was the guest of honor at an important groundbreaking of the future Olympic Stadium. With six other dignitaries arrayed in a line, Jordan thrust his shovel into the dirt with a luminous smile as three dozen photographers captured the moment.

The Barcelona events came off without a hitch. Michael first made a visit to the league offices of Spain's professional basketball association, the ACB. From there, we visited the site of the Olympic Village, then on to a press conference packed with local and international media. After lunch we took a tour of Nike's new offices in Barcelona. In the evening, Michael was one of the judges—and obviously the most influential—at a slam dunk contest with young Spanish league stars attempting to impress one of the great dunk artists of all time. Once again, Michael was the featured athlete in an all-star game with teams featuring top stars in the ACB. Honoring the ACB was a stroke of promotional genius for Nike. Michael played a half with each all-star team, scoring thirty-seven points on the night.

From Spain, we hopped up to Paris, where Michael did an exclusive interview with the European edition of *Sports Illustrated*. Though Nike had placed three-story-tall billboard images of Air Jordan in soaring poses on various Paris buildings, he went unrecognized on the streets as we went sightseeing along the Champs-Élysées and through the Montmartre district before standing awestruck in the Cathédrale Notre-Dame.

At dinner one night in an elegant Parisian restaurant, Michael was suddenly struck by the realization that Rob Strasser and Peter Moore were noticeably absent from this trip, no longer part of his team at Nike.

"We're all that's left of the original group," he said to Howard and me. "We're the last of the Mohicans. We've gotta stick together. You guys can't leave Nike until I leave."

"We're like the Three Musketeers and Rob's our D'artagnan," I said.

A momentary shadow of sorrow fell over our table lamenting Rob's absence. That dinner and *that* moment still touch me to this day.

Four days later, our group was in Munich for Europe's most important sports shoe and apparel market, the ISPO fair. Again, Michael drew a tidal wave of interest from shoe industry insiders. His whirlwind appearances helped increase Nike's international presence far beyond anything Phil Knight and others had anticipated. Upon our return, the European orders for Air Jordan shoes and apparel began pouring in.

By day ten of our trip, we were dragging a bit and anxious to return to the States. The return flight occasioned the longest card game of my life, a gambling marathon Michael had insisted on.

For the entirety of the nine-hour Chicago-bound flight, Michael and I played gin. At his suggestion, the ante was a hundred dollars a hand.

Estimating four minutes or so a hand, the math worked out to around fifteen hands per hour. I couldn't afford to risk losing at least fifteen hundred bucks an hour, or more if the cards didn't turn in my favor.

Jordan was a multimillionaire back then (a billionaire now). I was something along the lines of a dollar-aire.

"You know," I told him, "there should be odds on this card game, an over-under. This can't be no-limit."

"A limit? C'mon, you're *Vegas Sonny*, the hotshot gambler."

I told him $1,000 was my limit. As I shuffled, we made a couple of rules about meals and bathroom breaks. Then the longest cards marathon I'd ever been a part of began.

With the exception of a twenty-minute break for the first-class dinner, the flight was essentially nonstop cards from takeoff until touchdown. After each hand, we scrupulously marked down the winner, filling page after page in a Delta airlines notepad, one column for Sonny, one for Michael. Sometimes I'd be ahead by ten hands, sometimes Michael, an occasional verbal jab at one another, but mostly just dealing and playing in silence.

As the plane pulled up to the gate at O'Hare, we played the final hand. I had won—by exactly one hand. With a smile on his face, Michael paid me with an autographed ace of spades. I'm not sure whether he intended some cryptic message in picking that card or whether it was simply on top of the deck. Either way, it's a memento I still hold dear.

To this day I can say without hesitation that that ten-day European trip, that marathon gin game, and the Jordan comedy special remain among the most gratifying and personally enriching days of my life.

16

When Jordan Almost Walked

Though almost impossible to imagine, there was a moment when Michael Jordan was ready to bolt from Nike.

An *improbable* moment that had its origins when, somehow, a schism developed in Rob Strasser's relationship with Knight in early 1987, and they agreed to go their separate ways. This wasn't the first time Knight had looked askance at someone else getting a bit too much credit for Nike's success. A short time later, Peter Moore also departed. Neither severance was a pleasant *adieu*—no gold watches as parting gifts.

Rob and Peter then teamed up to form a sports/leisure marketing partnership in Portland.

Leading up to Michael's contract renewal negotiations in '88, Rob and Peter, whom I also remained in touch with, asked me what would end up being a multibillion-dollar question: Did I think Michael could exist as a brand separate from Nike?

I was wholeheartedly on board with the notion. Michael *should be* an autonomous brand.

Michael had certainly earned a spin-off. He could headline his own brand in sports or nonsports categories in a second. And have five companies ready to back him in less than forty-eight hours.

The marketing and design consultancy Rob and Peter formed was called Sports, Inc. "The guys who'd done the Jordan campaigns" had quickly established a successful client list in the industry based on their stellar reputations. They had also begun a line of sports apparel under the Van Grack label.

In the meantime, they had continued to develop a vision of an independent brand built around Michael. It was timed to coincide with the upcoming end of Jordan's contract in '88. Rob and Peter had remained good friends with Michael and stayed in touch after their exodus from Nike. They'd worked on their Jordan plan between their other marketing and strategic assignments.

They'd conceived a new vision of Michael as a premium brand beyond the limitations of Air Jordan high-tops. Beyond Nike.

After months of development, they laid out their plan in an expansive marketing document with charts, drawings, designs, categories, and projections.

I hadn't seen the entire plan in person, but they wanted my thoughts on how Knight might take it.

Knight can be very unpredictable in his perception of things. I knew for a fact the idea of Michael as a brand of his own would be a lot for Phil to chew on—especially if Rob and Peter were involved.

On one of Michael's visits to Portland, he met with Rob and Peter off Knight's radar at Rob's house where they spent nearly an hour and a half presenting the plan and discussing details. The master plan was in perfect alignment with Michael's own entrepreneurial aspirations. Jordan was rapt. They didn't have to convince Michael that he had the gravitas, brand profile, national recognition, and personality to be a business of his own.

With Rob and Peter involved, Michael felt it couldn't miss. He now saw on paper the chance to actualize ideas that had been rolling around in his head since his rookie season. The plan laid out the next ten years. Michael immediately loved the concept and bought in.

A flawless business plan for a multibillion-dollar future was there on Rob's dining room table. Grinning, Michael told them, "I've got a few ideas to throw at you, but I wanna make this happen."

I knew the Jordan brand idea was going to get done with or without Nike, with or without Phil's blessing.

Michael would help arrange a meeting with the X-factor: Knight.

Michael got hold of Knight and asked if he would mind taking a meeting with Michael as well as Rob and Peter to look at a brand idea they had come up with.

I can't imagine the shock that shot through Phil's mind upon hearing Michael's request. But he held on to his emotions long enough to do a favor for his premier athlete. He agreed to see the mysterious plan Michael was referring to.

Rob and Peter presented the idea to Phil Knight in his office later that summer. Phil listened, one hand over the other in front of his mouth, sitting stoically. Phil had a good poker face, but it failed him this time.

Revealing the beautifully conceived marketing plan, Rob and Peter laid out the Jordan brand definition, the product lineup, and an array of Peter's graphics with fresh images of Jordan. The vision included sportswear, fashion and business apparel, and high-quality business footwear. Rob and Peter would be in charge, managing the entire Jordan enterprise with Nike participating as a financial stakeholder and manufacturer. Nike would underwrite the operation and retain control of Air Jordan basketball shoes under a licensing arrangement, and Jordan would be an owner—not just an endorsee of the Jordan brand, which they envisioned being akin to Ralph Lauren.

They kept it brisk, well-aware of Knight's short attention span. As they laid out board after board, the trio began to sense Phil's mood turn darker.

Was this a plan to poach Jordan, a coup d'etat? And devised by two ex-Nike employees, no less.

Just the presence of Rob, Peter, and Jordan together probably smacked of betrayal and conspiracy to Knight. To Jordan, it was the future. To Knight, it may have looked like a blackmail plot.

Phil had never before launched any athlete as an independent or semiautonomous business. Even behind the tint of his shades, his eyes said what he must have thought: *Hand* Jordan his own company— never.

Knight's attitude was dismissive and insolent. He'd obviously been offended that anyone—particularly Rob and Peter (whom he now considered traitors)—would entertain a Jordan collaboration.

Years later, Peter Moore recalled that meeting: "Funny, in hindsight, we were a bit naive to think that Knight would have ever allowed this to happen. It would be an admission that he failed or Nike failed. One thing is for sure: We pissed him off."

Beyond just the politics of the situation, implicit in Knight's rejection was the suggestion that Michael was *only a great player*. With Jordan's NBA schedule and commitments, he wouldn't have time to be a business executive capable of running a burgeoning enterprise.

The subtext intoned that Michael was an ingrate for even entertaining the thought of his *own brand identity*. It's far easier just to take the millions you're already making.

Phil curtly thanked them, said he'd think about it, and walked out shaking hands *only* with Jordan. All three knew the plan had tanked.

Late that afternoon, we convened for a debriefing at Rob's home. I was with the three of them as they discussed the meeting. The mood was glum. Michael, a twenty-six-year-old, who was never to be underestimated, was angry and insulted. I perceived during that time that he never felt at ease in Phil's presence. To say that their relationship was strained during the months before he was up for his contract renewal is to put it mildly.

Knowing Michael's gambler's instincts and *mano a mano* mentality, I knew Phil's tepid response wouldn't be the last hand at that poker game.

The plan Mr. Knight saw that day was brilliant. It must have reminded him of the many great presentations Rob and Peter had made while at Nike over the years. They had, after all, helped create the Jordan mystique and now wanted to further evolve Michael's brand potential.

Michael's thinking at that moment indicated that he had no intention of "re-upping" with Nike without a contract that put him in command of his own destiny.

Shortly after that meeting, Phil let it be known in the inner circle that he was fine with Michael leaving. He firmly believed that Michael—and anyone else—was nothing without the Swoosh behind them. Knight convened a meeting with Fred Schreyer, the marketing director, and myself to explore a plan to supplant Michael. "What if we own college basketball?" he asked.

"We already do," I said.

"No, I mean *every* school, every college."

He was dead serious. "Get me some numbers. How much would it cost to make that happen?"

Knight envisioned having billboards strategically located in every college town in America. Nike would have a monopoly on the sport.

We did run some numbers and the cost was prohibitive. But Phil was seriously contemplating a future without Michael.

As it turned out, that dismal Jordan brand meeting may have worked in Michael's favor.

Once Phil cooled off and analyzed his dilemma, he knew he couldn't lose Jordan at *any cost*.

He probably realized the Strasser-Moore plan was not only unimpeachable but *doable*. Any competitor would jump at the chance to back Jordan.

If Michael had in fact escaped, Phil would have been faced with a new and potentially formidable competitor in a matter of months. He would have had to shut down the entire Air Jordan product line without Jordan at Nike.

Nike was Knight. But Nike was also Jordan. Knight couldn't afford to lose Michael. It was at that *improbable* moment that Knight asked for my opinion.

"You think Michael would leave?" Phil asked me.

I couldn't lie.

"It's not unthinkable," I answered. "He's the most self-assured person I know. . . . He's a gambler—and he's not afraid to go up against anyone. He'll bet on himself any day of the week, and he's already rich."

Michael Jordan was spoiling to call Phil's bluff and Phil knew it.

Tens of millions was a small price to pay to extend Nike's hold on Michael Jordan for life.

Michael's 1988 contract renewal gave him essentially everything that had been outlined in Rob and Peter's Jordan brand plan. That lifetime contract established what would become Brand Jordan as a sister (or brother) subsidiary. Michael was no longer an endorser, but an owner with a generous piece of the business.

Without question, the fact that Rob and Peter were involved had forced Knight's hand. Phil would never—could never—allow his most untouchable asset to reunite with two of the people most responsible for Michael's ascendance. Two people Phil was done with.

The '88 contract was, yet again, the richest contract in sports endorsement history. It assured that Michael Jordan would become not just a businessman, but a mogul—a business owner worth hundreds of millions. Generational wealth that made it possible for him to buy the Charlotte Hornets years later, which made him the world's first billionaire athlete.

I thought both Michael and I would continue our Nike adventure together for life. For a while, we did.

17

When Push Comes to Shove

Michael was as fearless as anyone I've ever known in the athletic arena and his expansive business affairs. But he steadfastly chose to remain squarely in a neutral corner when it came to his involvement in three thorny issues: politics, race, and family confrontations. And like most of us, he also resisted becoming involved in drawn-out legal matters best handled by lawyers.

Time has proven he was quite wise in choosing to sidestep such potential land mines, where Michael believed things could spin out of control, raise uncomfortable questions, hurt feelings, and alienate one side or the other.

As Michael once so famously opined, "Republicans buy shoes too."

So for his own peace of mind, he tried to stay in his lane, focused on sports and business deals.

But fame and unforeseen circumstances sometimes gave him no choice. When it was unavoidable, more often than not, I was on the other end of the line.

"Hey, Sonny, I need you to take care of something for me . . ."

The first such situation in the summer of 1990 had the potential to become a race-relations disaster for Nike. With "sweatshop" labor controversies roiling in various Asian production facilities, the last thing Nike needed in America was a racial public relations fiasco.

But that's what we got.

It began innocuously enough when Rev. Jesse L. Jackson, founder of Operation PUSH (People United to Save Humanity), a civil rights and social justice organization, asked a Nike executive to comment on South Africa's apartheid policy. PUSH had been founded nineteen years earlier on the South Side of Chicago by Jackson, a force of human nature wholly familiar with the power of speech. Economic empowerment was not only a guiding principle of PUSH; it stood as a pressure-building tactic to level the playing field for minorities in corporate America. A rumor had begun circulating that Nike had holdings in South Africa, which was inaccurate. Nike disputed the accusation. Jackson received a "We have no further comment" in response to the apartheid query.

The PR game was on.

Nike's *nonresponse* to PUSH became the ember that quickly fanned a public relations fire that drew national play in the media. Rev. Jackson then began a campaign targeting Nike in the culturally critical music industry. Jackson urged executives at Motown Records and other influential music industry companies, as well as artists, to speak out. The message: Boycott Nike! To up the ante, Jackson then took the stage in Atlanta at a rap concert to beseech the audience to stop buying Nike shoes. Phase II of the effort spread to inner-city streets through religious communities and churches.

As the "Boycott Nike" message was spreading, Rev. Tyrone Crider, the new executive director of PUSH, ramped up this five-alarm race-related firestorm by targeting the lack of diversity within the company. At the time Nike's minority employee representation was no worse than anyone else's in the athletic shoe industry, but it certainly wasn't above average either. There were no minorities on its board of directors, and I don't recall anyone of color at the vice-president level. Nike's public image was racially diverse and inclusive, but the corporate organizational chart was white from top to bottom.

I had signed some of the country's top Black coaches (John

Thompson, Georgetown; Fred Snowden, Arizona; Davey Whitney, Alcorn State; and John Chaney at Temple, the first Black coach to win more than seven hundred games). In the player ranks, we could point to Jordan, Bo Jackson, Carl Lewis, Michael Johnson, Charles Barkley, Jerry Rice, and David Robinson, all told, the largest assemblage of Black endorsers in the industry. But in the big picture, that meant little or nothing, especially in the eyes of Rev. Tyrone Crider, who proved an articulate and fiery preacher. Smartly, he coordinated his effort with Rev. Jackson and many other outlets in the Black-owned or Black-supported media, including newspapers, magazines, radio, and broadcast networks like BET.

Crider's "Say No to Nike" boycott, which Nike mistakenly thought would fizzle out, refused to subside. Operation PUSH had strategically timed their enhanced effort to crater Nike's 1990 holiday sales. "Don't buy a pair until we get our fair share" was the message played on its phone line.

PUSH's talking points claimed that the Black youth market represented an inordinately high percentage of sales for Nike's $100 to $130 top-tier Air Jordans, that kids were forced to sell drugs to afford those shoes, and that young Black kids were getting killed on the streets and robbed of their Air Jordans. The allegations were inflammatory but with enough truth regarding reported street crimes to incite the Black community.

In response, Michael released a rare written statement in opposition to the boycott, saying, "While I believe that all of corporate America needs to provide equal opportunities for qualified Blacks to advance into the corporate hierarchy, it is unfair to single out Nike just because they are on top."

Adding fuel to the inner-city fire, Jackson and Crider demanded that Nike do more business with Black-owned retailers, Black-owned banks, Black-owned advertising agencies, and other organizations, and that Nike increase its support of Black media with more advertising. They wanted stronger Black and ethnic representation in Nike's executive ranks as well. As Crider continued his onslaught, he developed his second theme: "It can be done in '91!"

"If Black folk in Montgomery could be disciplined enough to not ride the bus for a year," he told *The New York Times*, "surely African Americans, over time and through education, can be disciplined enough not to run in Nike shoes for as long as it takes."

Phil Knight, combative and competitive by nature, bristled at what he viewed as the extortionate aspects of PUSH's demands. Regardless of the ethnicity of Nike's executive ranks, we were certainly the furthest thing from a prejudiced organization. We paid Black athletes and coaches more than anyone else in history. Our commercials transcended race and portrayed the most positive Black imagery in the industry to a broader cross section of the culture than anyone previously had.

Still, it wasn't enough.

Knight initially went the predictable route, choosing to enlist lawyers and PR people in crafting Nike's response. A company spokesperson touted Nike's growing number of Black, Asian, Hispanic, and Native American people in the employee base. She pointed to efforts Nike had undertaken to communicate to Black youth that they should focus on education, where, the messaging went, they had a far greater chance of succeeding in life than by playing professional sports. To support that messaging, Nike ran public service announcements in inner-city Detroit, Philadelphia, New York, LA, and other markets. John Thompson had been the spokesman in one of those commercials in the mid-eighties.

In addition, Knight leaned on Nike president Dick Donahue, a political operative with strong ties in Washington, for guidance. He put out what was known internally as "The List"—only to see it backfire to the point of outright warfare.

That list included pages of questions phrased to sound exactly like the evidence-gathering phase of a grand jury. The questioning probed financial records, the details of state and federal investigations against PUSH, the conclusions the investigations had arrived at, and a request for its membership rolls. Nike also argued that the entire boycott was being orchestrated by Reebok, and wanted details of any contacts and communications PUSH had with CEO Paul Fireman's crew. According to several industry publications, Reebok had allegedly provided industry sales figures and segment statistics at a breakfast meeting they held with Crider before Nike was targeted. An allegation vehemently denied by Reebok.

Instead of cowering in the face of Nike's withering legal response, Jackson and Crider upped the ante and began a speaking and media blitz that called for a national boycott of Nike. The company's confrontational approach had backfired spectacularly and was clearly a strategic gaffe.

The reverends had another edge going for them too:

Michael Jordan played in Chicago, PUSH's backyard.

Phil Knight, realizing that the situation was breaking bad, called a meeting at headquarters to plot a more effective, less confrontational response to the boycott. Knight's anger had gotten the best of him and he'd blundered into an increasingly nasty, no-win race-focused showdown. Jackson and Crider felt disrespected. At that point we were just another lily-white company mustering a task force of white lawyers to deny economic equity to the Black community.

The reverends refused to deal with Knight, who they perceived as dismissive and contemptuous. Knight was, in fact, livid that his company had been targeted. He suspected PUSH was using him for publicity, wrapped around a social issue that wrongly tarred Nike with unfounded racist insinuations. The same tactics they had previously used against Coca-Cola, Ford, Burger King, and other companies.

Knowing my long association with notable figures in the Black community, including coaches, Knight reached out.

Phil called me directly to put together a crisis resolution team to get the parties talking again. It was not uncommon for Knight to call me on any matter, and the dimensions of this PUSH problem were becoming more and more uncontrollable. Because of my relationships with John Thompson, Michael, and Spike Lee, I was asked to intervene—in essence, to run into a burning building to get the parties talking instead of screaming—and to somehow convene a forum to put the matter behind us.

I had to enlist Nike's most potent and respected contacts to represent our interests at this summit. I called Coach Thompson first. He was a rock of respect—a good friend and a nationally known figure who had the intellect, credentials, and influence to be Nike's chief negotiator. He knew Jesse Jackson and had enough of a relationship to pull such a meeting together.

John and I agreed to hold the meeting in New York, rather than Jackson's home court in Chicago. I then called Michael, imploring him to join the negotiations. It would be a gesture of respect to Jackson and Crider to have him as part of any summit. I also invited Rudy Washington, at the time the basketball coach at Drake, who, in 1988, had founded the Black Coaches Association. Rudy was viewed as an outspoken activist for justice and equality in the coaching ranks.

When the dust finally settled, I was the only actual Nike employee at the summit, which took place in my suite at the Hyatt Grand Central hotel on East Forty-Second Street in New York City. I was there to greet all the participants. Because of my long history with Black coaches, generations of Black kids at my events, and my relationship with Thompson, Washington, Jordan, and Spike Lee, I was, thankfully, not perceived as the enemy. Once everyone said their hellos and settled in, I left and was not present as this roomful of respected Black leaders met to resolve the contentious outstanding issues.

One thing was unequivocal: John Thompson wasn't there to chit or chat. He was a formidable presence who fully understood the gravity of the situation. He and the others were intent on reaching a settlement. PUSH was most interested in what they called "*reciprocal economic agreements*."

Since I wasn't in the room, I can only relate what was communicated to me afterward.

It was genial but all business.

Thompson wanted to know exactly what PUSH's demands were. What was it going to take to end this harmful and acrimonious boycott?

At one point Jesse Jackson asked who Nike's Black representative was, and John answered, facetiously, "Sonny."

Following the meeting, I debriefed John, Michael, and Rudy, then relayed the results directly to Phil.

In the end, PUSH achieved their objectives. Nike agreed to extend more of its vast marketing and financial resources to the Black community and immediately changed its hiring practices, adding more than a thousand people of color in a matter of months and vowing that within a year no less than 10 percent of Nike department heads would be diverse. Nike promised Black representation on its board, and John Thompson was soon appointed as a member of its board of directors and executive committee. Prior to that decision, Phil had asked what I thought of the idea.

"Absolutely," I said. "You have no Black people on the board."

"Do you think the other coaches will mind?"

"What do you care?" I replied. "John's more qualified than anyone else I can think of. It's the right thing to do."

Knight also agreed to form an outside "minority advisory board" to track the company's progress in meeting its goals.

To be clear, I was a conduit, not an arbitrator. I had no negotiating role in that momentous meeting. I knew the key players and managed to put some of the nation's highest-profile African Americans in the same room to hash things out. Phil was savvy enough to realize that I was the only one in the company who could have arranged a meeting of that urgency.

In the end, what was perhaps the most explosive, rancorous, and sensitive public relations problem in the company's history quietly subsided—leaving a humbled but more culturally aware Nike in its wake.

18

The Crash of Flight 23

The name of the start-up was Flight 23.

At the time, Phil Knight probably saw it as a gesture of goodwill toward Jordan: allow Michael's folks to make a little extra income in a small business by setting them up with a T-shirt shop in their hometown of Charlotte, North Carolina, stocked with Nike apparel and gear, backpacks, posters, and the like.

Nike organized the entire deal, providing the family with a quick course in retailing, ordering procedures, and store fixtures and display racks, and extended start-up credit for the launch. Phil approved the idea, viewing it more or less as a hobby or diversion for the other Jordan family members. Capitalizing on the skyrocketing Jordan success, it seemed like a good idea, an accommodation to his singular star.

Peter Moore named the business, helped create the logo, laid out the store design, developed the signage, and even authored a clever newspaper ad campaign.

The only caveat: no footwear.

After it opened, Flight 23 didn't have people waiting in line up and down the block. Unfortunately, it never turned a profit. Given the cost of goods, shipping, setup—and not enough sales—Flight 23 eventually amassed more than half a million dollars in debt.

Even though the entrepreneurial enterprise was floundering, Michael's father, James Jordan, retained a grand vision for Flight 23's potential. He turned it into a brand of its own—a direct competitor to Nike. He had the Flight 23 logo on everything from T-shirts and sweats to caps and other merchandise. As such, the senior Jordan began producing and selling goods through sales agents around the country, using his obvious connection to Michael and the implied endorsement of Nike. Flight 23 began pulling in outside investors to expand the brand and selling a whole range of products. The idea of opening stores across the country seemed a logical next step.

That's when Phil Knight began getting "What the hell's going on?" phone calls from retailers.

Word began filtering back to Beaverton that Nike distributors were offering Flight 23 merchandise to retailers from Boston to Hawaii.

Knight was apoplectic.

It was clear James Jordan was in violation of the original agreement that stated Flight 23 was to be a single storefront, selling only Nike goods.

The issue blew up while Michael was on our Nike promotional trip to Europe leading up to the '92 Barcelona Olympics. He was certainly aware of what was going on but saw no harm in his family's enterprise. However, this competing line had the potential to create a rich brew of animus, threatening Nike's relationship with Michael, Michael's relationship with his parents, and Nike's relationship with its own retailers.

As one might expect, Knight was livid. He wanted Flight 23 grounded. Immediately. Permanently.

In a letter dated October 1990, he implored Michael to prevail upon his father to end the expansion plan and stop producing Flight 23 merchandise. Knight wanted Michael to make a statement, something to the effect of: "I believe my parents are getting bad advice from outsiders who do not have the best interests of my family in mind." Another theme Phil pushed Michael to stand behind was: "It is to be expected that some of our competitors would take a shot at this success, but I never expected one of those competitors to be my parents."

That last thread alone showed just how hapless and out of touch Knight and president Dick Donahue were in their understanding of Michael Jordan. Needless to say, the idea of any kind of public pronouncement from Michael against Deloris and James Jordan was ill-conceived, a nonstarter.

The request only served to piss Michael off.

Pushed into an untenable position, he sent word to Phil he wasn't going to turn on his family, and had no intention of intervening. Michael loved and respected his parents above all else. Phil's contractual arrangement in Michael's mind was between Nike and his father, James. Michael was an accessory after the fact and wanted no part of it.

Once again, Phil brought in his formidable legal team. He had them compose an ominous letter, which he wanted Michael to personally present to his family. No dice, said Michael.

Michael stayed at arm's length, believing the whole thing would play out eventually, likely through a settlement of some sort. He chose to sit out the brewing crisis. He had an NBA championship to win, not a squabble to settle. His focus was on unseating Isiah Thomas and the Bad Boys of Detroit and not intervening in Phil's T-shirt scuffle.

Complicating an already touchy situation was the fact that James Jordan owed Nike hundreds of thousands of dollars in back invoices for inventory, including products like tees, socks, sunglasses, and sweat outfits, plus loans, salaries, fixtures, and operating costs.

Flight 23 was tanking.

The situation had *bad choices* written all over it.

Knight, through company lawyers, threatened to immediately call in that debt as a wedge to get the Jordans to shut down Flight 23. Unquestionably, a lose-lose proposition was in the offing—one that could easily become an unflattering, embarrassing tabloid tale should it leak to the press. At stake: tainting Michael's reputation at the high point of his career and making Nike look like they were bullying Jordan's parents. Nike suing Michael's parents? Unthinkable.

The bad blood continued throughout the 1990–91 season, the Bulls' first championship year.

Enter yours truly, stage left this time.

At an impasse, both Michael and Phil asked me to intercede.

Michael told me, "Sonny, I'm not getting involved. You talk to my folks and Knight. See what you can do."

Michael trusted me and knew I had a cordial relationship with his parents. It felt like Phil was reluctant to trust anyone, but he knew Michael and I were close, and called on me again to intervene.

Both sides needed a resolution to this increasingly fractious interplay.

By this point, James Jordan, who possessed a rather robust ego of his own, had grown to dislike Knight, refusing to communicate with him or Nike lawyers. A series of threats—cease and desist notifications, collection proceedings—had only served to inflame the hostility.

So I stepped into the stalemate as the intermediary, dealing directly with Phil and the Jordans. By now Michael was completely immersed in a long season, fighting through a succession of playoff teams. I told him that things were progressing but leveled with him: His father was standing his ground and would rather go to court than give in to Phil Knight. Clearly, Michael got his pugnaciousness, competitiveness, and grit from James; I came to understand that fact fully as the negotiations dragged on.

The Flight 23 battle came to a head in Los Angeles in June 1991, with the Bulls in nothing less than the NBA Finals against the Los Angeles Lakers of Magic, James Worthy, Vlade Divac, and Sam Perkins. Michael's parents were traveling back and forth to the games between Chicago and LA. I was running from breakfast meetings at the Century Plaza Hotel to lunches at the Beverly Hills Hotel, on the phone day after day, every day, while trying to make headway with the Jordans between playoff games.

I reported each and every iteration of the conflict back to Knight, who hadn't traveled to the NBA Finals in LA, the near-daily meetings with James and Deloris, never wavering from my central negotiating premise: We've got to settle this matter to protect Michael—his image, his privacy, his mindset, his feelings. He's got his first championship to pursue and can't be distracted by this side-show. If any of this goes public, it could end up on the cover of the *National Enquirer*. It would be perceived either that Michael was turning on his family or that some serious schism existed between Nike and its iconic star.

Deloris was completely sympathetic to the implications for her son.

James, however, refused to budge. He couldn't bring himself to give an inch to Knight. Both men acted every bit as tenacious and competitive as Michael.

After days and days of negotiations, James Jordan proposed that Nike buy him out for $15.5 million—$1.5 million down and the remaining amount to be paid out over ten years.

I knew Knight was never going to pay anywhere near that amount, but I urged him to come up with some reasonable settlement offer that would allow James to save face.

"Look, Mr. Knight, in the end, you're going to pay more than you want and you're going to feel like you got screwed," I said. "You've already put a hundred million behind Michael. I'm talking to James every day and he's ready to fight to the end. Even if you win, you still lose. If you want my advice, I say it's worth paying a premium to make this go away."

Finally, Phil came to the same conclusion.

Deloris implored James to accept Nike's offer. With the persistent persuasion of his wife, a final take-it-or-leave-it offer from Phil landed somewhere in the middle. They made a deal.

I don't think James ever forgave Nike or Knight.

It wasn't a happy ending, but it ended.

. . .

I'D ALWAYS HAD A GIFT for negotiating deals with coaches, players, universities, and TV networks, but this affair—Jordan vs. Jordan, Jordan vs. Nike, James vs. Phil—was one for the ages in my personal experience.

When Flight 23 finally ended, Nike forgave over a half million in debt and payables, and purchased all rights to the brand for several million more. Nike then sent a crew to liquidate the retail store in Charlotte, leaving the walls bare and a "For Lease" sign in the window.

Knight wasn't willing to let bygones be bygones. The Jordans were never again invited to the annual coaches' conferences. I doubt he ever spoke another word to James or Deloris Jordan.

As Michael had predicted, the matter would eventually be resolved—but not without a residue of frayed relationships.

. . .

DURING THAT FIRST CHAMPIONSHIP RUN in the summer of 1991, Pam and I were away in Palm Springs on vacation. I had watched Michael's final two games on TV at the hotel as the Bulls wrapped up the title in game 5, Magic's final full NBA season.

I was so filled with joy for Michael. And for Nike . . . even more so for Phil Knight. It was the culmination of the Nike dream of supremacy and brand superiority. Now we had our "Michael Championship."

Though Nike Air Jordan's sales were unsurpassed in the industry, the NBA title was the final insignia of authentication that the '84 signing was a decision that justified itself a billion times over. In 1991, Michael was already making far more money from Nike than he did from his $2.5 million Bulls annual contract.

I remember the Sunday night game 4 at the Forum, almost as clearly as *The Shot* had struck me years earlier. Michael was twenty-eight years old and two games away from his first NBA title after seven long, tough, trophy-free years in the league.

Before the game, Michael had his right-hand man, Howard White, call and offer tickets for Pam and me to attend. It's always been difficult for me to enjoy games played by people I care about, especially critical games. When I do show up, I spend most of the time in the arena walking the concourse, only glancing occasionally at the game. I had walked concourses for games that Kobe and Michael and John Thompson's Hoyas played; I knew Michael's game 4 would have me tied in knots, so Pam and I politely declined the offer and decided to leave a few days early for the customary summer getaway at the Marriott Desert Springs in Palm Desert.

At some point, after scoring twenty-eight points in dispatching the Lakers 97–82, in the midst of all the hype and hysteria, Michael signed a pair of game-used shoes and passed them on to Howard White.

"Make sure you get these to Sonny," he said.

The next day, before the team headed back to Chicago to finish off the series, White phoned to tell me that he had left a box for me at the front desk of the Bulls' hotel, the Ritz-Carlton in Marina del Rey. A few days later on our way back home from Palm Desert I stopped by the hotel on Admiralty Way to retrieve them. In a neatly taped and wrapped box, the words "Hold for Sonny Vaccaro" were scrawled in black Magic Marker. Inside was an autographed pair of size 13 red and black Air Jordans. Game-used shoes. Vintage.

Opening the box, I was shocked to discover a slit cut in the top of the right shoe—done, I knew, to relieve the pressure on Jordan's throbbing big toe, which he kept aggravating during the playoffs. He had worn them at the start of the second quarter of game 4.

During the broadcast, the NBC Sports courtside reporter, Ahmad Rashad, focused a segment on the slit. Now the shoes were in my hands. A keepsake symbolic of the easy relationship Michael and I shared for six-plus years at Nike. He owned the world, and we watched it happen together—and now I had a treasured size 13 piece of it.

For more than thirty years, that gift served as a reminder of an irreplaceable period in my life. Then, in 2020, the shoes were listed in the Goldin Auctions catalog. Beside the photo of those high-tops was the blurb, "Michael Jordan 1991 NBA Finals Game 4 Used, Photo Matched & Twice Signed Air Jordan High Top Sneakers, Gifted to Nike Exec Sonny Vaccaro . . ."

I had kept them all those years as a touchstone that embodied one of the most nonstop exhilarating periods of my life in sports. They had carefully traveled from one storage unit to another for three decades before I put them on the auction block. As you shall see, words and actions exchanged in a brief public tiff five years earlier had soured a friendship that couldn't survive the influence of a billionaire CEO and a former best friend seeking no small measure of revenge.

. . .

FINALLY, IN THIS MEDITATION ON mediation, I'll offer one last example that delineates my role as a conduit in business dealings between Michael and Knight/Nike.

I say last because it would be, unbeknownst to me, the final Nike event of my career.

It took place during the annual Nike coaches' trip, this time at the resplendent five-star Broadmoor Resort in Colorado Springs, Colorado, from August 3 to 8, 1991—another of our spare-no-expense gatherings for our "Ministry of Great Coaches." For me, it was the last of our raucous respites where the game's top head coaches—Tark, Valvano, Boeheim, Rollie, Calhoun—could just relax, let their hair down, and enjoy a luxury vacation courtesy of the Swoosh.

Some of these soirees were more legendary than others, but to borrow an old Las Vegas axiom, "What happened at Nike getaways, stayed at Nike getaways." A flurry of diversions—golf, tennis, spa treatments, horseback riding, swimming, shopping trips, sightseeing—wrapped around grand dinners, the latest gossip, and a free-form social schedule the coaches and families shared with their top-ranked competitors. Some of the coaches were great friends; others would pass each other in the lobby without making eye contact or even a nod.

Prior to the Broadmoor, the '86 trip to the La Costa Resort & Spa just north of San Diego may have been the most memorable, and Michael had joined us that year. Nike, flush with success, spared no expense for these annual coaches' getaways. Each concluded with some lavish over-the-top dinner capping off a weeklong junket. Seemingly frivolous, but it may have been an affront to Mr. Knight how well-liked I seemed to be by Nike basketball people as well as the coaches on our roster. For every coaches' retreat, our team back in Oregon would put out an itinerary with the week's activities. The booklet had running commentary making lighthearted allusions to me: "Sonny impersonation contest . . . please bring your phone and then forget where you set it down," and "How about an hour in the sun—poolside with your legs covered, just like Sonny." Nothing profound to be sure, but once again, I was the focal point. At La Costa, the theme was a Prohibition-style speakeasy.

The coaches showed up in roaring twenties–style gangster attire, their wives flashily dressed to the nines. Each repeated the password to get in: "Sonny Sent Me." I'm not sure who came up with the idea of having water pistols, many resembling plastic machine guns, as party favors. Already filled with water, they were sitting on the tables when the guests entered. It's not difficult to imagine what happened next.

It started at a single table, when one of the coaches sprayed another coach and his wife. The second coach retaliated, spraying the first offender and his wife. The overspray hit someone at another table. In a movie script, it might say, "Chaos ensued." Within three minutes, there were dozens of grown adults caught up in the horseplay. About a quarter of the guests scrambled to flee the large, tented space, but those who remained engaged in battle. Warriors frantically attempted to reload their water pistols as the soak fest escalated. Wives in elegant evening attire had their sequined gowns drenched. Their coifs hung limp; some had eyeliner running in blackish smudges down their cheeks. One Nike exec's wife was pushed into a bathtub full of ice water and freezing-cold beer bottles. People chased each other around the tables to exact revenge. Soppy dinner rolls began flying around. Panicked waiters rushed around the room grabbing pitchers to remove the ammo. Michael, with the deft athletic skills of a Special Forces soldier, ran tactical maneuvers to ambush his targets and avoid being hit. People slipped and fell on the soppy wooden dance floor. Knight grabbed a water pitcher to fling water at an attacker. Everyone regressed to their child-selves, yelling as they ran for cover or pursued victims. After twenty minutes or so of chaos, Strasser went to the microphone to plead for a ceasefire to the riotous deluge. The famed resort was none too pleased with the evening's antics, but Nike was always good when it came to reimbursing damages.

. . .

FIVE YEARS LATER, AT THE 1991 Broadmoor getaway, a separate and very consequential meeting was to occur, which involved Knight, Dick Donahue, and a coterie of lawyers—all awaiting a decision by Michael, and whether he would come to Colorado and bring a monumental decision to a conclusion.

The purpose of this concurrent side meeting was to formally extricate

Michael's name, image, and likeness from the clutches of NBA Properties, allowing him to be the sole marketer of Jordan merchandise and clothing. Magic Johnson had the same desire but wouldn't opt out unless Michael led the way.

Michael's release couldn't happen without apprising him of the ramifications. Knight, Donahue, and the lawyers wanted Michael present to finalize and sign off on the plan. No Jordan, no meeting. He'd already turned down an invitation from Phil to join him at the Broadmoor. Michael's familiar first inclination was to "just let the lawyers handle it."

So Phil again asked me to pull a rabbit out of a hat.

I got Michael on the phone to implore him to join us at the coaches' gathering.

"Mr. Knight told me you're not coming," I said.

"Nah, I'd rather spend the time with my kids before training camp."

I told him Knight was really anxious to get this NBA licensing divorce wrapped up and that he (Jordan) stood to make substantially more money if he could take control of his signature NBA merchandise.

"I don't know," said Michael. The last thing he wanted was to get involved in more tedious Nike business interrupting the final month of his time off right before training camp. Plus, the issue with his parents and Nike had just wrapped up less than a month earlier. Tensions were still high.

I told Michael his presence in Colorado was crucial; everything was awaiting his go-ahead. I convinced him it would be fun, he could breathe some fresh Rocky Mountain air and play a couple of the Broadmoor's terrific golf courses.

"Look, Michael, it'll be less than two hours and you can spend the rest of the time golfing," I said. "You won't have to do any socializing with the coaches. A day and a half and you're outta there."

I used every angle I could muster, and he finally agreed.

Michael arrived by private jet, along with several of his friends, and showed up for the negotiations. It was at that meeting that the plan was finally laid out for him to break away from the NBA's merchandising arm. Nike's lawyers would represent him contractually and legally.

With the deal blessed by Michael, he and his friends got in thirty-six holes. Right before he took off, we hugged in the lobby and a limo took him and his group back to the airport.

Once again, by special request from Mr. Knight, I was the catalyst who brought together Phil's intentions and Michael's interests. Another multimillion-dollar business opportunity for both Nike and Michael materialized at that event as Michael formally opted out in January 1992.

And that, as I said, was my last official act at Nike.

Seven days later Phil Knight brought down the curtains. The whole time Knight and Donahue knew I was a dead man walking, though they pretended all was right with the world. The deceit of that fake conviviality only added to the nauseating sense of betrayal I would feel a week later in Oregon.

19

Fourteen Years and Ten Minutes

I knew something was up as soon as I walked into the reception area outside of Phil Knight's second-floor office on the Nike campus that muggy mid-August day a week later. A disquieting premonition shaded the otherwise ordinary occasion with a vague feeling of apprehension, a strangeness that had started earlier in the day when I was picked up at the airport by Ed Janka, the man I had hired to help manage Nike camps and events.

For some reason Janka seemed uptight and nervous, unlike the easygoing Ed whom I'd known for years. It didn't dawn on me until later that he was harboring an outsize secret. He was driving me to my last meeting at Nike.

I paused and said hello to Phil's assistant, Lisa McKillips, before walking into his office. *That's odd*, I thought. Lisa didn't ask me to take off my shoes—a gesture Phil required of everyone who entered his office. That customary act of respect in Asian culture was something Knight had picked up in Japan and consistently enforced. Outside the glass wall behind Phil's desk, the verdant hills of Oregon melted into the grayish clouds hugging the horizon. I was in my fourteenth year with the company.

Earlier, on the flight up to Portland, I had naively assumed that our annual August meeting would be about our plans for the upcoming basketball season. That said, I had another marketing deal that I couldn't wait to tell Phil about: I had worked out a possible partnership with DIC Productions to get top Nike athletes like Michael and Bo on television in an animated kids' series. When DIC called me, I thought the idea was brilliant.

Oddly, my direct boss, Fred Schreyer, didn't join us as he always had when I came to Beaverton. I knew he was in town, so why wasn't he around? Something was out of sync. This wasn't the same breezy vibe typical of my trips to the home office.

Ordinarily, I only came up to present ideas for future initiatives and to confer on upcoming marketing campaigns, budgets, grassroots events, basketball camps, and updates on colleges and coaches. After the Jordan signing, I was often consulted about potential endorsement deals. The state of the basketball division was in glorious shape—what the company called our "money line" helping to keep weaker performing lines afloat. The success of the Jordan brand pretty much precluded any further quarterly disasters, and we were flush with profits in '91. We owned the $2-billion-a-year athletic shoe market, selling in excess of $400 million worth of basketball shoes a year. Our dominance was so well established that in the basketball category the other companies essentially lost their grip. Basketball had become Nike's domain.

Sporting sunglasses indoors, Knight entered his office. *Why aren't we meeting in the conference room as always?* I wondered. After the usual offhanded pleasantries—How was your flight? How's Pam? Coaches looked like they had a great time in Colorado last week—Phil walked around his desk and settled into his chair. On his desktop were three side-by-side stacks of papers, which I soon found out were intended for me to sign.

Knight seemed more fidgety than usual. His cordialities betrayed something I couldn't put my finger on. *What's wrong with this picture?* Just seven days earlier at the annual coaches' gathering, he'd been his usual self. Affable but distant. Same as always.

...

IN A STRANGE WAY, Phil had never quite fit into our cadre of coaches and athletes. Though he appeared to try his best at the coaches' get-aways, he never really shed the odd amalgam of anxiety and awkward-ness that characterized him socially. He seemed an introvert thrust into a convention of unabashed extroverts. The coaches treated Knight with great deference and respect, but their conversations struck me more like the ones they'd have with a billionaire booster: friendly, more beholden, and slightly self-conscious.

   In his book, Knight described himself as "a person with personal idiosyncrasies." His odd eccentricities and carefully crafted mystique was him "Just being Phil" among the people who worked for him. Though gifted intellectually, his odd conceits—like wrapping rubber bands around his fingers, sunglasses indoors, staring at the ceiling as if he were off in space—always suffused meetings with a tinge of uncertainty.

...

I CONDUCTED CLOSE TO FIFTY meetings every year on various basketball-related matters and can honestly say I never ran into any-one with a more guarded and circumspect demeanor. Sports people in general are outgoing types, extroverts. For the most part, athletes and coaches, athletic directors and lawyers have some semblance of cha-risma. Phil, though commanding respect in his position as the Boss of Bosses, projected a shy awkwardness in business meetings and social gatherings. Conversely, with the rest of us, he preferred business dis-cussions and points of view be animated to the point of confrontation. He wanted the eventual decisions to be decided as the by-product of a heated, competitive debate. At which point Knight would afford all sides a nod of approval for a battle well fought—but no guidance on any specific direction. He'd leave everyone hanging, without a commitment one way or the other. Through some corporate alchemy, a decision would emerge and Knight's blessing eventually worked its way downstream to the combatants.

My meetings with Knight were different. I would breeze in for a short day-or-two visit every three to four months. We dispensed with small talk rather quickly and went straight to the numbers, projected targets, people, conferences, and universities we wanted to own.

Other than inquiring about the financial implications of my recommendations, he rubber-stamped virtually every idea I brought to him, from green-lighting the ABCD Camp to breaking the mold by securing exclusive million-dollar basketball sponsorships like Big Monday on a then fledgling cable network known as ESPN—a stroke of genius that elevated our brand to new heights. To his credit, he let me be me, allowed me to use my mind to Nike's full advantage.

. . .

KNIGHT SAT DOWN WITH A glance at the documents on his desktop. "So . . ." the tone indicating it was time for what this meeting was really about. Phil seemed uneasy but got straight to the point in a single sentence.

"I think it's time we go our separate ways."

I heard the words but their meaning was so incomprehensible they didn't immediately register. Shock, disbelief, and uncertainty was playing havoc with my brain. *Did I hear him correctly?*

"Wait," I finally said. "Are you firing me?"

"I don't want to put it that way," Knight replied.

Behind a veil of solemnity, the element of total surprise seemed to please him, a cherry on top of the relief and psychic release the act of firing me must have provided. It appeared he had unloaded a tractor trailer's worth of resentment in that moment, a feeling that had likely festered for years.

Put it that way. Well, how would you put it? I was bombarded by my own cascade of emotions: confusion, baffled bewilderment, numbness. Finally, raw anger.

"You can't fire me," I said in the most even tone I could muster. "I quit."

It was as if I hadn't even spoken. Knight just rolled on to the next densely lawyered document in front of him.

"We're just putting it out there that you've decided to stretch your wings, move on to new ventures on your own," he said. "I've got some papers for you to sign here. You know, we've gotta get square on that loan. The lawyers drew this up. You're welcome to read everything."

I had recently borrowed some money from Phil to bump up the down payment on our home in Pacific Palisades. Now that loan was clearly due.

"So we're done?" I asked, finally putting thought into words. "I guess I'm like the sheriff who rode into Dodge, cleaned up the town, and now that he's no longer needed, he's sent off on horseback into the sunset."

"Something like that," Knight said, flipping to the last page of another document for a signature.

Like that. Fourteen years. More than 125 schools and coaches currently under exclusive contracts. Dominance in a market the envy of everyone involved in athletics. *Like that.*

"There's another matter I'd like to talk to you about," he continued. "The ABCD Camp and the Roundball. We'd like to buy them."

The offer was six figures.

I'd just been fired, and in the same conversation, the dismissal included a final cleanse: He wanted to extricate me from the camp and all-star game that defined me. All I had to do was agree to sell my identity and disappear—the way Phil likes relationships to end.

Shocked or not, I was clearheaded enough to know one thing: I wasn't going to sell out to Phil Knight. I'd shut everything down before allowing him to march on with the events synonymous with my name.

"No, thank you. Those are going out the door with me."

"Look," Knight continued. "I know you're upset, but you should take a moment to reconsider."

"I don't need to reconsider, Mr. Knight. I want to thank you for everything. We had a pretty good run together."

I was stunned. We did not shake hands as I turned to leave.

Janka was waiting downstairs. He drove me back to the airport without saying a word. Only later would I find out he—and a small group of others—knew I was being fired and that he had escorted me to the firing squad.

Little did I know at the time, but the day before my dismissal Knight had walked into one executive's office and said, "There's something I want to talk to you about. Tomorrow your world is going to change in a big way," before informing him in twenty-four hours I would no longer be with Nike, no need to discuss the reasons why, and it goes without saying you keep this to yourself. The executive later recalled the news hit "like a death in the family."

"There had been no discussions, not even a hint," the executive added. "Basketball was carrying a lot of the load. Nike's recovery was on the shoulders of basketball. It was always, 'We need to find a Sonny in volleyball, we need to find a Sonny in soccer, football. Then, suddenly, there was no Sonny discussion."

I didn't want to call Pam from the airport in Oregon. All I could focus on was getting the hell home. On the plane, I was catatonic, silently suffocating in a shroud of trauma. *Fired? What do I tell everyone? Did Michael know in advance? What about all the coaches I'd been hobnobbing with for the past thirteen-plus years? What kind of press release had the PR department contrived to explain this?*

At that moment, the note Rob Strasser had taped to his door on the day he quit back in 1987 came to mind: *Tell the Truth* scrawled on Nike letterhead. I wondered whether they'd tell "the truth" in my case.

I landed back in LA, awash in anger, grabbed a cab, and somehow found Pam in a pew at Saint Monica Catholic Church on Lincoln Boulevard. She'd mentioned the night before that she was going to be there.

Catholicism's Assumption of the Holy Virgin Mary was the Holy Day on that August fifteenth. I whispered hello to her and we sat through the rest of the Mass. She was surprised to see me, overnight bag in hand. Something about my surprise presence furrowed her brow as we sat silently through the homily. She knew something on that trip up to Nike had gone wrong. She wanted me to explain what happened. I wasn't sure I could.

In the car, heading up to Pacific Palisades, I recounted the details of the meeting. A fourteen-year career brought to an end in ten blindsiding minutes. I didn't leave on my terms, I left on Knight's terms. Pam and I went over the details, trying to rationalize the result, attempting to somehow make sense of it. Pam kept asking, "Are you sure you heard him right?" If possible, she seemed more stunned than I was.

When we arrived home, a full answering machine answered that question. A red blinking light signaling panicked calls from coaches across the country. We listened but were not in the frame of mind needed to accept calls. One other glaring fact stood out as we listened to the messages: Janka had been on the phone right after he dropped me off at the airport, before I'd even landed in LA, notifying the coaches that Sonny was moving on and he'd be replacing me. The official talking points were that I had quit and was off to pursue my own ventures. "Why didn't you mention that last week at the Broadmoor?" more than one message asked.

The only phone call we picked up was from Juanita Jordan, Michael's wife. She called to make sure we were okay. Michael got on the phone to ask the same thing. "Are you alright? Can I do anything?"

I asked how he found out, since I hadn't been the one to break the news to him.

"Janka called."

In the aftermath, Pam and I both endured a wild ride of emotions and feelings, with myriad unanswered questions to process.

Why? What went wrong? Who's behind this? Was this Phil's idea? One thing was certain: The entire episode had been orchestrated in advance. Press releases, the legal paperwork, the notifications. But from a business standpoint, it made no sense. We owned the game, for God's sake. How could this have happened?

I had worked for Nike and Phil since 1977. In all that time, there was never a cross word between us, never any divergence in vision, strategy, or contract negotiations. Of course we had spirited discussions on budgets and university A versus university B debates. But we always ended up on the same page, with the same horizon line in our sights. I became Sonny Claus to coaches and universities across the land. I did deals on handshakes. They made sense; they built the brand and increased our dominance. That made everyone—coaches, athletic departments, conferences—richer than they'd ever been.

Phil had a reputation over the years—well earned—for cutting off at the knees anyone who developed too much power or profile. Knight could easily have stepped into the media spotlight, but he was camera shy and reclusive. Clearly, I wasn't. I had become the face of Nike basketball.

I was on *60 Minutes* twice. I was on *Nightline*. Bob Costas interviewed me. I was quoted hundreds of times in the media. In a 1988 *Sports Illustrated* profile Curry Kirkpatrick had described me as "the most influential force in athletic footwear, period," eliciting this quote from Knight: "When these massive orders for shoes began pouring in . . . we gave him [Vaccaro] all the room he needed."

To make corporate matters worse, I wasn't going through the PR or marketing department for permission to sit for *60 Minutes* or to do an interview with Costas. The media came to me directly. If a paper or magazine or sports outlet needed a quote, Sonny Vaccaro, always direct, outspoken, and unfiltered, gave you something you could use. I was knowledgeable and accessible.

My sense now is that my presence in the media spotlight implied I was taking too much credit for Nike's success. Maybe Knight considered it an affront—the equivalent of standing in front of him while his photo was being taken. After my firing, Nike lawyers told me that "with the company's money anyone could have done what I did." To which I responded, *"Let me set the record straight, it may have been Nike's money, but it was always my ideas."*

More than thirty years later I've settled on a far less personal and more parochial reason for my dismissal. The Nike I'd gone to work for in the late seventies had dramatically changed and I no longer fit its Fortune 500 protocols.

After Nike went public in December 1980, the company naturally became more and more sensitive to its stock price. Remaining in the good graces of Wall Street far outweighed the old freewheeling band-of-misfits mentality. Management with master's degrees and PhD pedigrees were as essential as a strong balance sheet.

In truth, I was one of the last vestiges of the original Nike. With each trip back to Beaverton, the company became more and more alien and unrecognizable to me—there was a completely different feeling. In my early days, Phil Knight *was* the human resources department. By the nineties, HR sprawled across one and a half buildings in Beaverton and locations across the world. As new managers filtered in, they had their own vision of how Nike was to be run in the future.

My isolation from the power source—more psychological than geographical—frayed any threads of support I retained in Beaverton. I was an anachronism, the old guard. Yesterday.

I had no Wharton MBA. I didn't want to run a division from an office nestled in a row of offices in a row of buildings. I wanted to be where the games were played with the people who drive the game and the players who play it. I did business face-to-face or on my phone.

Knight had always been very accommodating, allowing me free reign to grow basketball.

That autonomy, though unorthodox, appeared to rub Nike's new president, Dick Donahue, the wrong way. He became Nike's president and COO in July 1990.

Years before in the early seventies, Donahue had helped Nike dodge a huge financial hit when attempts were made by the United States government to place tariffs on Nike products produced overseas—duty taxes that could easily have put us out of business. Though Donahue—the former head of the Massachusetts Bar Association—wasn't remotely connected to the shoe business, Knight was impressed and hired him for a slot at Nike International to help with expansion issues. Knight saw value in Donahue's connections to the Kennedys and corridors of Congressional and West Wing power. As president, Donahue wanted a menu of new "disciplines" instituted at all levels. This was now his show and it would be run with the proper consulting-firm-approved organizational charts, oversight, and controls. That's a president's prerogative and you either fall in line or make other plans. I wasn't adapting well and wasn't about to.

To me, Donahue was just another president in a rotating carousel of presidents, some I'd never even met. Yet, Donahue was, I suspect, a key catalyst in my firing. With that in mind, I can tell you he wasn't the least bit impressed with a sweatsuit-attired, fast-talking Italian who didn't fit the corporate paradigm of the Washington, DC, elites so prevalent in his legal career.

He was right. I didn't.

From what little he knew of me, I think Donahue perceived me as a rogue operative, untethered to the executive suite. To Donahue, who had no connection to Nike's origins, Sonny Vaccaro was an outlier. Companies are given to stamping out any deviations in structure, and I was an anomaly that had to be addressed. No one in any other department or position at Nike had the autonomy that Strasser and Knight had granted me. I knew basketball from the inside; they knew it from press clippings and the sports pages. I had my Rolodex but nobody to watch my back once Strasser left with Moore to start their own company four years earlier.

The new Nike was not the Nike I signed up for fourteen years earlier.

In truth, Phil didn't fit the new Nike either.

Knight and I both knew the company had lost forever the crazy, spontaneous experimentation and camaraderie that once represented a counterrevolution in sports.

He and Nike had become everything Knight hated about the industrial-size manufacturing giants, like Adidas, of his earlier years. Nike was now the kind of company he once detested.

I chuckled at the notion, a conceit really, that Nike's brand profile—how they thought of themselves—was still that of a small core group of free spirits dedicated to testing their own limits in athletic competition. They'd spent millions to foster the illusion of individuality and athletic iconography even though Nike itself had become a vast industrial sports shoe marketer, international in scope and with a presence in every sports market segment. They probably had a department to keep track of departments.

In retrospect, after a great deal of thought, the firing isn't the most interesting or consequential part of this hinge event in my life. As it turns out, it was merely a standard transition that occurs in everyone's business career. Jobs come and go—you quit, change companies, pursue other opportunities.

This story is bigger than that.

Though Knight had no idea at the time, it marked the beginning of a new escalation in the Shoe Wars. This time it was Sonny Vaccaro against the 10,000-pound gorilla he helped create—and the industry icon on top of it. By firing me, Knight had unleashed forces of opposition that would have unintended consequences.

Nike was about to go from the job of my life to my archenemy. After spending fourteen years helping drive Nike to the forefront, I was about to spend most of the next fourteen in mortal combat with Knight/Nike.

Yes, Knight/Nike had an unlimited war chest, global scale, and a huge head count advantage. No one could match its resources. On the other hand, I had a nationwide network of ground-level contacts—an unmatched collection of names and numbers. I knew the ins and outs of the game better than anyone at Nike, period. Going into battle, I knew I would be outmanned and outspent, but Nike had no one capable of outthinking me or more adept at tactical maneuvers. Their strategy was a brilliant one: *Copy anything and everything Sonny does.*

As the next phase of my life was about to begin, Phil Knight had provided his basketball people with the best advice he'd ever given: *"Never underestimate Sonny Vaccaro."*

Especially one extremely motivated, emotionally driven Sonny Vaccaro.

Whether Phil Knight liked it or not, I would be indelibly etched in Nike lore, one way or another, for decades to come.

20

Team Jordan Reconvenes
to Save Adidas

On a freezing November day in 1992, I was in Detroit ironing out some last-minute details for the upcoming Roundball Classic, which after twenty-eight years in Pittsburgh was moving to the Palace of Auburn Hills, with Magic Johnson as the marquee name of the rebranded event. That day I got an unexpected phone call from Rob Strasser. Literally out of the blue.

"We've got a pretty-exciting opportunity we want to talk to you about. Can you meet Peter and me in New York this week?"

"What's up?" I asked.

"It's big news. Can you make it?"

After Rob and then Peter Moore split from Nike in the summer of 1987, they had started a new company, Sports, Inc., that quickly picked up some noteworthy clients. Right off the bat they created a stylish line of apparel for Adidas known as "Adidas Equipment" and a line of footwear for Foot Locker called ITZ—short for In the Zone. Tag line: Be Your Own Hero. Thanks to Rob and Peter, the Roundball and ABCD Camp were going to be the flagship events to introduce the ITZ line to the grassroots market.

"I gotta change my flight," I said, "but I'll be there."

In New York I met with Peter and Rob at Pete's Tavern off East Eighteenth Street near Gramercy Park. Rob's great appreciation of history gave him a taste for old-time New York bars and alehouses, which made the hallowed premises of Pete's a logical choice for our meeting. Though I'd kept in contact with Peter and Rob steadily since I'd left Nike, I hadn't seen either of them in person in more than a year.

When Adidas had the opportunity to work with Nike's former marketing and creative brain trust, the Germans wasted little time making a deal—for good reason. The company was in sad shape.

Adidas America, the German brand's American subsidiary, had been run by Peter Ueberroth for the previous ten years. Though Ueberroth had made his name as the head of the organizing committee behind the hugely successful 1984 LA Summer Olympic Games (and later as commissioner of Major League Baseball), his management of Adidas America was largely viewed as a failure. The Adidas brand in the States was getting pummeled. Though they were the premier powerhouse in soccer in Europe, their lack of attention to the US market had left them staggering and shrinking—with only about a 2 percent market share in the $10 billion American market. Incredibly, they were even far behind LA Gear, a fashion shoe upstart.

I found Rob and Peter parked in a booth at the back of Pete's. We hugged mightily as dear friends do, and I was genuinely elated to see both of them. Something big was afoot and I couldn't wait to hear the details.

"You don't need a menu, just get the prime rib," Rob said.

"So?" I said. "What's the big news?"

"We've been in negotiations with Adidas about running Adidas America," Rob replied. "We're going to take over the American operation."

That was big news. Strasser and Moore taking control of an iconic brand. *My God.*

"We've been to Germany a few times," Rob said. "The financing's lined up. Shit, I can even spell Herzogenaurach." (The city where Adidas was headquartered.)

What a change from only a couple of years earlier, I thought, when Adidas was our archenemy, our prime adversary when the three of us were at Nike

"Look, Sonny, it's gonna happen," Strasser said. "We want you to come join us."

I have to say that caught me off guard. I was well into my second full year post-Nike, and Pam and I were actually thriving. I had partnered with DIC, the animation and television production company, to develop an animated TV series for kids featuring athletes in heroic action roles. I was working with athletes like Dikembe Mutombo, Billy Owens, Stacey Augmon, and Jimmy Jackson with my new company, Vaccaro Sports Partnerships, marketing shoe deals, trading cards, and other endorsements. I felt like I was beginning to stand on solid ground. I was still running the Roundball and ABCD Camp; I'd reinvented myself post-Nike. It was scary but exhilarating.

"I don't know, guys," I said. "Pam and I have got a good thing going. I don't know if I want to jump back into it all again."

Did I really want to go to war against the company I'd helped build? Go head-to-head against a $3 billion money-making machine, an army of employees, and $300-million-plus a year in operating income? A dominant force led by a man with a particular animus toward former employees fighting for the hearts and minds of young athletes and major universities now owned by Nike.

Strasser had the knack for uttering just the right line at just the right time. And damn if he didn't do it again.

"Sonny, listen—very few people have the chance to climb the same mountain twice."

That line struck a chord with me. Over the coming days, I couldn't get that thought out of my head. The opportunity had another thing going for it: If I decided to join Adidas, it would help me release the simmering resentment for Nike that rankled me like a pebble in my shoe.

Over the next hours we talked strategy, the waiter hovering nearby looking to wrap things up. In response, Rob just kept ordering food and drinks. (His tip at the end of the night more than covered the cost of our three-hour meal.)

"Did you get any marketing money in the deal?" I asked. "You know Knight will do everything in his power to crush us."

"We've got a little—basically squat. That's why we want you."

I'd already locked up the college game and most of the major coaches for Nike. I told them we would have to go younger.

"Whatever you need to do, do it," Peter said. "We'll back anything you want to do."

I flew back to California with one hell of a decision to make.

Did I really want to go head-to-head with Phil Knight? Indeed, it would be the greatest challenge imaginable. Obviously, we knew how formidable they were—we're the ones who'd helped make that happen. The prospect of "climbing the same mountain twice" was tantalizing . . . only this time, it would be like climbing the same mountain with a fearsome Swoosh-driven blizzard howling in our faces.

I had to sleep on it. And talk with Pam. I couldn't make a decision on the spot.

Of course, the prospect of bringing back the Three Musketeers was tantalizing. If Rob, Peter, and I were as good as we thought we were, then we could hold our own against Knight and Nike's money machine.

A decision was made.

Game on.

February 1, 1993, Sonny Vaccaro rejoined Rob Strasser and Peter Moore at their new home, Adidas America. And with that, I strode full force into what would become known as the Shoe Wars, this time with three bold stripes on the battle flag instead of a Swoosh. But I had no delusions—this war, without question, was destined to spark some serious ill will. I knew Nike couldn't be beaten on the macro level, so I would have to rely on guerrilla warfare—a less-is-more strategy designed to strike quickly at the heart of an open opportunity.

Sounded like fun.

And it was.

The day it was announced in the press that Rob Strasser had taken over Adidas America, Nike's stock dropped.

• • •

ON ITS OWN, JUMPING BACK into battle would have made 1993 a notable year. Instead, week after week, it became one of the most tumultuous, heartbreaking periods of my life.

To begin with, if Nike was a well-oiled machine, Adidas was in the midst of transition chaos. No sooner had I signed on than the entire company was sold to a group headed by Robert Louis-Dreyfus, an ex-advertising agency executive. In the wake of the purchase a new organizational structure was put into place. Rob and Peter spent hours each week interviewing prospective hires, reviewing résumés, and pinning index cards on Rob's handmade organizational chart. It was gratifying to see résumés and calls pouring in from people at Nike, who loved and respected Rob and wanted to come help him climb the mountain. Industry publications touted the news as a legitimate challenge to Nike. No telling what the impact on Phil's ego was, as story after story lionized Strasser as the driving force behind Nike's march to success. The credit was well-placed—and accurately attributed. But those stories only stirred Phil up.

To put some personal muscle behind the Adidas resurgence, Rob, Peter, and I hit the road. Face time was a critical component in our strategy to schmooze industry buyers and executives. Two days after my start date, we were in Atlanta for the 1993 Super Show, shaking hands, renewing acquaintances, and giving Nike an old rival with some familiar faces to worry about. A couple of weeks later, we hit the NBA All-Star game in Salt Lake City sporting Adidas gear. In March, we were on scene for the Big East tournament in New York, rebranding ourselves as the "New Adidas." Next, it was on to Seattle for the Western regionals of the NCAA tournament. A week later, we were in New Orleans for the Final Four. The Adidas hospitality suite was in the same hotel as Nike, symbolically, one floor above. We entertained virtually around the clock with coaches, the media, and key retailers, continuing to establish that Three Stripes were now embodied in Rob, Peter, and me.

I saw Phil Knight briefly at the championship game between the heralded Fab Five of Michigan and North Carolina. We shook hands and barely spoke, although I recall telling him, *"Michigan may be your team, but they're my kids."*

Of course, he wanted to lay a marker down.

Phil's first act of retribution was separating Mike Krzyzewski from Adidas and bringing him to Nike, making sure he timed the news for maximum impact at the Final Four. In typical Knight fashion, he signed Krzyzewski, who'd been with Adidas for years, with a reported million-dollar signing bonus, a $375,000-a-year consulting fee, plus stock options—a sum that was unheard of at the time. Although Duke had appeared in Adidas gear during the tournament, they'd spend the next twenty-five years and beyond clad in Nike. As *The Washington Post* wrote, "The only difference between Coach K and the others playing this game is that he's going to get more money than anyone else. He may not have won the NCAA, but where it counts he's Coach of the Year."

Later that month, on April 28, 1993, as Pam and I were gathered in a private room with Michael and Juanita Jordan and a group of his friends and business associates to celebrate the grand opening of

Michael Jordan's restaurant in Chicago, we received the soul-crushing news that our dear friend Jimmy Valvano had succumbed that night to cancer at the age of forty-seven. News that brought us all to tears, leaving the rest of the evening a blur.

If that wasn't enough pain and sorrow, three months later, James Jordan, Michael's father, was found murdered in North Carolina in a random roadside attack at the age of fifty-six, another staggering blow to the entire basketball community.

And then, in early October, the ongoing horror show reached a new low.

Officially, in the FBI's records, it's listed as case #196B-PD-37319, the "PD" referencing the Bureau's Portland Division. In summary: a Justice Department investigation leading to a federal grand jury considering allegations of "corporate espionage" by John Vaccaro and Howard White, Michael Jordan's righthand man at Nike. You read that right.

Post-Nike, I had kept in touch with Howard, who I'd known dating back to his high school days when I had considered him as a potential Roundball invitee. Howard later helped Lefty Driesell recruit Moses Malone at Maryland, though Malone skipped college and signed with the Utah Stars of the ABA in 1974. Howard and I, as I've said, were tag-team partners crisscrossing the world with Jordan from '84 until '91.

When Knight evidently caught wind of our continued contact, all hell broke loose. Knight, or someone in his inner circle, picked up the phone and called the local FBI field office. As a result, under the RICO Act, three years of my bank and phone records from the period between January 1991 and December 1993 were subpoenaed and friends and associates interviewed.

Imagine how much clout someone must have to open an FBI RICO case against you and to have years of bank records and phone bills subpoenaed in evidence. This was before digital files. You're talking about literally going and packing your personal files in boxes at the bank and phone company.

According to court records, Howard was suspected of "funneling proprietary information to John Vaccaro," which would "allow Adidas to outbid Nike on contracts and use the players to endorse Adidas products."

As if I needed inside information from Nike on marketing, signing players, strategy, or anything else.

Fortunately, Brian O'Neill, a personal friend, brilliant lawyer, and former US attorney, was more than up to the challenge. To its credit, the grand jury examined the "evidence" then dismissed the Federal-level accusation. It never went to court.

Through a Freedom of Information Act request, after three long years we eventually received a heavily redacted file—and I mean blacked out.

Still, even that kind of small-minded revenge act paled to the devastating news that arrived before dawn on Saturday morning, October 30, a Halloween weekend horror show that ended the most cherished male relationship of my life.

* * *

WILDFIRES A FEW MILES UP the California coast, both north and south of us in Pacific Palisades, had enveloped the air in an acrid, hazy pallor, a faint smoky odor penetrating our home, when I was startled awake by the insistent ring of the phone beside me. I took calls seven days a week, but everyone knew not to reach out before 7:00 a.m. Something was wrong. Still groggy, I fumbled to grab the handset.

A distraught voice was on the other end of the line.

"Sonny . . . Owen."

Owen Clemens was officially a marketing manager at Adidas, but more importantly the "fixer" for all matters organizational. He was also Rob Strasser's executive assistant. Whatever the issue or assign-ment, Owen got it done—for the company or for Rob personally. You name it: a trade show, travel, a real estate transaction, a meeting with a retailer, an executive retreat, or a hundred other corporate contin-gencies, Owen was the go-to person. Normally quick with a light-hearted, prickly jibe, his voice was uncharacteristically frantic.

"Owen, you okay? What's wrong?"

"Son . . . he's gone. Rob's gone. He died at the hospital last night."

Rob Strasser, the CEO of Adidas America, our burly over-three-hundred-pound bearded bear of a man, had always enjoyed life to the fullest—too many deep-into-the-night business dinners across the globe compounded by too much stress, too much travel, too many cigars, and too many missed signs. Now, at forty-six, it all imploded with a thunderous, irrevocable finality at an Adidas conference out-side Munich.

I'd had friends and family die. But as I've said, Rob was like an-other brother. Now he was gone. Forever. This was as deep an episode of grief and disbelief as I had ever experienced. Some events in life overwhelm you to the point where the enormity is beyond compre-hension. This was that kind of moment.

Sickening waves of nausea and numbness poured over me. Whatever those speckled light flashes are called, they were dancing around my head.

"Wha . . . what? How?"

Pam, now fully awake, knew something was terribly wrong.

"Sonny, what is it? What happened!?"

"It's Owen in Germany. Rob died."

"Oh my God." Pam immediately burst into tears. I was sobbing along with her. We couldn't speak.

"We think it was a heart attack."

We later found out it was an aortic aneurysm. Rob's high blood pressure and frenetic global pace had finally come calling.

Owen continued with details, how Rob was to be brought home to Oregon, how Rob's wife, Julie, was doing, where Peter was, and a blur of other information. I hung up. I thought of the utter devastation that would sweep over Adidas when the news got out. I spent most of the day sitting on the stairs at home, inconsolable, broken.

In the world of athletic gear, Rob Strasser's sudden death was a seismic event. No one in the industry, not even Phil Knight, was of more consequence, held more gravitas. *The New York Times* published an obit. *The Oregonian* ran the headline, "Death Staggers Adidas America" and "staggers" was the right word.

Still in shock, I flew to Portland, where Peter and I addressed the entire company, which happened to be located in Nike's backyard just across the Tualatin Valley on a bluff overlooking its twenty-building corporate campus featuring six-acre man-made "Lake Nike," Rob's way of informing Phil Knight we were right there, hovering over his corporate shoulder. Peter and I put on a brave face, but we both knew the company was at a crossroads. The abject sadness was made even more morose when Knight chose not to attend Rob's funeral and ultimately only a handful of brave souls ignored Knight's example and came to pay their respects anyway. Regardless of what Phil Knight may have said afterward to mitigate that venal act of pettiness, I have never experienced a more stomach-turning act of retribution. Beyond reprehensible.

Peter Moore would immediately take over the company. For Adidas America, it was a life-altering leap into the unknown. "I'm not Rob Strasser," Peter told the assembled crowd, "but I can do this job. We have a long way to go, but everybody here knows they are part of a team, and we're depending on all of you to step up and help me."

Truth be told, losing Rob proved a breaking point I've never spoken publicly about until now. There are very few people in my life, other than Pam and my parents, I think of more than Rob. Even today, lying on the couch or staring at the water, I'm overwhelmed by his loss, a loss that has never left me.

In the wake of Rob's death, Pam spoke privately of the "deafening silence" in our home. Little or no talk. No music. Just dead air for a long period of time. Time after time I would go out and have a meeting or give a talk—put up a good front—then come home and fall into a deep, dark well of depression, where just getting out of bed took every last ounce of energy.

Yet, in the end, I couldn't dishonor Rob's memory by letting my mourning lead to disengagement from the world or Adidas. Rob, the history buff, would have recounted a string of wars where one general or another went down and the nation went on to achieve victory. I knew instinctively what he would have wanted us to do. In his spirit, I got up and didn't back down. I soldiered on. In a note to employees at Adidas I wrote, "No one can replace Rob Strasser's flare with people and his genius in the marketing world. I want you all to know, however, that all of us at Adidas will be driven with passion to fulfill Rob's dream."

To this very day, October 30 is a personal day of mourning, a trigger of unfathomable loss. In a small gift box tucked in a bedroom drawer, I still have the faded rose I wore the day of his funeral.

• • •

DESPITE THIS SUCCESSION OF NIGHTMARE events in 1993, a clear tactical business plan had solidified. An action plan that harkened back to my roots, where I had first found success.

In the grassroots basketball world, I had one tremendous advantage: Nike had flat-out abandoned high school and summer teams, their coaches, and leagues in cities across the country. In essence, they had left one of the key marketing doors wide open for me. Nike had pulled up stakes and left town.

I immediately pounced. Everywhere I looked, virgin territory was out there—great programs hungry for shoe, uniform, and gear deals. Nike's stunning abandonment meant the next generation was there for the picking. The premier teams in summer basketball, stung by Nike's and Reebok's inattention, welcomed me with open arms. For the most part, entry-level grassroots basketball was Sonny Vaccaro's domain, and I saw tremendous upside. Nike spent their time renewing colleges and chose to terminate summer travel teams. I didn't have to sneak in through some back door—their blinders opened the door for Adidas to get a foothold in an area Nike once owned.

In ways that mattered to me, Adidas and Nike had suddenly transposed mindsets. Nike was the ungainly, ponderous behemoth, bureaucratic and slow-footed. Adidas was the guerrilla band of street fighters, attacking vulnerable frontiers in Nike's blind spots. The arrogance that Knight had so abhorred in his "revolutionary" days was now his company's trademark feature.

I had advantages: a nationwide network built around the Roundball and the ABCD Camp—events that still outshined Nike's attempts to supplant my games despite being outspent a hundred to one.

In Strasser's cavernous absence, I redoubled my efforts. His memory, his words playing on a loop in my mind, rekindled my passion. In grief, I channeled Rob's words: *The high school is the birthplace, the first stop; it's where dreams are born. Be the brand today's ninth grader grows up with."*

Using the Roundball and ABCD Camp as a base of operations, we'd extend our brand to future stars, those emerging in high school, on summer teams, and across inner-city playgrounds. The next generation of coaches and players were my beachhead. The formula I began with never died. I signed twenty-five or thirty talented young coaches—Herb Sendek, Fran Fraschilla, Kevin Bannon, and Kevin Stallings—for nominal amounts, maybe $5,000. As with Jimmy Valvano at Iona years earlier, I looked to sign assistants and smaller-school head coaches destined to work their way into coaching prominence in the decades to come.

In addition, I immediately began signing the high schools and summer programs Nike had cut loose or missed. Programs like the New Jersey Playaz, Team Breakdown in Florida, the Long Island Panthers, and dozens more. From California to Texas, Louisiana to Illinois, New Jersey to the Northwest, I picked off teams and gold-star high school coaches like Bobby Hurley Sr., Saint Anthony's in Jersey City, New Jersey; Jim Haley, Vanguard High, Ocala, Florida; Gary DeCesare of Saint Raymond's in New York; and Bobby Hartstein of Lincoln High in New York, where Stephon Marbury played. I had Tenis Young, a recreational director from Philadelphia, and Willie Boston from Albany, Georgia. There was Mac Irvin, who ran Chicago's top prep league. I could fill half this book with the terrific grassroots people from across America who kept me apprised of every up-and-coming prospect wherever basketball was being played, including those who played on crumbling concrete outdoor courts or ancient oak floors at inner-city YMCAs.

Once Nike saw the retrenchment happening on the ground, they scrambled to jump back in. Too late. I was not just masterminding Adidas' strategy but Nike's as well. Their entire grassroots game plan, on orders from Knight, was to watch what Sonny Vaccaro did and counter my every move.

Once again, Nike simply threw money at people without any genuine, organic connection to the community itself. They scrambled to recoup some semblance of credibility by hiring George Raveling, a former friend of mine, to run their summer programs. Nonetheless, despite the budget disparity, I took great pleasure in outmaneuvering Raveling and Nike with our grassroots strategy. In turn, one after another, *Parade* All-Americans chose the ABCD over Nike-sponsored camps. Felipe López, Jason Kidd, Randy Livingston, Rashard Griffith, Dontonio Wingfield, Zendon Hamilton, Rasheed Wallace,

Tracy McGrady, Stephon Marbury, Charles and Ed O'Bannon, Jamal Mashburn, and hundreds of others chose ABCD and the Roundball as the place to showcase their talent.

From the ABCD Camp and Roundball, I saw a trend emerging: The preponderance of talent appeared to be clustered on the East Coast. The pendulum always swung back and forth, but the talent seemed to be aggregating in New York, New Jersey, Philadelphia, Chicago, DC, Detroit, and further south in Florida and Atlanta.

I found living three thousand miles away in California—a continent away—to be too far removed from the concentration of emerging players now on the East Coast. I knew instinctively we had to be there. I had to meet the players' parents, watch the kids play, have lunch with them, build relationships with coaches, right there, person-to-person, on the scene.

So I spent a good part of the final months of 1993 and early '94 traveling back and forth between Los Angeles and New York to scout out a new location for ABCD, which had previously relocated to UC Irvine in California, then Eastern Michigan University near Detroit. I visited Rutgers University's Newark campus, Hofstra University, and Manhattan College in the Bronx. Rich Kosik, an academic advisor who had supervised the educational curriculum at the ABCD Camp since its inception, and Bobby Hartstein, camp codirector, suggested we check out Fairleigh Dickinson University (FDU) in New Jersey. FDU had a great location, the Rothman Center gym, and easy access to hotels and other facilities. Not to mention talent-rich DC, Philly, Baltimore, Chicago, and New York within a day's drive.

"I want to move the ABCD Camp to Fairleigh Dickinson in New Jersey," I told Peter Moore. "We'll get tons of media coverage and the best kids and their coaches can just drive to the camp."

"Okay," said Peter. "Do what you got to do."

The relocation was set. The ABCD Camp would take place at Fairleigh Dickinson University beginning in July 1994.

I had a markedly different conversation with Peter after our first-year success at FDU.

"I've got to set up shop on the East Coast. I've had my ear to the ground for a few months now and Adidas must have a presence back East," I told him. He pondered it for a moment and then approved the move on the spot.

"One more thing," I said.

"Yeah . . ."

"I got him."

"You got who?"

"Michael." I was speaking in metaphorical terms.

"Michael who?" Peter asked.

"Our Michael Jordan."

His mind assumed I was talking about a college player.

"Who? A college player?"

"No," I said. "It's a high school kid."

Peter pressed me. "Is it Garnett?"

"No, it's not Kevin."

"You've been talking to him, right?"

"Yeah, but it's not Garnett."

"Who are you after?"

"Kobe Bryant. That's the main reason I need to be in New York, so I can make sure. I need to be close to Philadelphia without being in Philadelphia."

And once again, without hesitation, Peter said, "Go for it."

He might as well have said "Just do it."

21

Jellybean's Kid

I was on the floor in the main gym at FDU in July 1994 amid the chaos and clamor surrounding Registration Day when, from a short distance, a familiar voice called out.

"Sonny, hold up."

The voice belonged to Gary Charles, the founder of the Long Island Panthers, a force in East Coast youth basketball. While most people who attended camps showed up in jeans or sweat suits, Gary always dressed to the nines, on this day festooned in an expensive white fedora and dapper suit. A systems programmer and assistant vice president at Citibank, he had devoted an equal share of his life to keeping the Panthers a feared opponent in youth basketball. Over the years he'd sent a steady stream of terrific players to ABCD and the Roundball. Adidas now sponsored his team and we'd become fast friends.

As always, we hugged hello. I quickly noticed Gary was standing next to two other people.

"Sonny, you remember this guy?" he asked, gesturing to a tall, thin bespectacled Black man I couldn't quite place. Seeing the puzzled look on my face, the man said, "Joe Bryant."

I hadn't laid eyes on Joe "Jellybean" Bryant since he won the MVP as a seventeen-year-old from Philly's Bartram High School at the 1972 Dapper Dan Roundball Classic. Now nothing less than this thing called sports and the confluence of opportunity and happenstance had brought us back together.

"Jellybean!" We hugged. "How've you been, young man?"

"I've been great," he said.

Nodding to the six-foot-ish wiry kid next to him, he said, "This is my son, Kobe. Can I get him into ABCD this year? He's a sophomore at Lower Merion in Philly." I shook Kobe's hand and welcomed him to the camp.

"Hello, young man. Gary tells me I should keep an eye on you."

"I hope you do, Mr. Vaccaro," the self-assured teenager said with conviction.

"Good. Maybe this'll be a 'like father, like son' thing—your dad was one of the best, young fella," I said. A father-son MVP story— that would be a nice headline, if it happened.

"He's pretty good, Sonny," Joe said. "In Italy, he held his own with some of the guys I played with."

At the time Joe Bryant was an assistant coach at his alma mater, La Salle University, in Philadelphia. He'd gone from college to the NBA and been lucky enough to play with the 76ers when they went to the 1977 NBA Finals on a team that featured Dr. J and Doug Collins. Joe went on to play for the Clippers in San Diego before ending his NBA career with the Houston Rockets in 1982–83. From there he spent a few seasons overseas in Italy, playing with a variety of clubs in the Italian pro basketball league before retiring in '91. Kobe had been born in 1978 while Joe was still with the Sixers and spent most of his childhood hanging around his dad's practices and games. Blessed with natural athletic talent, Kobe had been brought up with a basketball in his hands practically from birth.

Searching for the future of Adidas basketball, I'd focused my attention on Coney Island's Stephon Marbury, on his way to being named New York State's Mr. Basketball and already known by his nickname "Starbury." But at the 1994 ABCD, it took Kobe all of a week to blast to the top of my "gifted" list. Competing against the top 160 American players, along with a handful of prospects from places like China,

France, Australia, Canada, and Russia, Kobe was intimidated by no one. Although future NBA star Tim Thomas won the camp MVP award, Kobe's ballhandling, shooting, passing, and knowledge of the game went far beyond his years. And he carried a look in his eye that caught mine, like the one he held as he approached to say goodbye at the end of a breakout week.

"I want to apologize, Mr. Vaccaro."

"Apologize? For what? What'd you do?"

"It's what I *didn't* do, Mr. Vaccaro. I wanted to win the MVP and I didn't get there. But I guarantee you, I'll win it next year."

I've never forgotten that moment. Imagine a fifteen-year-old who had just established himself as one of the premier players in the country against a torrent of other talent . . . disappointed he wasn't the absolute best.

The timing of our interaction could not have been better. After two trying years at Adidas, we'd finally achieved a certain sense of calm and momentum. The Roundball Classic and ABCD Camp had been reinvigorated. By July '95, we were in the second year of sponsoring the Big Time Tournament in Las Vegas, destined to grow from thirty-two original teams into hundreds of teams. Slowly, we had found our financial footing and signed some key endorsement deals: Jerry Tarkanian, who was now coaching at Fresno State; Norm Stewart at Missouri; and Gene Bartow at Alabama at Birmingham. We also locked up team deals with the New York Yankees, Notre Dame, Tennessee, and Nebraska.

Still, we needed a *star*. Not just any star but someone in the Michael Jordan galaxy. And, as I outlined in this May '95 memo to the executive board, that star would not come cheap:

I sincerely believe that we need a blockbuster player—but in order to get this person, we have to be able to commit a lot of money to the project. Not only money to pay the athlete, but money to back him *up with advertising regionally, nationally, and internationally. We must get a player that means something both on and off the court. We must not lose sight of one very important thing: This player has to be a **great player**. One who the public will take to, talk about, and most important, try to imagine in their minds what his next move will be. There must be a greatness and an elusiveness to this player/person. America needs heroes and the world worships them! I will not and cannot emphasize to you the importance of getting the right player. He has to be someone who translates his very presence into a near mythical being. You can imagine what it is to be like him, but you know that you can't. That's what it's all about.*

. . .

AS PROMISED, KOBE BRYANT WON the Senior Class ABCD MVP award in '95 before heading back to Lower Merion for his senior year in high school. By now Kobe was no longer just a local phenom; he'd collected an avalanche of honors—All-State, All-American, and state champion.

After watching every one of his games at ABCD for two straight years, I *knew* Kobe was someone Peter and I could work with in much the same way we had with Jordan. Now all I had to do was make it happen—and make sure Phil Knight never caught wind of my plan.

From speaking with Gary Charles, I was well aware that Joe Bryant had been exploring the possibility of his prodigal son going pro straight out of high school. Joe was sure Kobe was up to the challenge, and Kobe himself had wanted to fulfill the NBA dream he'd carried since he was five years old—and do it as soon as he could.

The courting of Kobe Bryant proved to be something out of the movie *Mission: Impossible* . . . so stealth that I never attended a single game at Lower Merion. His father helped with the mission, offering comments that Kobe might sign with La Salle, Michigan, Duke, North

Carolina, or Villanova when he signed his National Letter of Intent. Joe insinuated time after time his son was going nowhere else but college. But a small group of us were positive he'd never make a single lay-up on any college campus. When 6'11" *USA Today* National Player of the Year and future Hall of Famer Kevin Garnett entered the 1995 NBA Draft straight out of Chicago's Farragut Academy, we figured it was a foregone conclusion Kobe would follow in his footsteps.

With Gary Charles as my envoy, a series of back-channel discussions continued through '95 and '96. Over that year or so, I met frequently with the Bryants and we became quite close. I also met with Kobe's extended family, his aunts and uncles, the composite group known as "Team Bryant." They didn't owe me anything but a chance to land Kobe.

Only once did I see Joe and his wife, also named Pam, down in Philly. We went one time to catch a Villanova game during the '95 Christmas holidays and joined them occasionally for dinner in New York or New Jersey. My cover story for our apartment on the Upper East Side was that I was keeping a close eye on the burgeoning East Coast grassroots scene. (Nike was off the trail since I hadn't signed a billboard player up to that time.)

I was well aware that the Bryants were leaving their options open with other shoe companies; we never negotiated directly until Kobe graduated high school. I never once laid my cards on the table, only letting the family know Adidas had sincere interest. I told them, *"Your son has the chance to become the Michael of his generation."* Nike, Converse, and Reebok, meanwhile, showed little interest—unwilling, it seemed, to sign an untested high school star.

. . .

IN THE SPRING OF '96, Arn Tellem, a Philly native on his way to becoming one of the biggest sports agents in the business, arranged a secret workout for Kobe in front of Lakers' GM Jerry West at a gym in one of the beach cities south of the LA airport. Not just any workout, but a full-on NBA test, an hour and fifteen intense minutes. When West arrived, we introduced him to Kobe, who gave him a firm handshake, a future NBA legend greeting the iconic guard whose image adorned the league's logo. *The* Jerry West, who sadly passed away in June 2024 at the age of eighty-six.

During the workout Kobe was to go one-on-one against Michael Cooper, the recently retired ('91) Lakers' guard specifically brought in that day by West. Cooper was an eight-time member of the NBA's All-Defensive team, including five times All-First Team. In the end, Kobe surprised Cooper, the teenager giving much more than he had anticipated. Ankle-breaking crossover dribbles, pull-up jumpers, fakes, spins, deep three-pointers, graceful scoops and floaters, a preview of the pyrotechnics to come. Not an iota of nervousness in front of the league's premier front-office executive, who was watching intently in the stands.

West sat, arms crossed, watching Bryant for the first time. He never said a word, and neither did we. No need for us to elaborate on what was unfolding before his eyes.

After just fifteen minutes, West had seen enough. "Arn," he said, "see what you can work out with some of the clubs ahead of us. The kid is going to go before [pick] twenty-four. I've got a player or two I could move. See if you can work a trade."

We shook hands again and walked with West to the exit. He waved goodbye to Kobe on the way out and disappeared. I walked on the court and gave a budding superstar one big hug.

"You killed it, Kobe," I said.

For the next twenty minutes or so we fooled around on the court. I think we played a game of Horse, leaving me the second victim Kobe had that afternoon.

That private workout was the one and only Kobe would do for any team. West had advised us to lay low and Arn agreed. He restricted access for every other NBA team inquiring about Kobe, knowing they'd be reluctant to draft a high school kid without first talking to him or working him out. In the meantime, Arn got to work. With the free-agent signing of center Shaquille O'Neal to a seven-year, $120 million contract, current Lakers' big man Vlade Divac became a kind of accessory after the fact. Working below the radar, Tellem worked out a deal with Charlotte to take Kobe at number thirteen and trade him to LA in exchange for Divac.

. . .

ON MAY 21, 1996, fresh out of high school, a month shy of the NBA Draft, with Kobe wearing a black-and-white Adidas warm-up suit and twirling an Adidas-logoed basketball on his fingertip, we announced a multiyear deal in front of the media for the then astronomical figure of $1 million a year. Even the Bryants had no idea I was going to come in with a figure that rich. As part of the package, Joe would be paid $150,000 a year as a consultant.

As a one-time gambler, I'd gone all in more than once in my life—but never for $5 million over five years. In many ways, the Kobe deal was far more fraught with risk than the Jordan signing. At least with Michael, everyone had watched him win a national championship at Carolina and an Olympic gold medal. He had performance markers that could justify his signing. Even with Jordan's proven potential, I had to put my job on the line to get it done. With a seventeen-year-old who hadn't even played for a college team, the leap of faith was monumental. Once again, I was putting my reputation on the line to secure a star that I believed capable of carrying an entire brand.

Thankfully, Peter Moore was on board from the moment I'd given him my evaluation. As Peter said in the "Sole Man" *30 for 30* documentary: "If Sonny told you that a fifteen-year-old in China was the next big thing, you go after him."

Steve Wynne (not the Las Vegas Steve Wynn), the Adidas America president at the time, may have been a little nervous at the start. After all, this was a basketball moon shot. But once he was in, he was *all in*. His comment to the *Philadelphia Daily News* that month proved prophetic: "Kobe's one of a new generation of athletes who will help transform sports in the next decade. There's a generation of kids coming into sports that have grown up loving it in a way that brings an enthusiasm to the game that I think will be significant."

Naturally, not everyone agreed. Across the industry, the signing was derided, universally panned by the media and so-called experts. Boiling down to trolling along the lines of *Did you hear what Vaccaro did this time? He just paid a high school kid a million bucks a year!*

. . .

JUNE 26, 1996. CONTINENTAL AIRLINES Arena, East Rutherford, New Jersey, site of the fiftieth NBA Draft, widely considered one of the deepest and most talented in league history.

Point guard Allen Iverson went number one to the 76ers in a draft loaded with future NBA All-Stars: Steve Nash, Ray Allen, Stephon Marbury, Jermaine O'Neal, Antoine Walker, Marcus Camby, Shareef Abdur-Rahim, and Kerry Kittles.

At number seven, center Lorenzen Wright's name was called by the LA Clippers.

The Nets owned the next pick.

I'd known New Jersey's new head coach John Calipari for years from my camps and all-star games. Cal knew I knew the Bryants and Kobe very well. Earlier in the night, as I sat in the green room with Kobe and Arn, I had conversations with both Cal and Nets general manager John Nash. When they queried me, I mentioned the possibility—nothing more, nothing less—that if drafted by the Nets, Kobe might opt to play in Europe for a year.

"Seriously," said Calipari, "the kid would go to Italy instead of the NBA?"

"John, all I can tell you is, there is a possibility that could happen."

Every second seemed interminable as we feigned nonchalance awaiting the Nets' selection. As David Stern approached the podium, my heart was pounding its way through my shirt and tie.

"With the eighth pick in the 1996 draft, the New York Nets have selected . . . Kerry Kittles, guard, Villanova."

We jumped out of our seats and cheered, hands raised in the air, momentarily forgetting Kittles was seated right behind us. We turned to congratulate Kerry, elated he had been New Jersey's first pick. Kittles would become a very good NBA player, but he wasn't Kobe Bryant.

A half hour later we watched Kobe walk onstage and shake hands with Commissioner Stern after being drafted thirteenth by Charlotte. Later that evening we watched him swap his Hornets hat when Stern returned to the podium and announced that Kobe Bryant had just been traded to the Los Angeles Lakers for center Vlade Divac.

Getting Kobe signed and traded to LA was unquestionably the single most important basketball move in Adidas's history. A moment that reaffirmed my decision to jump back into the Shoe Wars, the culmination of a bitter battle with Nike that had only intensified over the preceding five years. Along with the signings of first-round picks Tim Thomas, Jermaine O'Neal, and Antoine Walker, Adidas America was no longer an also-ran. We were seriously back in the game with our *Michael* signed, sealed, and destined for greatness.

In the aftermath of Kobe's signing, Knight vowed he would never be put in that position again. I soon received word that Knight had assembled his troops and repeated the same ominous warning to them:

"Don't ever underestimate Sonny Vaccaro. Don't ever let him out of your sight."

...

I KNEW KOBE WOULD BE *very* good. But would I have predicted he'd be an eighteen-time All-Star, selected eleven times to the All-NBA first team, win five NBA championships, be named to the NBA's All-Defensive first team nine times, earn two NBA Finals MVP awards, and end up a lock for the Basketball Hall of Fame? Not in your life.

The same way I could never have imagined the unspeakable tragedy in which Kobe would lose his life, the result of a helicopter crash into the side of a fog-shrouded mountain on January 26, 2020, at the age of forty-one. We watched a nation grieve, an outpouring of praise and sorrow at his shocking passing, along with his thirteen-year-old daughter, Gianna, and seven others, including six family friends, that fateful Sunday morning in Calabasas, California.

God rest his immortal soul and those who perished with him.

22

T–Mac: 175 to 1

Sonny, you can't invite this kid. He comes from a bad family situation. If you take him at the ABCD, you're in for a heap of trouble."

Tracy McGrady's former high school coach (who shall remain nameless) had passed on the warning.

I ended the phone call saying, "Okay, Coach, thanks for your input."

Two follow-up calls came in from other coaches imploring us to do the same—jettison McGrady before it was too late. To me, this went beyond actionable information; it was beginning to feel personal. Some kind of vendetta.

I had been considering inviting Tracy Lamar McGrady Jr. to the 1996 camp based on the recommendation of Alvis Smith, one of our trusted summer coaches and a guy who had a knack for finding talented players over the entire state of Florida. McGrady, a rising senior at the time, was a tall, gangly kid with a slight droop to his eyes. Since Tracy hadn't played for a well-known high school and none of the "official" rating or scouting services had heard of him, he was off the grid.

Once again, I checked with Alvis down in Florida.

"Sonny, you think I'm gonna recommend a kid who can't play? I'm telling you, I ain't seen a kid with this much talent in a while."

At most I only had room for 175 kids at ABCD. The top-tier players were no-brainers to invite. It was always the last fifty or so where the choices between who goes and who doesn't got granular. Alvis, whom I trusted, was effusive about the 6′8″ small forward / shooting guard. Tracy's ex-coach's warning was just as strongly considered.

During his junior year in high school, Tracy had averaged twenty-three points and twelve rebounds in Auburndale, Florida, about forty miles northeast of Tampa, not exactly a hotbed of high school basketball.

I was mulling a decision when my most trusted advisor brought me to my senses. "I cannot believe anyone is that bad," Pam said. "I want you to trust Alvis on this. Any coach who'd go to such an extreme to stop a young person is the problem. You're the one who always gives kids chances. You invite him."

Out went an invitation. McGrady was the last player to make the cut, literally number 175. He was assigned to a team. Nobody had the slightest idea about whether he was going to rise or fall in a gym full of the top talent in the country.

I was curious, so I kept an eye out. Year after year, whether it was LeBron or Kobe or some unknown in the rankings, the mission for the players is: *Do something*. Blending in was the equivalent of not being there.

You could say Tracy proceeded to *do something* on a jaw-dropping scale more dramatically than any unknown we'd ever invited. I remember one game in particular. McGrady's team was playing against a team starring Lamar Odom, one of the most highly touted players at ABCD and across the country—"the next Magic Johnson," some said. Odom was a powerful 6′10″ center from Queens, New York, a big kid with big skills, the kind of player who could make you look sick and send you home with a fractured ego, a lock to be a pro very soon. My curiosity piqued when I learned Tracy had told his ABCD coach, "I'll take him."

At every camp we had matchups between two "real deal" players whose shoot-out created some serious buzz. LeBron against Lenny Cooke. O. J. Mayo versus Derrick Rose. Kevin Love versus Greg

Oden. The Odom-McGrady face-off was different, unanticipated—a marquee player versus an unknown quantity.

On this particular day McGrady emerged as someone ready to step into rarified air. Lamar got his shots in but his overall performance was lackluster. McGrady not only gave Odom problems, he threw his game off, badgered Lamar until he lost his cool. On offense, Tracy proved every bit Odom's equal. He drove past him, pulled up for a series of jumpers, passed to other players as Odom lunged. Fast, fluid, creative, and fearless.

I found myself thinking this is happening again—another one of those "zero to hero" breakout stars is making his debut.

Naturally, with so many eyes in the stands, I was hardly the only one taking notice. A "Who is that kid?" curiosity swept through the bleachers like a hurricane, assistant coaches frantically taking notes, flipping through the camp booklet to find more information on who?—McDuffy, McGuffy, McCauly?

By the end of the week, they all knew the name McGrady after Tracy solidified his new stature with one of the immortal all-time All-Star Game moments. Midway through the second half Tracy made a steal and headed up court to dunk home free. Glancing back, he could see James Felton, a 6'10" center and damn good player, closing in.

No one captured the moment better than Bruce Feldman, then working for ESPN, who wrote:

Everyone in the gym took notice as [Tracy] slowed at the top of the key to wait for the much-hyped Felton. When the big man caught up, McGrady stared him down, then took off a couple of strides inside the free throw line. Felton jumped too, but just as his fingers grazed the ball palmed in his opponent's right hand, McGrady whipped it down to his waist. In the next instant, he grabbed it with his left and windmilled it through the hoop so fiercely that it

should have dented the floor. By the time the unheralded prep
landed, he [McGrady] was the next big thing. Dozens of fans and
players tumbled onto the court, yelling and high-fiving, temporarily
halting the game. All Felton could do was shake his head, scratch his
cheek and try not to look the victim. But the damage was done. The
country's most-sought-after big had been owned.

From those five spectacular days on there was no looking back for
Tracy. In New Jersey's sweltering summer heat, T-Mac had *arrived.*
He came to his first-ever camp as a nonentity and left with professional scouts making note after note on number 175. Only now that
number had changed.

"Nobody had a clue who Tracy McGrady was," Tracy later said.
"Sonny Vaccaro gave me that platform. I left that camp the number
one player in the nation, 175 to number one."

Those droopy eyelids, his soft smile, and quiet demeanor may have
left some with the impression that Tracy played without passion, that
he didn't give it everything he had—and as he soon proved again and
again, nothing could be further from the truth. McGrady was one of
the greatest natural athletes I've ever seen. His execution was vicious,
precise, decisive, and often artful. Sure, he needed some polish because he lacked the level of coaching requisite to reach greatness but
that would change soon enough.

After his performance at the ABCD, McGrady left Auburndale
High behind and played his senior season at powerful Mount Zion
Christian Academy in Durham, North Carolina, for coach Joel
Hopkins. Mount Zion ended that season ranked number two in the
nation. McGrady averaged 27.5 points and was named *USA Today's*
High School Basketball Player of the Year.

A steady stream of college coaches and pro scouts had brought
their notebooks to Durham as McGrady became the biggest blue
chip on many a team's charts. I knew a certain shoe company that

wasn't about to pass on this up-and-coming star, my encore to Kobe Bryant.

Only this time, Nike wasn't sitting on the sidelines. By now Phil and the Swoosh knew what I knew. Tracy was destined to become the first pro prospect Nike and I would fight over. And if Phil was going to steal him from me, the Swoosh would have to reach deep to pull it off.

After Tracy graduated from Mount Zion, I brought him out to California for a visit. He'd never been west of North Carolina and may have been a bit starstruck, though he handled it with his customary aplomb and graciousness. Tracy's demeanor was invariably respectful and polite. There was a gracefulness and kindness about him that made him a joy to be around. He was curious, listened, and had an engaging presence that was beautiful to experience.

I knew he'd be a first-rounder—if not a lottery pick—if he chose to skip college and turn pro. Given his generous soul, he was anxious to help his family rise above their humble status. Every major college program in the country was hot on his tail, but my sense was Tracy had the athletic tool kit and scoring skills to make the jump straight to the pros. While he was in town, we introduced him to Kobe, who was just finishing up his first year in Los Angeles. His family had settled a few blocks away from us near the Pacific Coast. Tracy and Kobe had an immediate affinity for one another, and, of course, Tracy admired Kobe's accomplishments. They talked shop, hoop, shared stories, Kobe opening Tracy's eyes to the road ahead.

Business is business, though, and Tracy wasn't going to sacrifice the best shoe deal possible just because we'd become close. I advised him to maximize his deal, whoever the bidder. Players deserve the highest dollar they can negotiate.

In a matter of days, Nike flew Tracy up to Portland, giving him free rein to load up on gear at the company store, then waltzed him around the impressive promenade of buildings sporting famous Nike athletes, topped off by a two-story-tall Jordan poster. Undoubtedly they filled his head with visions of someday having his "own" building overlooking Lake Nike. Nothing can light up the imagination or provide ego gratification more than the full Swoosh VIP experience.

All I had was the experience of bringing Tracy to the ABCD Camp and watching him ascend from a nonentity to the number one player in America.

. . .

I WAS IN PALM SPRINGS, a resort city about 120 miles from LA, where Pam and I routinely went for a getaway, when Alvis Smith, Tracy's summer league coach, called.

"Sonny, full disclosure . . ."

"Yeah, Alvis, what's up?"

"Listen, Nike came in with a big offer. Biiiggg offer. If he goes with Nike, we'll still be okay, right? This won't mess up anything with Adidas?"

"What's the number, Alvis?"

"A million five."

"That's fantastic!" I was elated for Tracy. Life-altering money.

But I was going to beat Phil Knight whatever it took.

In a press conference broadcast on ESPN News from Mount Zion, Tracy McGrady, in suit and tie, announced he was going to enter the NBA Draft. After watching Kevin Garnett in '95 and Kobe in '96, his time had come.

On June 18, 1997, Adidas America made Tracy one of the richest teenagers in America, signing him to a six-year deal at $1.7 million per year, nearly double what they had paid Kobe a year before. Nike never countered.

A week later, the '97 NBA Draft took place in Charlotte. Tim Duncan was the first selection by the San Antonio Spurs. Tracy was drafted ninth by the Toronto Raptors. In July 2000, he was traded to the Orlando Magic. The next year McGrady made his first of seven NBA All-Star teams. Two years later he won his first of two scoring titles. As part of the Class of 2017, he was inducted as a member of the Naismith Basketball Hall of Fame. Over the span of his first contract, Adidas produced six signature T-Mac shoes. We later signed Tracy to a lifetime deal. As I told one sports business publication at the time, "If you believe in the kid, why would you go through the trouble of having to renegotiate every six years? It's like free agency, when there are renegotiations, there's always a chance your guy can leave. Now Tracy is tied to us both monetarily and spiritually forever."

It was the first time I'd gone head-to-head with Knight to sign a player he wanted. I won that round.

I wouldn't be as fortunate in 2003.

23

A Betrayal in Malibu

I got a call in my hotel room during the 2000 Final Four in Indianapolis from one of my grassroots "eyes and ears" guys, another of the people I had come to know in the urban basketball hotbeds across the country.

"Sonny, it's Chris Dennis."

I'd first met Chris at the Final Four in Tampa a year earlier when he joined our group for dinner and I got to know a little bit about his background, particularly his immersion in the AAU scene and helping kids in and around Akron, Ohio.

"Good to hear your voice again, young man. Where are you?"

Chris told me he had made the three-hundred-mile trip from Akron for one reason—and it wasn't to watch the Final Four.

"I'm here to see you," he said. "I've got a tape I want you to see. A kid named LeBron James. He's a freshman. It's highlights of the game against VASJ [Villa Angela–Saint Joseph's in Cleveland]. Do you have a moment to take a look?"

I'd heard bits and pieces about James but had no particular knowledge of him—or his game. I got tips every year on young up-and-comers that coaches insisted I needed to see. So this was nothing new.

Dennis said LeBron was a fifteen-year-old freshman that had just led his team to the championship game in Florida at the AAU Nationals. And had starred on a high school team that went a perfect 17–0 that season.

"Sure, Chris. Come up to my suite around three?"

"Great, Sonny, I'll meet you then. I've got one of LeBron's friends, Maverick Carter, with me. You mind if he tags along?"

"Not at all, I've got a roomful of people. Call me when you get over here."

By 2000, I'd been a fixture in grassroots basketball for nearly forty years. I knew that Chris Dennis had a keen eye for talent and had great rapport with kids. He had played out in California when he was younger and still kept abreast of talent on the West Coast.

When Dennis arrived at my suite, fifteen or twenty people were already milling about, snacking, drinking, and swapping stories, some of the dozens of invitees who passed through my door that day. It was my long-standing tradition—a Final Four "meet and greet"—prior to heading over to catch the NCAA semifinal games.

I honestly never knew who was going to show up. A few years earlier, at the Final Four in Atlanta, a 6'9" or 6'10" gentleman approached me and said hello. At first glance, I couldn't place a name with the face. He introduced himself as Leon Douglas. I hadn't seen Leon in twenty-five years, not since the 1972 Roundball. He was a stellar talent who'd played center for the University of Alabama, earning all-SEC honors for four straight years and playing in the NBA with Detroit and the Kansas City Kings before departing for Italy, where he played professionally for a decade. Leon was coaching in high school when we met again. We hugged and laughed. Then he offered up one of the most flattering compliments ever directed my way.

"See this guy!" he boomed to a suddenly quiet room. "He was ESPN for us before there was an ESPN."

. . .

INVARIABLY DURING THE FINAL FOUR, a few coaches would come to the hospitality suite and ask if I could step aside to chat privately for a moment, many of them young assistants on the rise, seeking counsel: Am I doing the right thing? Do you think it's time to move? Can you get my name in front of coach A or B? It was very personal. Truth be told, over the years, at one point or another, virtually everybody who was anybody in college, high school, or summer league basketball passed through my Final Four suite.

I always understood how shoe money could alter people's lives, change the trajectory of a program, or boost a career. I lived and worked in a highly competitive business for a long, long time, trusting my convictions and instincts, rarely misjudging who the good guys were—or weren't. Sappy as it may sound, I cared about opportunities for coaches and kids. I had more than my share of fateful, fortuitous breaks, and if I could help someone else's career along the way, I rarely said no.

. . .

WHEN CHRIS DENNIS AND LEBRON'S young friend Maverick Carter arrived, I introduced them around the room. In addition to the old cartridge video tape in his hand, Chris had brought a xeroxed stack of clippings and articles from Ohio papers touting young LeBron. Chris handed out a few of them to the coaches and left the rest on a table for anyone interested.

"Okay if I play the tape?"

"Yeah, let's see it."

Without any preamble he slid the cassette into the VHS player. The room quieted down.

After eight or ten seconds a highlight reel began playing. The tape had about twelve minutes of low-quality handheld footage edited together.

When it was finished, LeBron James had done something only a few kids his age had ever done: Impress me.

Understand, I was inundated with people touting kids year-round.

State champions, Mr. Basketball of this or that state, all-this, all-that from every corner of the country. This was different. The kid on that grainy video was someone I wanted to see more of.

Chris Dennis just stood over to the side trying to gauge the reactions to a tape he'd seen probably thirty times before.

"I know it's a little early, but I hope you'll consider him for the ABCD when he's old enough," he said, knowing we didn't take freshmen at the camp.

"I'll definitely keep tabs on him," I said. "I appreciate you bringing the tape. That tape says all I need to know."

"I've got copies. You can keep it," Chris offered. With that, we hugged, then he shook a few hands and left with Maverick.

At that moment, I already knew LeBron James would be on the ABCD invite list for 2001. Now, I wanted a closer look.

A few months later as I was winding down from the ABCD and the Big Time Tournament in Vegas, Chris Dennis contacted me again.

"Sonny, Dru Joyce and I are going out to Oakland to have LeBron work out with the Oakland Soldiers. I was hoping you could fly up to catch him live. Calvin Andrews arranged for him to play against some older players and college guys."

The Oakland Soldiers were one of the better Adidas-sponsored West Coast summer travel teams, and Andrews, the Soldiers' founder and head coach, was a close friend. Along with LeBron, Chris, and Dru, the group coming to California included LeBron's high school coaches; Dru's son; LeBron's mother, Gloria; and family friend Eddie Jackson. I wanted to meet LeBron.

I hopped on a Southwest flight out of Burbank with Pam and headed for the Bay Area. After we arrived, we went straight to the Oakland hotel where the LeBron crew was staying and I had breakfast with LeBron and his mom. Right from the start I was impressed with how he carried himself. I felt an immediate, quiet comfort with the entire group.

A couple of hours later I was at the War Memorial Gym off Golden Gate Avenue at the University of San Francisco (USF) to watch the scrimmage. I said my hellos and exchanged hugs with the Soldier coaches and made my way to the bleachers to watch LeBron and the other kids warm up. Then the whistle blew and Calvin Andrews quickly divided up the squads and began the workout.

Both teams were composed mostly of college athletes. I knew one of the players on LeBron's team, Johnny Cox, Kobe's cousin, who had played for USF. There were just a handful of people in the stands, the sparse crowd reminding me of another workout—the one Arn Tellem and I had arranged for Kobe Bryant in front of Jerry West four years earlier.

LeBron got off to a slow start in a pair of oversized shorts that kept slipping down. His coach called a time-out and LeBron quickly switched to a smaller size. When play resumed, I watched the 6′8″ sophomore-to-be make a series of basketball moves with unusual skill and complete confidence—the same type of moment unfolding in front of me that I'd witnessed in Kobe's workout with the Lakers, Jordan's winning shot against Georgetown, and McGrady's moves at ABCD. I instinctively knew LeBron had the same exceptional qualities each of them possessed.

In less than fifteen minutes, I'd seen all I needed to see. During a time-out I rose and approached LeBron's entourage.

"I've seen enough," I said. "He's everything you said he was. You can tell him I think he's phenomenal. We'll definitely be in touch."

I gestured goodbye to LeBron, and hugged Gloria, Eddie, Calvin Andrews, and Chris Dennis. The scrimmage continued as we headed back to the airport. Gloria teared up. Elated that *Sonny Vaccaro* had not only made a special trip up to the Bay Area but had confirmed everything that had been written about Gloria's son.

I've been fortunate to have what one might call quite a few seminal moments in my eight decades of life. That day in Oakland ranks close to the top, as it would soon define the next three years of my life. That day I also knew there wasn't a remote chance in hell that *that* kid was going to play a single minute of collegiate basketball.

In a preview of the turbulence to come, the flight back to Burbank was terrifying. Our plane somehow flew into a thunderstorm, pitching and weaving uncontrollably to the point where our flight attendant was thrown to the floor and the person next to Pam started vomiting. Pam was beyond frightened, reciting one Hail Mary after another. Meanwhile, I'm thinking, *Oh my God, I just saw the greatest high school player I've ever seen—and I'm not going to live to talk about it.* I'm not certain if God answered Pam's prayers, but that short jaunt up north would immediately rearrange my professional priorities.

From then on, I had only one mission: to get LeBron James's signature on a lifetime Adidas contract.

. . .

THE FOLLOWING SUMMER LEBRON MADE his debut at the ABCD Camp at Fairleigh Dickinson University. Fresh off a season where Saint Vincent–Saint Mary was shredding mere high school mortals, LeBron was about to shed any semblance of anonymity on the national stage. In short order, "King James" would emerge atop the wish list of every A-list college coach in America.

Jump-cut to LeBron's senior year in high school, where his team was ranked number one and played a national schedule. Three days after New Year's Day 2003, Pam and I arrived for the featured night game of the Pangos Dream Classic at UCLA's Pauley Pavilion. The Saint Vincent–Saint Mary Irish against one of California's elite schools, the 15–1 Santa Ana Mater Dei Monarchs, the game nationally televised on one of the ESPN channels.

Pauley was beyond sold out—nearly thirteen thousand jammed to the rafters. The UCLA basketball team hadn't drawn more than seven thousand the entire season. Back home in Akron, they no longer played Saint Vincent–Saint Mary games in the school gym: They had long since moved to an arena at the University of Akron to accommodate the crowds.

On one side of the court I couldn't help but notice that none other than Phil Knight had decided to make a rare public appearance, sitting beside George Raveling and Howard White. For some reason Knight and I were introduced to the crowd that evening, and I must say, I received what sounded like a louder ovation—at least to my ears. If I needed any more evidence that the Battle for LeBron was going to be the most contested Shoe Wars confrontation of all time, Knight's presence had just confirmed it.

Despite his worst shooting performance of the year, LeBron still scored twenty-one points to lead all scorers and gave enough assists to his talented teammates to secure a big win over Mater Dei.

After the game Pam and I met with Gloria and LeBron back at their hotel. On that occasion, I posed arguably *The Question* of their life.

"What would you guess is the amount of money LeBron will be getting for his shoe contract next year?"

LeBron spoke first. He guessed around $5 million.

Eddie Jackson, on a speakerphone back in Ohio, thought that sounded about right. "But we can always reach for the stars," he added.

"I don't know," added Gloria. "Five to seven wouldn't be out of the question."

I paused for a beat to allow them to absorb what I was about to say.

"The number is ten million a year . . . for ten years," I said. "LeBron is going to get a $100 million deal."

LeBron's jaw dropped. Eddie yelled out on a speakerphone from Cleveland. Gloria could barely catch her breath.

"That's the number," I said. A number I quite purposely soon put on the street, and that's the figure that appeared in most of the media. This kid, I said, would get a richer shoe deal than NBA MVPs, NBA champions, NBA All-Stars, Michael Jordan, Tiger Woods, Bo Jackson, you name it. He would become an instant mogul.

To underscore my point, I literally built the 2003 Roundball Classic around LeBron James. His photo was plastered on the cover of the *Chicago Sun-Times* special section supplement we published to promote the game. The headline read, "The King James Game." All of our promotional materials and street posters featured LeBron.

It was our thirty-ninth annual game, played at Chicago's sold-out United Center—19,678 fans—our biggest crowd since the Pittsburgh era. In a show of respect, LeBron chose to wear Jordan's immortal number 23. Then, in pure Jordanesque fashion he scored twenty-eight, hit the game winner, and won the West team's MVP.

For the previous three years, I had built what I regarded as a genuine close relationship with Gloria, LeBron, and Eddie. I had visited Akron, shared dinners at the Sheraton in Cuyahoga Falls, been to their home, and remained in constant touch. We'd become friends, not acquaintances. We saw them at the Final Four and at the Big Time Tournament, where they stayed a few extra days after LeBron's summer team had been eliminated. They had visited us in Calabasas, shared meals, laughed and talked on the back patio along with Calvin Andrews and his wife, Kacy.

But it wasn't just me. The entire Adidas sports marketing department was deeply engaged. We sponsored the high school team, staying close to all the coaches.

Given that I'd already put the $100 million number into the ether, I knew I had to have Adidas "corporate" on board. So fully a year and a half in advance of an actual offer, I'd begun having meetings with the executives in the top echelon at Adidas. In June 2002, I met Erich Stamminger, the CEO of Adidas America, who'd recently moved from Germany to the States. We set up a lunch in Santa Monica to discuss the importance of the LeBron conquest and what a LeBron signing would portend for the future.

The Germans at Adidas international headquarters were preternaturally soccer-centric, of course, and didn't grasp what basketball had become in America. They perceived the game the same way it was viewed in Germany—a second-tier sport. Peter Moore had tried to impress upon them that LeBron would soon be the equivalent of a Beckham or Beckenbauer in soccer. Stamminger showed no concerns with the $100 million commitment LeBron would require. He was unfazed.

"This sounds like a good move," he said. "I support you, of course."

A few days later, on June 8, 2002, the worldwide CEO of Adidas, Herbert Hainer, flew in from Germany. Stamminger and I met Hainer for breakfast at the Ritz-Carlton in Marina Del Rey so I could detail the action plan. Again, there was no pushback with the $100 million number. The only hesitation was whether we had a legitimate shot. I told Hainer I believed we were the front-runners.

"Okay," he said. "Let's go for it."

Two months later, I had yet another meeting, this time with Ross McMullin, the forty-year-old president of Adidas America, to discuss the deal. Now everyone that mattered was on board. I had confirmed our strategy face-to-face with all the top leadership—no uncertainty, no caveats. They had almost a year to do whatever forward planning was necessary to consummate the deal.

Meanwhile, there was a parallel drama unfolding regarding the state of our relationship with Kobe Bryant. For reasons known only to Kobe, he had grown dissatisfied with his shoe deal. As his stature in the league had grown, he began to feel undervalued or undermarketed or who knows what? We tried to assuage his discontent. In 2001, Adidas had flown him to Germany to wine and dine and express our deep appreciation. We then made a proposal to extend Kobe's contract for another nine years, from 2003 to 2012, for more than $100 million. Adidas was already heavily promoting Kobe products and new models were in the pipeline. Adidas made clear it wanted to keep him in the family for another decade. But despite our enthusiastic push he wasn't satisfied.

In any case, Bryant bought his way out of the remainder of his Adidas contract and agreed not to sign with any other shoe company until the end of the 2002–03 NBA season, giving Adidas time to wind down production of his shoes and unload inventory. Our three-time NBA champion was on his way out—eventually, to Phil Knight and Nike—adding even more pressure to the importance of signing LeBron to fill the upcoming void.

But then as we headed into the home stretch in the spring of 2003, word rolled in from Germany that the company was exploring various permutations of the forthcoming LeBron offer and how it might be structured. From what I could gather, company lawyers or accountants were waffling on my $100 million number and had passed their concerns up to Hainer.

We were sitting in Portland at the first video-conference meeting I'd ever been to, with a satellite hookup back to the Adidas home office north of Nuremberg, when I was assured that $100 million was still the number; the only issue was how we were going to serve it up. For me, the only way to make sure we stayed in the game was to keep it simple: $10 million, ten years. No vacillation, no timidity, no clauses, incentives, or equivocation.

"No, no, Sonny," I was told. "The whole company is behind you. We want this as much as you do."

I wasn't so sure. All the words sounded reassuring, but I could sense something was off.

. . .

IN MAY 2003, THE KING James Sweepstakes were hurtling toward the Act III climax. Adidas, Nike, and Reebok were acutely aware that

LeBron James would be a magnum opus–level sports signing. Quite possibly the most important shoe and apparel deal anyone would see for the next two decades.

In preparation, the Big Three pulled out all the stops, mobilizing entire departments to craft recruitment presentations tuned to the tiniest detail for this once-in-a-generation teenager. It was rumored that Nike had more than a hundred people handling various aspects of their pitch, complete with a Phil Knight cameo.

While Knight usually refused to get into bidding wars, I knew he'd do anything and everything to make sure Adidas / Peter Moore / Sonny Vaccaro or Paul Fireman, the CEO of Reebok, weren't the ones outfitting LeBron's feet for the next two decades. Still, all things being equal, I felt my friendship with LeBron and his family would give us a slight edge in the end—if we had a captivating, creative, powerful parity offer. The summer before Knight hit on a nice gambit to get an insider lobbying for Nike: they brought Maverick Carter, LeBron's best friend, out to Beaverton for an internship in 2002.

Aaron Goodwin, LeBron's agent, had put together the order of the presentations. Reebok, the long shot, would go first, essentially to benchmark a baseline deal. We batted second. And the billion-dollar Swoosh-beast would go last—hoping to beat out everyone by millions.

Prior to the meeting, Adidas had posted a series of billboards in Akron to get LeBron's attention (along with his team and Gloria) and begin building a campaign around our pursuit of LeBron. Our pitch, expressing our commitment, began on his home turf, leading up to our formal presentation. Peter Moore's vision for LeBron's platform wasn't just to present him as a great basketball player or athlete but an iconic brand—a cultural icon who stood for more than basketball victories or championships. We saw him becoming not a heroic star of athletic exploits, but a culture-altering figure with the impact of a

Muhammad Ali or Jesse Owens, someone who transcended the sport but in a different way than Michael Jordan had.

But our marketing would be meaningless if the money wasn't right.

After several years, the moment was at hand. All the effort was down to presentation week. We flew LeBron, his high school teammates, and Gloria on a private jet out to LA. They arrived on Friday, May 9. That night we arranged for the group to catch game 3 of the Western Conference semifinals at the Forum, Lakers against the Spurs. I called their hotel upon their arrival and welcomed Gloria and LeBron to California. This was a full-court press: limo, a lavish dinner, red-carpet treatment orchestrated down to the smallest detail.

The following day, May 10, 2003, a sunny Saturday, we brought the group to a Malibu mansion—a stark white, contemporary California seaside trophy home with a spectacular ocean view overlooking Zuma Beach just west of Point Dume. Handshakes, introductions, and a catered lunch opened the festivities before the spectacle of our presentation and the $100 million contract reveal. LeBron's entourage mingled by the pool, attended to by a group of Adidas account executives and PR people. LeBron and his agent and mom were invited inside to the presentation that I'd been building up to for three solid years.

The final pitch took place in a large, well-appointed living room we had staged to act as a conference room, featuring state-of-the-art audio-visual equipment and custom display screens.

Goodwin had invited as a consultant Fred Schreyer, whom I had worked with at Nike and liked very much. Fred was a lawyer known for his expertise in player endorsement contracts. Adidas's global basketball vice-president, David Bond, anchored our presentation, a show Peter Moore had personally developed and overseen back in Portland, the same role he had played nearly twenty years earlier for the Jordan pitch. In the room, along with me, LeBron, and Gloria were Bond;

Kevin Wulff, Adidas's director of sports marketing; Paul Ehrlich, the top Adidas legal affairs guy; and Travis Gonzolez of public relations.

As with the billboards in Akron, our pitch positioned LeBron as an athlete bigger than the game itself, someone akin to an iconic social justice warrior. A platform built on stature and gravitas—a meaningful and substantive through line that represented him and the brand in a transcendent way.

Of course, we showed prototypes, lofty graphics featuring LeBron, thematic variations, clothing, marketing ideas, and mock-ups. It set a high bar for our competitors. Our plan had sophistication, philosophical overtones, and brilliant graphics. It should have. It cost tens of thousands of dollars to produce. The creators and designers of the show, Peter Moore and David Bond, had done us proud.

It was down to the only detail that really mattered: the number.

As someone—I can't remember who—handed out the book with the financials, Bond spoke of a package that represented a very substantive investment in LeBron's future and what he would and could become . . . and then segued into a monotonous discourse on the particulars, which quickly strayed into a verbal fog that somehow "lost the room" and became a convoluted mish-mash of platitudes and provisos that seemed to have an asterisk after every completed sentence.

I opened the book and my heart jumped out of my throat.

The big number was $70 million. The "ifs" and incentive clauses and bonuses for this and that didn't matter; $70 million was what jumped off the xeroxed page.

A down payment.

The deal wasn't the deal I'd been on record for—or at least not the way I'd headlined it to LeBron and Gloria. I flushed, tried to conceal my gasp.

$30 million short.

Below that, in a dense series of paragraphs that resembled a Supreme Court brief, came words like *incentives, performance benchmarks, ifs, thens, time frames.*

As I scanned the document, all I could think to myself was: *What happened? Why are they doing this?* And I knew instantly, in a blinding flare of realization . . . that we'd lost.

Not only had I been ambushed, but so had LeBron and Gloria.

They sat impassively, peering down at the document, a lawyer-concocted financial word salad that numbed my mind, much less that of a fresh-out-of–high school eighteen-year-old.

They had my word on this.

Now my word, *Sonny Vaccaro's word* meant nothing.

The tone and tenor of the room had changed in a matter of seconds—the air sucked out like an open hatch on the space station.

The Adidas guys may have been waiting for LeBron to jump for joy in appreciation, but we'd already lost the day. The week before, when Reebok presented, Paul Fireman had placed a $10 million cashier's check in LeBron's hand, leaving tears in Gloria's eyes.

Now a week later in Malibu, they had been presented with contract terms that had the net effect, psychologically, of making LeBron *prove himself to us*, rather than the other way around. I don't know if they were insulted but I certainly was.

It was over.

In less than five minutes, three years of intense pursuit, effort, and credibility had vaporized. I struggled to maintain some semblance of composure—we'd spent tens of thousands of dollars to reach this presentation, and fizzle had replaced dazzle. I was stunned. I turned my head toward LeBron and Gloria. She nodded, signaling she wanted to talk off to the side. I got up, told our team we needed a moment, and excused myself before following LeBron and Gloria outside to regroup.

I hugged them both. Then Gloria said, "Sonny, we know what

you did to position everything. We know what you intended to do. This isn't anywhere near what we talked about, but it's not your fault. We're going up to see Nike and we'll let you know what's happening."

"I know, I know. You've gotta do what's best for your family," I said, or something equally lame and banal. That was all I could muster, my loquaciousness absent in that moment of crisis. And then I added quietly to Gloria, "My last advice to you is, don't tell Nike what the offer here was—let them bid." The least I could do was help them to end up with the figure we'd been expecting from the outset.

"Okay, Sonny, we won't."

I hugged them and went inside to repeat the same advice to LeBron's agent.

Within days, Nike announced it had signed LeBron James to a seven-year contract worth $90 million. We had the future number one draft pick and certified all-time great *right there—this close*—and let him slip away.

Life has always been comme ci, comme ça for me. Take a hit, get back up, bounce on to the next idea. Win some, lose some. This was different. The stakes couldn't have been higher. This wasn't simply a misunderstanding. This was a *betrayal*.

Words flooded my mind, negative words that rarely occupy my thoughts: *Debacle. Implosion.* A backstabbing in broad daylight. I had just witnessed the single most stupid blunder ever recorded in the annals of sports marketing. The dumbest and most dumb-founding *nonsigning* in endorsement history. (And I would never put those harsh words in print if I didn't believe they are the absolute truth.)

I had failed. Not in my planning or strategy or tactics or effort, but in convincing the Germans of how *monumentally consequential* LeBron James would be for the fortunes of Adidas.

Adidas would never recuperate from our failure to close the deal with LeBron James. And Nike, once again, has never looked back. They had their successor to Michael Jordan—a monumental signing that has paid incalculable dividends to this day.

I thought it was ours to lose. And we did.

• • •

I WENT TO FETCH PAM and said a few quick goodbyes and left.

One of the Adidas guys came outside and asked me to stick around for a debriefing and evaluation of the presentation. I begged off. "Catch up tomorrow," I replied curtly. I was in no mood to analyze. I wanted to get out of Malibu as fast as I could.

Pam could see the rage I was struggling to contain. Oscillating between seething and shaken, it was as if there'd been a death in the family. In a way, that's exactly what happened.

"Sonny, what's wrong?" Pam asked. "Are you okay?"

"We'll talk on the way home."

Before we left, I took one last look at LeBron. His body language was 180 degrees different from his usual force of nature presence. This wasn't the meeting he'd expected either.

Heading south on Pacific Coast Highway, we took a left onto Malibu Canyon Road, heading east over the Santa Monica Mountains toward our home in Calabasas.

"You know what I'm gonna do, don't you?"

"I know what you're going to do," Pam answered, both aware of and resigned to the dark, irrevocable inflection point we'd reached. The finality of moving on from Peter Moore and a group of people we had grown to love was sinking in.

Two months later we finished the 2003 camp season. I resigned in August just after speaking with Peter. We had always been far more friends than business associates. He understood when I told him I could no longer represent Adidas, stand behind the brand after the LeBron collapse.

They had lied to me, undermining my credibility. And even though I did my best to hide the disappointment and my psychological estrangement from Adidas around the camp kids and crew, my mood had settled into muted shades of gray. Same old Sonny outside, not so much on the inside.

I had no employment options in my back pocket. Today, I don't have one iota of shame in admitting that losing the LeBron deal was the most bitter disappointment of my entire time in the shoe marketing business.

This wasn't something I was going to get over easily.

At least not in this lifetime.

24

Reebok: My Shoe Wars
Swan Song

Tom Shine was the founder and driving force behind a clothing company called Logo Athletic, headquartered in Indianapolis, that held licenses to sell branded team merchandise with all the major sports leagues. I'd known Tom for years from seeing him every April at the Final Four and various industry shows and summer events. Back in 1990, he had reached out to me about moving the ABCD Camp to Indy with a tantalizing offer: Through his local contacts he guaranteed the facilities at IU–PUI (Indiana University–Purdue University Indianapolis) at no cost. Even though Nike had rented gyms for years, the offer was too attractive to pass up. Adios, Princeton; hello, Indy in the summer of 1991.

About ten years later Paul Fireman, the CEO of Reebok, brought Shine on as senior vice president of global sports and entertainment. At which point Tom approached me about switching shoe companies. I had just extended my contract with Adidas so I politely declined. I liked the gregarious and affable Shine immensely, but I just couldn't bring myself to make the leap. Maybe because I'd never been part of a shoe company where Rob Strasser and/or Peter Moore weren't integral. Maybe I was just too comfortable with the status quo. In any case, I wasn't going to jump ship on Peter.

In the summer of 2003, two months after the LeBron debacle in

Malibu, when rumors began circulating that I was about to say sayonara to Adidas, Tom contacted me again and we met at the Peninsula Hotel in Beverly Hills. His message: Now's the time. He told me Reebok would provide all the resources and support staff I needed to bring my entire grassroots operation over to the Vector (the name Reebok had assigned to its logo)—that vote of confidence and a chance to start anew suddenly looked very attractive to me.

At the time, Reebok was a distant third with a tepid 15 percent market-share after being on top in the mid-eighties. Nike's share stood at 40 percent, a predominant number evidenced by the most recent college basketball season, when forty-nine of the sixty-five teams invited to the Division I men's tournament were Nike schools, including all the Final Four teams.

Shine said Fireman wanted to finally meet face-to-face and figure out how to regain some momentum in the category. I already knew Reebok had point guard Allen Iverson as its star NBA endorser and, as of the 2004–05 season, the company (sometimes branding itself RBK) would, for the first time, have the exclusive rights to design, market, and sell products for all NBA teams. A private jet was arranged for a meeting with Fireman at Willowbend, Cape Cod's premier private golf club.

In September Tom and I met with Fireman for a late lunch in the dining room at Willowbend, overlooking one of the lush fairways surrounding the clubhouse. Fireman proved incredibly charismatic—not just smart and accomplished, but extraordinarily persuasive. I already had enormous respect for the man who'd made the whole industry stand up and take notice in the mid-eighties with Reebok's white soft-leather "Freestyle" aerobic shoes. Moreover, he was familiar with my camps, the Roundball Classic, and my Jordan, Kobe, and McGrady exploits. Our affinity for one another was immediate. And I fervently shared his preoccupation with challenging Nike's near-insurmountable dominance.

Shine had previously asked me to put together some numbers to "bring the whole show" over to Reebok. By now that show included my latest creation—the Big Time Tournament in Las Vegas that I'd founded in 1994. The Big Time was a natural and logical extension of everything that I'd been doing from the start, a continuation of my strategy at Adidas to expand our power and reach where it mattered most—youth basketball.

If the ABCD Camp brought in the best individual players, it only made sense to expand the concept to teams, further showcasing teenage talent to college coaches on a national stage that we positioned as "The Championship of Summer."

Before Big Time, summer tournaments were either regional or confined to specific cities, like Issy Washington's Slam-N-Jam in Carson, California, near Los Angeles, and various other tournaments in Arizona or New York or down South. Big Time exploded that provincial model and took summer tournaments to a national and international stage in a city tailor-made for A-list entertainment and media attention. In short order the Big Time established Las Vegas as the summer destination for team tournament play. Following our lead (as usual) the other major shoe companies rushed in to compete for venues and summer teams in the city every July.

The teams we invited represented the cream of the crop from every corner of the country. The D1 Greyhounds featuring O. J. Mayo and Billy Walker; Mean Streets Express with Derrick Rose and Eric "EG" Gordon; the Atlanta Celtics with Dwight Howard and Josh Smith; Long Island Panthers with Lamar Odom and Malik Allen; and the Southern California All-Stars led by Kevin Love, Brandon Jennings, and Taylor King. Once the word spread, applications poured in. From thirty-two original teams, we quickly jumped to sixty-four, then to more than a hundred. By 2003, in excess of six hundred teams participated, some seven thousand players from all over the country: the Crusaders from Nebraska, the New Orleans Jazz, the Portland

Panthers, the Playaz from New Jersey, the Long Island Panthers, the Northeast Texas All-Stars, Maryland's DC Assault, Team Breakdown from Florida, Positive Image from Pennsylvania, the Red Shield Cohawks from Colorado. You name the superstar, they all added their luster to the Big Time Tournament, including LeBron, Kobe, Carmelo Anthony, James Harden, and Paul George. As teams progressed pool by pool, the competition reached Final Four intensity, the winners fighting their way through a total of ten games to capture a championship. I'd always put the word out that, "There's a player for every program at the Big Time."

At its peak, Big Time had ten Vegas high school facilities plus UNLV's courts under contract from morning till night. A staff of more than two hundred people helped manage the enormous confluence of talent and teams. Thanks to the Roundball, ABCD, and Big Time, Adidas had become the uncontested "Big Dog" in the summer game by 2003.

Now Reebok would lay claim to the gravitas my events represented if I went to work for Fireman. At Willowbend, I watched silently as he thumbed through the pages of my report between questions, his fingers scanning the promotional figures, the camps, all-star games and tournaments, the assortment of coaches and AAU teams I believed I could attract over the next few years. Obviously a quick study with a prodigious intellect, he was absorbing my action plan in real time. When Fireman finished reading the numbers, he turned his eyes toward mine and said three words destined to alter my now-sixty-four-year-old identity yet again.

"This is doable."

And in the span of a midafternoon country club lunch, the deal was done.

Before I said yes, however, I had one proviso. I wanted all parties to understand I reported directly to one man across the table.

"Just so you know, Mr. Fireman," I added, "I'm the furthest thing from a corporate type. I don't do office hours and weekly status meetings. I do a lot of media and spend a good deal of my time on the road meeting players, parents, and coaches. I've spent my life keeping the elite quality of the Roundball and the camps a priority."

"That's fine, but I want you to always keep Tom in the loop."

"That I look forward to," I said.

"Then we've got a deal," he said, extending his hand toward mine.

My move to Reebok was officially announced on October 8, 2003, and made national news from ESPN to *Women's Wear Daily*. The headline on the front page of *The Boston Globe* business section read, "Reebok Brings in Dealmaker Vaccaro."

"Grassroots basketball is one of the most exciting and relevant elements in youth culture," Fireman said in a statement announcing my hiring. "With Sonny on our team we can develop this initiative and firmly position Reebok for long-term and sustainable growth in this critical area."

Shoe Wars III was suddenly on.

. . .

THE FIRST TIME I WALKED into Reebok headquarters, a glass-walled architectural marvel in Canton, Massachusetts, I felt reenergized and proud to be associated with the brand. I met the new support team who proved equally energetic and talented. Our mission was to make as much trouble as humanly possible for Nike and Adidas.

Under Tom Shine's watch, the Roundball, ABCD, and Big Time Tournament continued to flourish, giving Reebok an immediate, dominant presence and instant legitimacy based on my decades-long reputation and credibility.

The first two years I could not have asked for a better working environment as Tom and Paul were delightful to work with; always positive, they more than lived up to their promises. In return, Reebok made a splash when 6'7" shooting guard Shaun Livingston, a *Parade* All-American, signed to a shoe deal straight out of Peoria High in Illinois on his way to the Los Angeles Clippers as the fourth overall pick of the 2004 NBA Draft. Like so many players before him, Shaun had sought my advice and counsel. He had earned a scholarship to Duke. As always, I never pushed any of the kids I talked to one direction or the other; I just laid out the facts and prerogatives as I knew them, allowing the players and their families to come to their own conclusions. Shaun—and many former Roundball Classic players—generously donated year after year so we could buy tickets and rent buses to provide thousands of kids and parents from the Chicago area the thrill of a lifetime by bringing them to the United Center to watch the Roundball Classic at no cost.

. . .

IT WASN'T UNTIL LATE 2005 that I sensed something was amiss at Reebok. The once open and genial lines of communication somehow became less flowing and frequent. I sensed a subtle distance developing with management. I wondered how things that had been so open and cordial had suddenly gotten out of sync.

The reason for the change revealed itself in January 2006—and rather dramatically: the industry-altering news that Fireman had sold Reebok to Adidas for $3.8 billion, a monumental restructuring of the entire athletic shoe apparel landscape.

For the first time in decades, this blockbuster merger represented a force with the scale and financial resources to offer a compelling challenge to the giant in Oregon. Nike feared no one, but they couldn't deny this was a formidable new player they would have to "game plan" against. That was the theory at least. What I couldn't quite understand: What was the benefit to Adidas, my new (old) employer?

At that point, I'd been doing camps and games for more than forty years, thirty of those for shoe companies. That had been my world since 1964. I had done everything I had hoped to accomplish in grassroots basketball and beyond—breaking the mold by signing coaches, colleges, and future NBA superstars; championing Jordan; helping reverse Nike's trajectory; and putting Adidas in serious contention. By now the idea of doing another camp, another all-star game, had become rote. I'd already done them—and better than anyone else in the industry.

This change in ownership back to Adidas seemed like a lightning bolt from the heavens. At sixty-four, was I really going to go back to work for Adidas and pledge allegiance to a brand I'd only recently left?

Nothing about that sat well with me. I thanked all the people at Reebok, wished them well, and sent my resignation letter.

I had arrived at another inflection point. The course of my life had shifted on its axis.

Sitting at home on the West Coast, I thought back to the night some ten years earlier when I found myself watching Dwayne "Pearl" Washington, the ethereal point guard for Syracuse in the mid-eighties, perform his magic on ESPN Classic. Here was Pearl, long after his college career was over, entertaining me—and possibly millions of others over the years—and the thought suddenly occurred to me: *I wonder if he's getting paid to fill out ESPN's programming schedule.*

That thought led me further back in time, to 1991, to another economic rights brouhaha during UNLV's heyday. UNLV had just finished the regular season 34–0, a basketball team for the ages led by Greg Anthony, Larry Johnson, and Stacey Augmon. The previous year the Runnin' Rebels had overpowered Duke by thirty points in the NCAA championship game. I was close to that team, not only because of my long-standing relationship with Tark, but because I was doing local television as Chick Hearn's sidekick and colorman on the Rebels' syndicated telecasts that aired back in LA.

Point guard Greg Anthony was the unquestioned leader of that

UNLV team. The president of a Republican student group, he harbored hopes of one day becoming Nevada's first Black senator. A deep thinker and articulate speaker, Anthony had continued to question why players were precluded from enjoying any of the economic riches associated with a nationally famous team. The NCAA, the networks, and countless businesses were certainly cashing in on UNLV's extraordinary success. *Why not the stars of the show?*

Greg also had an entrepreneurial instinct and (tiptoeing at the fringes of NCAA rules at the time) had begun selling T-shirts on the side. He was a partner in the business, which naturally led to the notion of selling "Back-2-Back" or "2-peat" championship tees around the 1991 Final Four. Greg and Stacey's idea was to unveil the shirts in front of the cameras after the team won another national title. For months Greg had talked back and forth with NCAA officials about selling the shirts around the tournament, only to have the monarchy in Indianapolis repeatedly reject the idea as impermissible under the rules of "amateurism."

In late February, I met Greg and Stacey at a restaurant near the Thomas & Mack Center, home of UNLV basketball to hear more. At that lunch Greg revealed a bold (even mutinous) plan to sell the tees at the Final Four *with or without NCAA approval.* Then he went even further.

"We're prepared to make a biiiggg statement, Mr. Vaccaro," he confided.

"That being?" I asked. He had my full attention.

Greg laid out what was clearly an act of defiance bordering on insurrection—in front of a national television audience. He explained that as the Monday night championship game was about to start, the UNLV team would refuse to take the floor for tip-off. A sit-in that would delay the broadcast—not for an hour, but perhaps five or ten minutes. Just long enough to sow panic in the broadcast booth, certainly for Jim Nantz and Billy Packer to be wondering aloud in front of millions of viewers what had sparked the unannounced delay, as cameras panned the current national champions on the UNLV bench refusing to get up. Then cut to a shot of some CBS floor producer in headphones, pleading with Tark to order his team to go on court. When asked what was going on—as they inevitably would be—Greg's answer would describe the action as a silent protest over the autocratic, monopolistic ways of the NCAA—*injustice for all* (including their head coach, still under investigation by the enforcement staff). The incident would be the lead story on the national news on every network. And if they'd won, Greg and the team vowed to sell their T-shirts despite the NCAA warning them against it.

Only one problem with their master plan: UNLV fell one game short of the title game. In a semifinal marred by one questionable officiating call after another, the Runnin' Rebels, favored by 9.5 points in a rematch against Duke, lost by two, ending their forty-five-game consecutive win streak and any hope of their rebellious and historic statement making it to national television.

Can you imagine the repercussions and retributions had that coup taken place at the NCAA's annual crowning event?

• • •

MY FOCUS JUMPED TO ANOTHER "rule" that made my blood boil: These powerful sports organizations routinely imposed discriminatory rules that felt like restraint of trade to me. I'd been stewing over the proposed Article X language in the NBA's collective bargaining talks with its Players Association. In precise terms Article X stipulated that any prep basketball player had to be at least nineteen years old or one year removed from high school before becoming eligible for the NBA Draft. Strangely, Article X did not apply to international players.

Translation: Yet another restrictive, nonsensical rule perpetrated on the players. The "one and done" rule was about to be implemented with the backing of the NBA, the NBA Players Association, and the NCAA. It wasn't enough that Kobe Bryant, Tracy McGrady, Kevin Garnett, Moses Malone, Jermaine O'Neal, and LeBron James were lighting up the league; for a variety of billion-dollar reasons the NBA and NCAA had decided it wasn't good business for owners, the players association, and colleges to have US high school graduates in the league—even the truly gifted ones. When I discussed the matter with NBA Commissioner David Stern, he laid the blame at the feet of the Players Association wanting to protect its veteran players (and their salaries), although his hands weren't exactly clean in the matter (nothing went down in the NBA without the approval of Stern). When a Congressional hearing was scheduled in DC to investigate the Article X matter, Stern claimed he was unavailable to attend, citing work duties. The hearing never took place. In my view, three corporate entities had constructed yet another barrier to limit opportunities and economic freedom for young players clearly qualified to jump directly to the NBA.

Article X was eventually adopted as part of the 2006 Collective Bargaining Agreement. With it, players like Kevin Love, Derrick Rose, Kevin Durant, and a host of others over the future years would have to pretend to be in a university degree program for literally half a semester.

The hypocrisy and injustice of the new rule sickened me.

I had arrived at another inflection point. It was time to reprioritize and rethink—to actualize what had been eating at me for more than a decade by then. After talking with Pam, I decided to reconfigure the direction of my life and fight full-time for the civil and economic rights of the young athletes who'd been the bedrock of my success from the beginning. If I didn't commit now, right now, well into my sixties, I knew it might never happen.

Most importantly, it was time to right a collective wrong. To help put an end to what Taylor Branch later described in his seminal 2011 article in *The Atlantic* as a form of modern-day slavery. In my mind, I owed the kids who'd provided me with a lifetime of opportunities, excitement, and a modicum of fame I could never have dreamed of as a young man. Without those teenage athletes, there would have been no Roundball Classic, no ABCD, no Nike, no Rob Strasser, no Air Jordan, no Kobe, no Big Time, or any of the other opportunities I had a backstage pass to at the epicenter of modern sports marketing.

I knew I needed the space and time to do something to stop the endless exploitation. I believed the players I had outfitted in those millions of pairs of shoes had civil rights—*human rights*—that were being trampled. If my voice could help change that pattern of economic suppression, I was going to speak up. With Pam's full support (though not without trepidation) there was no choice but to sever my shoe company ties and chart an improbable new course.

So, I put an end to the Roundball, ABCD Camp, and the Big Time. I left Reebok, cutting my last corporate connection (and the basis of my long-term financial security) to go on unpaid leave. Some burning gravitational force was drawing me to a more important role—a higher calling, if you will.

There would be no more Shoe Company Sonny Vaccaro. From that point forward, no matter how long I lived, I committed to become an outspoken proponent for current athletes and those to come.

When PBS correspondent (and legendary former *60 Minutes* producer) Lowell Bergman later asked me in the 2011 documentary *Money and March Madness* why I left the business, these ten prophetic words were all I could muster in response: "I had to do it. . . . I had to do it."

25

Barnstorming Academia

"The NCAA and amateurism in the world we live in today is a one-way street—the kids have no vote and no say. The numbers now—what were millions—are going into the billions. The runaway train does not stop. . . . If these lawsuits don't win now, I don't believe there'll be another time in history that they [the NCAA] can be held accountable."

—*Sonny Vaccaro, keynote speaker, March 25, 2011, Harvard Law School Symposium*

At sixty-seven years old, I was headed back to college. Actually, many colleges.

Not to get another degree, mind you, but to seek out a forum that was fertile ground for my message above. I wanted to go to the bastions of higher education—not to address a coaching staff or administrators—but to reach the next generation of legal minds, sports journalists, university leaders, and business and industry executives that might be open to the idea that college athletes deserve their fair share of the NCAA's riches.

The idea of going on a speaking tour had been churning in my mind for the better part of five years. For decades I had witnessed NCAA leadership repeatedly and cynically use "amateurism" and "student-athlete" as a dog whistle to protect their fiefdom and deny a subjugated class the right to receive fair value for their efforts.

I had given up hope trying to bring about any substantive change within the system; I was, after all, the NCAA's personal piñata— the archenemy of higher education and amateurism. The association's counternarrative, laden with its self-righteous claims, had proved enormously effective in drowning out calls for change. Casting me as the Darth Vader of college sports, they repeated their go-to retort— "Consider the messenger"—in one public statement after another.

Without a doubt, I'd been more than slightly responsible for turning major college basketball into an unabashed money-making machine. Long-term television contracts for essentially three weeks of March Madness alone were now more than $11 billion. When you're a beneficiary sharing in a profit bubble that large—the conferences, coaches, school administrators, athletic directors—you're simply not going to risk alienating the overlord by demanding that a group of teenage athletes share in the largess. Who in their right mind would stick their neck out?

. . .

IN RETROSPECT, THE SPEECH THAT put me on the map and a target on my back came in front of the Knight Commission on Intercollegiate Athletics back in 2001.

The commission, with a mandate to "clean up" college athletics and protect amateurism, heard from a variety of high-powered individuals, including the heads of sports networks, athletic directors, economic professors—each one more esteemed than the next—bemoaning the negative impact "outside" money was having on the purity of collegiate programs. I meant no disrespect with my words in front of that august group of luminaries that day. They just don't like hearing one of the universal truths of collegiate athletics spoken out loud: They unequivocally lived off sponsors and broadcast dollars—an addiction they had no hope or desire of ever breaking.

The most incisive description of my testimony that day would be written ten years later by civil rights historian Taylor Branch in his seminal "The Shame of College Sports," which appeared in the October 2011 issue of *The Atlantic*. With permission, here's an excerpt:

> *"I'm not hiding," Sonny Vaccaro told a closed hearing at the Willard Hotel in Washington, D.C., in 2001. "We want to put our materials on the bodies of your athletes, and the best way to do that is buy your school. Or buy your coach."*
>
> *Vaccaro's audience, the members of the Knight Commission on Intercollegiate Athletics, bristled. These were eminent reformers—among them the president of the National Collegiate Athletic Association, two former heads of the U.S. Olympic Committee, and several university presidents and chancellors. The Knight Foundation, a nonprofit that takes an interest in college athletics as part of its concern with civic life, had tasked them with saving college sports from runaway commercialism as embodied by the likes of Vaccaro, who, since signing his pioneering shoe contract with Michael Jordan in 1984, had built sponsorship empires successively at Nike, Adidas, and Reebok. Not all the members could hide their scorn for the "sneaker pimp" of schoolyard hustle, who boasted of writing checks for millions to everybody in higher education.*
>
> *"Why," asked Bryce Jordan, the president emeritus of Penn State, "should a university be an advertising medium for your industry?"*
>
> *Vaccaro did not blink. "They shouldn't, sir," he replied. "You sold your souls, and you're going to continue selling them. You can be very moral and righteous in asking me that question, sir," Vaccaro added with irrepressible good cheer, "but there's not one of you in this room that's going to turn down any of our money. You're going to take it. I can only offer it."*

I would never have called out the Knight Commission or the NCAA if I didn't wholeheartedly believe thousands of young men and women were being denied a reasonable share of compensation in a vast sports machine, particularly from the royalty-free use of their names, images, and likenesses (NIL) in a multitude of sponsored rights, content, and merchandising deals the NCAA was profiting from—*years after they were no longer in school*.

So it was in 2007 that I set out on my knight-errant quest: challenging what a lower court had previously called a "classic cartel" with the same zeal, energy, and sixth sense I'd employed to sign coaches and schools—another banzai blitz, this time designed to reach fresh minds.

Veering into the great unknown, I began accepting invitations to speak at some of the best schools in the country. Some invites came from professors or department heads; others extended by students—the head of one campus organization or another. We agreed beforehand that I would never take a penny, not a single cent in speaker's fees. My essential theme never wavered: *It was long past time to share the wealth with the "workers" largely responsible for creating that wealth.*

. . .

MY ADVOCACY TOUR OFFICIALLY BEGAN in April in Durham, North Carolina, home to Duke University, 2,600 miles east from our home in Calabasas, California. *The New York Times* summed up my speech under a headline that read, "Shoe Marketer Who Enriched N.C.A.A. Takes on His Creation."

I might've allowed my detractors to label my unfiltered soapbox arguments as *pontification* were it not for the fact that the real, relevant, and persistent injustices were in full force at that very moment. Eyeing those injustices from street level, I came to the conclusion that universities have never made a substantive change in their financial arrangements with athletes, whether it be practice length, stipends, or snacks, without lawsuits being involved—many of which are settled before a verdict is rendered to avoid embarrassing revelations or legal precedents.

At my basketball events, we had a term for the athletes who would soon be stars at the next level. We called them "Next Factors." That's how I viewed this cross section of law, business, and journalism students. Hopefully, they would be "next factors" in determining whether athletes themselves would have a seat at the table, a voice for change. I wanted those faces in the crowds and classrooms to feel the same sense of indignation and disgust I felt. I was looking for outrage—a contagion—similar to the emotion of Peter Finch's Howard Beale character in the classic 1976 film *Network*, when he screamed: "I'm mad as hell and I'm not gonna take this anymore!"

On their own, teenage athletes had zero chance of overcoming the untethered power and hubris of the NCAA. And to be honest, my chances weren't much better—but at least I had a platform because of my history and media relationships. One critical component I could contribute to the athlete's cause was *visibility*. The young athletes needed advocates with media access, and I vowed to be one of them. This is not to say I was alone on this journey. By now a legion of authors, sports columnists, reporters, and lawyers had been pounding away at the association's monopolistic practices, with exceptional writers like Dan Wetzel at Yahoo Sports and Joe Nocera at *The New York Times* leading the way. As Jay Bilas, the esteemed ESPN basketball analyst, lawyer, and ex-Duke star, put it:

> *Here's the NCAA's entire amateur scheme, in case you're wondering: Convince the public that amateurism is noble, win legal battles, maintain the tax dodge, claim poverty, cite Title IX, keep government from interfering, generate billions of dollars, don't share money with athletes. Rinse, then repeat.*

The only difference, as I saw it, was perspective and commitment. No one had been more involved in as many different levels of basketball with as many shoe companies as I had. I'd seen the issues from inside the executive suites of corporate America to grassroots summer events, but most importantly, from the perspective of athletes who had achieved great success as pros and businessmen and those who had little or no money to live on while their jersey was being sold for a hundred bucks or more in the campus bookstore.

The college kids I talked to weren't even born when the Roundball Classic was formed, when Michael played for the Bulls, or when I was building my success, brick by brick, in summer basketball. If nothing else, I knew I had a proven knack for communicating with young people.

In the beginning, I figured I'd do maybe ten or fifteen speeches a year and keep the thread alive with media interviews in between. But that wasn't the case. Right from the start I struck some kind of chord; one invitation led to another and then another. And another.

By the time I wrapped up my cross-country tour in 2012, I had shared my observations and opinions at nearly forty of the top institutions in America, some more than once. I spoke at law schools ranging from Duke to Harvard to Columbia to UCLA to Berkeley to Yale. At business schools from MIT to Wharton, Georgetown to UMass, and symposiums and town halls at Northwestern and Drexel and Howard University. It was exhilarating, exhausting, and flattering.

I found interacting with students just as energizing as interacting with previous generations of basketball players had always been. From one school to the next, one stop to the next, the energy in the room rekindled my determination to raise awareness, to rabble-rouse, to convert agitation into action.

I welcomed the students to challenge me on any issue they chose; I wanted their opinions and feedback. Most of all, I wanted them to gain an awareness of the way the NCAA did business—a far different picture than the carefully crafted public service spots the association ran for free (thanks to the networks) during regular and postseason games.

In my speeches I never for a single moment drifted from the incontrovertible facts found on the ground: The record-setting D1 football and basketball media rights deals. The hypocrisy of the NCAA's "Academics First" message. The constant court battles over the prima facie ruse surrounding the word *amateurism*.

Interestingly, only one head basketball or football coach was present at any of my appearances—James Jones of Yale. I was persona non grata in the NCAA's eyes, and coaches, by and large, had decided not to roil those waters by being present at my speeches, but rather chose to adhere to the party line that paid so well.

. . .

AS WEEKS TURNED TO MONTHS and months to years, my goal changed: My audience was no longer just college students and lofty commissions but the halls of Congress. I needed to find some senator or congressperson willing to hold a hearing on the state and fate of *athlete-students*, especially given the revenue stream flowing into the NCAA's account from the unchecked use of NIL. I wanted Congress to examine the NCAA's preposterous claim to be a "nonprofit" education-based association as well. How grotesque to think that a multibillion-dollar organization had rules so onerous, controlling, and mean-spirited that, for many years, they denied late-night eating privileges to hungry, growing young athletes who put up to fifty hours or more a week into training, workouts, and practicing for their individual sport along with studying for classes.

Who does that?

Who puts athletes on year-to-year scholarships instead of guaranteeing all four years as was customary until the early seventies? Who would demonize young people and derail their careers for meaningless petty rule violations? Who would abandon kids who suffered major injuries to fend for themselves when it came to insurance coverage?

Who does that?

Who has teenagers sign away their financial rights for the rest of their lives as the basis for eligibility without the benefit of a lawyer or parent being present to advise them?

Who the hell does that?

Experiences with the NCAA, the NBA, and half a century in the game gave me a rich array of topics to try to condense into an hour-long talk. But whether I was in front of a five-hundred-seat auditorium or seated at a dinner table with ten members of the business club, I didn't care. If this crusade had to unfold just one mind, one other human at a time, fine by me. Change was my only measure of success.

Suffice it to say, the NCAA was well practiced in the art of alternative facts long before that phrase entered the vernacular. College athletes were getting their message drowned out by a vast, fully staffed PR machine. Expecting justice from the halls of power in Indianapolis voluntarily was a fool's errand.

I knew we were gaining traction when *The New York Times* reported that an NCAA spokesperson named Bob Williams stated: "Time has shown that Mr. Vaccaro's vision of intercollegiate athletics is fundamentally at odds with the N.C.A.A.'s—and reality for that matter."

Reality?

This coming from an organization whose former president Myles Brand (now deceased) once stated—with no irony whatsoever—*"College basketball is not a business."*

In the aforementioned PBS documentary *Money and March Madness*, correspondent Lowell Bergman asked the bestselling author and journalist Michael Lewis, "Why should I care [about the plight of athletes]?"

Lewis answered, "You shouldn't care—*unless you have some weird obsession with justice.*"

I certainly did.

Given my outspoken opposition to one of the most powerful organizations in sports, one with an almost limitless supply of legal firepower at its disposal, I had no expectation that change would occur in my lifetime.

Turns out, I was completely mistaken in that assumption.

26

The Tide Turns:
Hausfeld Takes the Case

I was in Washington, DC, in March 2009, for two important events. I had a meeting with Jonathan Godfrey, a senior aide to Michigan's long-serving Congressman John Conyers, a staunch civil rights proponent who had helped pass the bill authorizing the Martin Luther King Jr. holiday. Godfrey had been instrumental in organizing the Congressional hearings that investigated the NFL's CTE (chronic traumatic encephalopathy) brain injury crisis. I wanted Conyers to examine the NBA's "one and done" age restriction on US high school players, and, to our delight, he was willing to hold a hearing (a hearing, as I said, David Stern later scuttles).

The other reason I was in the Washington area was a speaking engagement at Howard University. It was the last leg of a trip that had included speeches at Indiana University Law and Business schools followed by being one of the panelists at the prestigious MIT Sloan Sports Analytics Conference in Boston. HBO's *Real Sports with Bryant Gumbel* had sent a crew to film at both the Indiana and MIT events. Having been among the first to advocate for athlete's rights, Gumbel was doing a segment on high school superstar Brandon Jennings, who had recently decided—with my counsel and overseas connections—to play professionally in Italy rather than subject himself to the NBA's draconian age limit.

To my surprise, that evening at Howard, one of my dearest friends came to catch my presentation.

His name is Rob Ades, and it turns out his presence at that lecture was the first dot that connected to a series of other dots that proved integral to the launch of the historic *O'Bannon v. NCAA* case.

I had known Rob since the mid-eighties. He had what I call "a presence"—handsome, quirky, a unique personality, articulate, eccentric, and full of life. In his younger days Rob had worked as a counselor at Camp Robin Hood in New Hampshire, a haven for kids ages seven to sixteen. Later he was a member of the famous "Tuesdays with Red" lunch roundtable with legendary Boston Celtics coach Red Auerbach that convened each week at the China Doll restaurant in DC. Rob's lavish Final Four party on the Thursday before the semifinals on Saturday was a coveted invite attended by a who's who of basketball aficionados. Rob had thousands of friends and I was proud to be counted among them.

Rob's professional life was equally eclectic; as an attorney he represented the DC police and firefighter unions and worked as an agent representing high-profile coaches and local media personalities such as Jim Boeheim and then *Washington Post* columnist Tony Kornheiser. Rob had also been the spark of creative genius behind the first "all-sports" or "all-school" rights deal. An alum of the University of Miami, he was providing legal counsel to then athletic director Sam Jankovich when, in 1987, ten years into my career at Nike, he called with a proposal that changed the face of collegiate sports marketing.

"Sonny," he said, "I just talked with Sam. We've got an idea we want to bounce off you."

"What's the idea?"

"What do you think of Nike outfitting every team, every varsity athlete at Miami, not just basketball, everybody?"

"Wait a second—the whole school?"

"The whole school."

Just my kind of idea. Audacious, innovative, game-changing.

"Jankovich is on board?"

"Sam's on board."

"I love the idea," I said. "Lemme call Knight. I'll get back to you."

I called Phil, and it was one of the best conversations we'd ever had. I was ecstatic. I told him, "This is it, Mr. Knight. We hit the mother lode. We'll own the whole school. Every sport. One hundred percent."

Knight approved the concept, and I called Rob back to set a meeting with Sam—a meeting that would restructure corporate investment in college athletics. From that point on, every deal we did was for the whole enchilada at every university. That's when schools became "Nike schools" or "Adidas schools."

. . .

I WAS IN FRONT OF the room at Howard, mingling with a group of faculty members, when I felt a hand on my shoulder.

I turned.

"Oh my God, Rob! I didn't know you were coming!"

"I wouldn't miss a Sonny Vaccaro performance. You kidding me?" he joked. We hugged. I introduced him to the head of the business school. Later on, I paused to single Rob out to the audience as the catalyst in the "all-school" deals.

Whenever Pam and I were in Washington we would invariably join Rob for lunch or dinner. We arranged to have a late lunch at one of his favorite restaurants in DC, Famous Luigi's, a tiny, two-story Italian kitchen on Nineteenth Street near Dupont Circle, a few blocks from the White House.

The conversation that afternoon wasn't basketball gossip and hot prospects. Instead it was focused entirely on my NCAA crusade. I told Rob about my plans to one day sue the association in federal court. As a lawyer Rob validated my premise that the NCAA was likely engaged in a range of unconscionable actions and rights-related gray areas—some more egregious than others. Ever the friend, he apprised me of the "pain and torture" I would face if the case were ever certified to proceed.

"Tort cases, especially those with class action and antitrust implications, can take five, ten years or more to reach a conclusion," he said. "And you're going up against an organization with tens of millions to spend on lawsuits. I don't want to discourage you, 'cause I know how much this cause means to you . . . but suing the NCAA would be one of the most formidable challenges you've ever undertaken, my friend."

I sat silently for a moment, contemplating his words of warning.

"Well, I'm gonna keep talking until some senator or congressperson takes notice," I responded, undeterred.

Rob understood nothing was going to stop me.

"Listen, I know someone you should talk to; he may be able to help you. His name's Kenneth Feinberg." Those two sentences were the beginning of a sea change for American athletes.

From that late lunch in 2009, what would become known as the *O'Bannon* case was born. By sheer chance, Kenneth Feinberg happened to be Rob's next-door neighbor in Bethesda, Maryland. The same Kenneth Feinberg who had been chosen to oversee the delicate matters surrounding the September 11th Victim Compensation Fund, a task he handled with authority, grace, and dignity.

Rob called Ken, a fellow attorney, and asked if he happened to know Sonny Vaccaro.

"No," replied Feinberg. "Who is he?"

"He's a legend in the sports world," Rob said, before adding that he thought I had a pretty compelling story that needed to be told, not in a magazine or on *Real Sports* but in a court of law. Once Rob finished explaining my theory on the NCAA's reign of terror, it was Feinberg's turn to speak.

"You're a good advocate," he said, "but what Sonny's going to need is a creative—and tenacious—class action litigator. Someone willing to take chances and frame the case in terms of a monopoly and anti-trust. And one other thing: someone unafraid to take on the NCAA."

. . .

TWO DAYS LATER, PAM AND I were down in Chapel Hill, where I was to deliver a talk at the University of North Carolina for the College Sport Research Institute Conference. We were unpacking our bags at the hotel when my phone rang, signaling a 202 area code.

"Sonny Vaccaro?" the caller asked.

"Yes, speaking. Who's this?"

"Sonny, I'm Ken Feinberg. Rob Ades suggested I call. Is this a good time?"

"Mr. Feinberg, thank you for calling. I didn't expect to hear from you so quickly."

"Well, Rob related your desire to pursue litigation against the NCAA. I wanted to make sure I understand the things he mentioned in your conversation. He seems to believe you've got a reasonable—"

I cut in. I couldn't help myself.

"Mr. Feinberg . . ."

"Ken, call me Ken."

"You're a lawyer. Just hypothetically, let me ask you a couple of questions."

"Go."

"How is it legal for a big-time sports business that's worth billions to keep selling . . ."

I relayed a short-form summary of my view on the NCAA's incorrigible practices—like the nefarious "Student-Athlete Statement," the seven-page form young athletes needed to sign every year according to NCAA Constitution rule 3.2.4.6 and NCAA Bylaw 12.7.2 and then deliver to their athletic director in order to be eligible to play. Beginning at the bottom of page 4, in "Part IV: Promotion of NCAA

Championships, Events, Activities or Program" is a section that includes the following contract language:

"You authorize the NCAA [or a third party acting on behalf of the NCAA (e.g., host institution, conference, local organizing committee)] to use your name or picture to generally promote NCAA championships or other NCAA events, activities or programs."

That specific section of the form essentially gave the NCAA the right to use a player's NIL without royalties or compensation in perpetuity—long after they were no longer students at the university. Hidden in the contractual legalese was nothing less than a carte blanche financial heist.

The NCAA protested that a student-athlete could still play whether or not he or she signed that particular form—but not in actuality. Rarely—if ever—was a lawyer or advisor present to help the young athletes understand the consequences of signing that document. Instead, NCAA attorneys inserted this caveat: "Before you sign this form, you should read the Summary of NCAA Regulations, or another outline or summary of NCAA legislation, provided by your director of athletics or his or her designee, or read the bylaws of the NCAA Division I Manual that deal with your eligibility. You are responsible for knowing and understanding the application of all NCAA Division I bylaws related to your eligibility."

Imagine a seventeen- or eighteen-year-old, fresh out of high school, trying to decipher a mind-numbing 450-plus-page rule book of NCAA regulations handed to them by some graduate assistant. "Sure, gimme a minute to thumb through this, would you?" No counsel, no parental consent, NO WARNING that a teenager was about to sign over the rights to his or her NIL—for life—with their signature at that moment.

. . .

MY PHONE CONVERSATIONS TENDED TO mirror my speaking engagements—a zig here, a zag there, seemingly disconnected rambling. Ken Feinberg understood my Don Quixote–like pursuit and that it would continue, whether it found its way to court or not. My soliloquy went on for about twenty minutes before Ken was satisfied nothing was going to deter me—not the odds of success, not those who believed it was a fool's errand, nothing.

"I'm going to have someone call you," he said. "He's a lawyer that specializes in these types of issues. His name is Michael Hausfeld. Are you going to be in your hotel room?"

"Yes, we'll be here."

We hung up.

Ten minutes later, the phone rang again—another Washington, DC, number.

To this day I can still feel the first tremors of that call—the initial rattles of an earthquake that, within three months, would shake the foundation at 700 West Washington Street in Indianapolis to its core.

• • •

BASKETBALL AND SPORTS WERE AN alien world to Michael Hausfeld but he was willing to listen to an argument that had interesting—and important—legal implications, particularly regarding antitrust. Our initial call proved to be a slightly longer version of my conversation with Feinberg. Michael's questions were more from a rights perspective. Obviously interested in my premise, he spoke in soft, sometimes halting terms, no small talk, asking precise questions that got to the core of the injustice the NCAA's practices *literally reeked of.*

"Listen, Sonny," he said. "Would you be available to show us some of your materials if I sent a couple of lawyers from our San Francisco office down to meet with you?"

That was the moment I felt, with all my gambler's instincts, that this case had a chance of coming to life.

When I hung up, my heart felt like it was beating in double time, my hands were literally shaking. *Oh my God,* I thought, *this could be it.*

Afterward, out of curiosity, Pam and I researched Michael

Hausfeld. As we suspected, he was a legal force to be reckoned with—he was *world famous*, renowned as a voice for the voiceless, focused on righting wrongs in cases of international significance. In the 1990s, he had won his first major class action case—against Texaco—for discriminating against thousands of minority employees, resulting in a monetary settlement of $176 million. He later sued Exxon on behalf of Native Alaskans after the *Valdez* oil spill, and later a bank in Switzerland on behalf of Holocaust survivors.

"You know what just happened here . . ." I said to Pam.

"I do. . . . I think this is it."

My mind jumped ahead, thinking about all the boxes of material we'd need to gather for the lawyers who'd be meeting with us in a short week or two. Materials I'd been accumulating (thank God) for more than three decades, hoping they'd be relevant someday in just this kind of moment.

If a lawsuit happened, this wasn't going to be some fly-by-night nuisance case—this was an honest-to-God federal antitrust litigation. It was the first time I had allowed myself to credibly believe that we just might be able to hold the NCAA accountable, a chance to reverse a string of abuses that the overlords of college sport had been imposing on young athletes for seven decades.

On the flight home from Charlotte to LA, I couldn't sleep. There are only four or five times in my life I'd felt the kind of energy surge Hausfeld's interest had given us. It was like that glowing Arc Reactor energy device that Robert Downey Jr. had plugged into his chest to restore his powers in the first *Iron Man* movie. I could feel it in my blood. The same kind of inspirational jolt I'd felt the second we signed Michael Jordan at Nike.

. . .

ON A BREEZY, COOL TUESDAY afternoon in April 2009, Pam and I walked into the Loews Santa Monica Hotel on Ocean Avenue for a four o'clock meeting. Passing through the lobby, peering out the four-story atrium windows, we saw a picturesque scene unfold in front of us. A narrow swimming pool framed by neat rows of loungers, and beyond the breakers lazily crashing onto the sand, a glorious Southern California sunset in the making.

We asked for directions to the "Malibu" room, where we met Jon King and Megan Jones for the first time. Both of these young Hausfeld associates were bright, serious, accomplished attorneys. Jon asked if he could help carry one of the two storage boxes Pam and I were carrying. The boxes contained decades of articles, clippings, and NCAA-related material I'd collected and organized over the years.

After the cordialities, it was time to tell the tale. About me, and the NCAA's shameful history dating back to the early fifties and the days of Executive Director Walter Byers, who ruled college sports like a Third World despot for thirty-six years. I gave Hausfeld's two young associates the extended two-hour version of the issues I'd been shar-ing around the country the last couple of years—stopping occasionally to let them peruse some of the articles and documents they casually pulled from the dozens of those loosely arranged or paper-clipped in the boxes.

When the meeting ended Jon and Megan asked whether we'd mind if they took the boxes with them back to San Francisco. "Of course," I said, "but please don't forget them at baggage claim. I've been collecting those for half my life."

Pam and I drove home with a mixed feeling of anxiety and excite-ment. Now we had to wait for the lawyers to go through and analyze my collected clippings and reading material. I could only pray that they would conclude we had a case worthy of their involvement.

Just over a month later, Pam and I were in Greece, our trip organized by Angelos Kotaridis, the owner of a European ath-lete management agency who reached out to me at the request of the Angelopoulos brothers, owners of the Olympiacos basketball team. We were invited over to discuss the possibility of securing additional high school players of Brandon Jennings's caliber to play in Greece. In the midst of that adventure, I received a call from Michael Hausfeld.

In his quiet, reserved tone Michael asked if we could change our itinerary to include a stopover in Washington on our way back home.

At 11:00 a.m. on Friday, May 15, 2009, with little if any sleep we entered the law offices of Michael D. Hausfeld, a richly paneled space in dark walnut and glass, Washington gravitas with an *L.A. Law* vibe. Jon King and Megan Jones greeted us and showed us to a well-appointed conference room.

As we were getting settled, Michael, trim and graying at the temples, entered the room, impeccably tailored. He extended his hand quite formally. I briefly shook it, then heartily hugged him. Though he seemed too reverential and distinguished to hug, I hugged him anyway. Laughing, Michael broke the hug and smiled. I was struggling to contain the sense of elation that came from my realizing—in the moment—the monumental importance of this meeting.

We assembled around the walnut conference table to expand on my indictment of the NCAA and answer any questions. I welcomed the inquisition; I wanted them to hear about my experiences, about the decades of NCAA deceit and denial of workers' compensation for injured athletes or, worse, those who had died on the field; and what Walter Byers himself once called the "economic camouflage for monopoly practice" that had been perpetrated on young athletes for far too long. It was a lively, animated session. Michael kept the proceedings moving, questions asked, often in disbelief.

Hausfeld's people had done their homework—scouring the internet, reviewing legal journals and previous court cases. They were fully up to speed and had previously presented their written evaluations to Michael. I was there to see a man of immense reputation—who, in all likelihood, was weighing dozens of other potential injustices his firm might confront around the world—deciding whether or not to take on an abusive, arrogant, imperious organization that some talkative Italian guy had embarked on a crusade against.

As morning shifted well into the afternoon, there was no lapse in the flow. I could tell my stories and anecdotes had clearly offended Michael's sensibilities and sense of decency, especially given the NCAA's claim to both legal and, almost laughably, moral standing. I'd always felt that anyone with a semblance of common sense knew the NCAA was operating a multibillion-dollar confidence game, where the players are pawns—their quid pro quo limited, at the time, to room, board, books, tuition, and incidental expenses. Meager in contrast to the deluge of monies coming in to the NCAA.

George Carlin, the legendary comedian, once quipped, "Some people have no idea what they're doing—and a lot of them are really good at it." But the NCAA knew exactly what they were doing.

I told the lawyers across the table that the NCAA's "amateurism for you / profit for us" business model depended on them keeping the players a permanently subjugated class—compliant, contained, intimidated into nonaction. They wanted athletes to believe that any serious legal challenge was going to be long, ugly, expensive, and personal—the most unpleasant, exasperating experience of their lives.

For his part, Hausfeld couldn't believe that the fraudulent guise of "amateurism" gave the NCAA the freedom to lock the athletes—its labor force—out of even a miniscule slice of a billion-dollar pie.

To prove my point I handed Hausfeld an essay in *The Atlantic* written by Donald Yee, a sports agent whose career at the time had spanned more than thirty-five years.

Do you see who is not invited to this feast? The players. To put it bluntly, the players are getting screwed. In exchange for their labor, they receive scholarships—but nothing commensurate with the contribution they make to colleges' bottom line or to the lavish lifestyles of coaches and administrators. No other country puts athletes through a system that essentially declares, "You do the work, we keep the rewards, and you get nothing." It's a cruel and unjust system, and American sports fans tolerate it, right out in the open. That talented young Black men have been unable to share in the bounty of college-football revenues is a stark illustration of inequality, particularly when a majority of the people in power in college athletics are white.

With fingers of each hand touching at the tips, Michael listened intently, his face furled into a pained mixture of anger and empathy. Without pause, I recounted story after story, stopping only to take a sip of water or answer questions. His comments and asides showed he was convinced the NCAA was an organization, as he would describe it later, conceived in collusion, operated in collusion, and protected by collusion, obviously attempting to create a mystery and immunity around "amateurism," all the while spending tens of millions in legal fees to defend what a lower court in the pivotal 1984 *NCAA v. Board of Regents of the University of Oklahoma* antitrust case had deemed a "classic cartel."

"These teenagers had to sign that form to play in college? They ask teenagers to sign that statement—with no counsel present?! I've never heard of anything like that," Michael said.

"They own the rights to their images forever? No royalties, no rights releases, no prior approvals?

"You can't be serious—teenagers with no legal advice signed away their rights ad infinitum?

"They claim they're not a business? Did they say that on the record?

"How can they get away with these practices? Who is overseeing these people?" he asked, shocked as he was curious.

"This goes on at colleges? In America? That can't be."

We had definitely achieved what you want in any meeting: rapt attention and an emotional response.

By the time our conversation concluded, it was well past midday. The meeting concluded with Michael's four-word acceptance speech: *"Let's take them down."*

I could have cried when I heard those four words! Finally. Maybe I wouldn't have to wait for an entire generation to see the NCAA's modus operandi exposed.

Hausfeld had taken on powerful banking, multinational companies, and governments. He was not the slightest bit intimidated.

Over the next few days, Michael handed me the first of many critical assignments, something that had to happen before any court case could even be filed.

"Now you have to find me a lead plaintiff."

Nothing to it, I thought to myself. My Rolodex was chock-full of NBA Hall of Famers and former college stars.

"You can count on it, Michael," I replied, assuming several would volunteer to be that "face of the case."

I was right; someone would step up—but it took considerably longer than I had anticipated to find the warrior willing to lead us into what was about to become a tortuous seven-year battle for justice.

27

Mr. O'Bannon, Please Raise Your Right Hand

My search for a lead plaintiff began by flipping through the tabs of the old but pristine Rolodex that Pam kept on her desk. We were looking for phone numbers that hadn't yet made it into our iPhone contacts.

I jotted down the names and numbers of at least six Hall of Famers, ten ex-NBA All-Stars, and about a dozen or so other players who had made their name at the Roundball or ABCD. I called former players I'd known spanning a lifetime in basketball and business. I worked the cards from A to Z to produce a short list of people—well-known, accomplished athletes—who had made significant contributions to the game. Someone willing to commit what would likely be significant blocks of time out of their personal life to participate in what I anticipated would be a contentious battle against the NCAA that could drag on for years. Against very long odds. And with no guarantee that it would end in victory.

Making calls one by one to the former players was, in a way, a trip down memory lane—reconnecting with my basketball roots. Explaining the case, informing them about Michael Hausfeld, gently imploring them to join me, and revisiting old war stories made for a series of wonderful nostalgic conversations, each free flowing and warm but in the end bittersweet. Time after time, ending with the same bottom line: "I'm sorry, Mr. Vaccaro. Please understand, I'm totally on board with the mission—that cartel's been making bank off us forever. But I wish you luck finding someone willing to step into the ring against the NCAA for the next 'X' number of years. They've got more money than God and they play dirty. Sorry I can't help you more. You know how they operate. I'm worried I'll be blackballed from TV work and coaching jobs."

The NCAA had a built-in intimidation factor. A vicious, protracted fight with the NCAA was scaring people away.

Just because I had chosen to devote the next stage of my life to the cause, didn't mean a famous former athlete would make the same choice.

And then, nothing short of divine intervention occurred—*again*.

With Las Vegas playing a pivotal role—*again*.

. . .

IN 2009, ED O'BANNON LIVED in a suburb southeast of Vegas called Henderson. I had known Ed and his family—his younger brother Charles and parents, Madeline and Ed Sr.—dating back to Ed's days as a standout at the ABCD Camp and his MVP performance at Roundball. He'd been invited to both following a stellar four-year career, including a state title, at Artesia High in Lakewood, California, just west of Anaheim. As a senior at UCLA, Ed had received the John R. Wooden Award after leading the Bruins to the 1995 national championship. After college, he had played a couple of years in the NBA (1995–97) before finishing his pro career in Europe. UCLA eventually welcomed Ed into its Athletic Hall of Fame. They retired his number (31) to immortalize him as one of college basketball's greatest players at a university known for Hall of Fame players.

In April 2009, just as my search reached perhaps its bleakest point, the theory of *improbability* once again intervened.

Ed happened to be enjoying a beer after a round of golf at the home of Mike Curtis, an associate at the Las Vegas car dealership where he worked, when Curtis offhandedly mentioned that his son, Spencer, had role-played Ed in EA Sports' *NCAA Basketball 09: March Madness* Xbox 360 video game.

"What? What do you mean he was playing me? In what video game?" Ed asked, dumbfounded.

Like most college athletes of his generation, Ed had no idea that the NCAA had licensed collegiate players' "likenesses" to EA Sports as part of a sixty-dollar video game. To ensure some semblance of legal immunity, EA had chosen to remove the names from all the players' jerseys. Everything else—weight, height, left- or right-handed, even the jersey number—was spot-on.

Young Spencer was more than happy to show the real Ed his video game reincarnation. Sliding the game cartridge into the Xbox, he skipped to various sequences of a 6′8″, thin, bald-headed, left-handed forward wearing number 31 in a blue Bruins jersey, sinking jumpers, blocking shots, and high-fiving teammates.

"Damnnnn," Ed drawled, observing the obvious: "That's me alright." Pausing for a moment, he asked, "Can you run that for me again, Spencer?"

O'Bannon had never been contacted for the rights to his image and likeness nor received a single cent in compensation. The NCAA and EA Sports had simply helped themselves to the profits from one of the video gaming industry's blockbuster hits without even the courtesy of a phone call or an email. The same was true for hundreds of other players portrayed in the game. The NCAA had blatantly appropriated all their likenesses, turned it into a mega success—and kept the proceeds for themselves.

In the real word of rights management, that's called theft.

One association president after another (and their legion of lawyers and spokespeople) had long maintained that "likeness" was defined by how the NCAA defined it. While, at the same time, ruling it impermissible—impossible—for players to promote their own name, image, and likeness (NIL).

Nice trick if you can get away with it. And it had gone on for decades.

. . .

AS FATE WOULD HAVE IT, I happened to reach out to Eddie within days of him seeing himself in that video game.

"Ed, I have a favor to ask—a big favor," I said. "It will require more time than you have, and more aggravation than you need. But it's a chance to make history."

"Whoa, Mr. Vaccaro, that's a lot to take in. What are you about to ask me?"

"Ed, the lawsuit against the NCAA is going to happen. It's real. We're going to take them to court on antitrust grounds. They've denied you and the other players your share of the profits for fifty years. We've got one of the most famous lawyers in the world on the case—Michael Hausfeld—he's agreed to handle it. I want to talk to you about getting involved."

"You want me to be one of the plaintiffs?"

"Eddie, I want you to be the *name at the top*. I want you to be the face of the case."

There was a moment of silence on the other end of the phone. Clearly, Ed was caught off guard. I knew he must have been thinking back on the video game.

"I don't know, Mr. Vaccaro . . ."

"Look, Ed. . . . Pam and I want to fly to Vegas to talk to you and Rosa. Don't make a decision now. I just want to meet, answer your questions, tell you where things are—and what you can expect. It's not a decision anyone would make on the spot. We'll call you back to set a date that works for everyone."

Less than two weeks later, Pam and I had dinner with Ed and his wife at a restaurant in Las Vegas.

At dinner, I did more talking than eating, explaining to Ed and Rosa how Michael Hausfeld had come on board. I talked about his involvement in the major international cases. I described Michael as a fearless, brilliant litigator—a man of compassion, deep conviction, and integrity, fully up to any challenge the NCAA might pose. We both spoke of all the ways players had been cut out of the NCAA's profits. How its rules always found ways to disenfranchise or disadvantage the athletes responsible for the vast majority of the revenue. Something Ed now had firsthand knowledge from his video game experience a few weeks prior. No one understood more about the underhanded ways the NCAA had capitalized on players' NIL than the O'Bannons.

As the evening wore on, quite naturally the issue of family came up. By this time the O'Bannons had three children and Rosa was growing in her own career. The kids were involved in sports. No one was blind to the implications of signing on to a case of this magnitude. A commitment brimming with the potential to turn their happy, suburban life upside down with a loss of anonymity and swarm of media attention. Not to mention that they might be opening themselves up to random unhinged callers and online trolls questioning Ed's motives.

As the conversation wound down, we found the O'Bannons deep in thought, pondering the impact his involvement might have. While excited, I refused to sugarcoat what lay ahead. Not a single word I spoke masked the *enormous commitment* this would entail.

There was no pressure on my part that evening; I only asked for their consideration. I'd been rejected so many times already, another refusal would have been no more disappointing than all the times I'd heard "Sorry, no" before. But I had an inkling something was different this time, a good feeling.

In a word, hope.

The evening ended with nothing more than an invitation to call if there were any more questions. Now all we could do was wait—anxiously—for their decision. The future of tens of thousands of college athletes and the basic principle of fairness and justice hung in the balance.

About ten days later I got a call.

"Mr. Vaccaro. It's—"

"Eddie, good to hear your voice."

"Listen, Rosa and I talked everything over."

Then, the most interminable pause hung in the air for three or four of the longest seconds of my life. . . .

"I'll do it. I'll be your lead plaintiff."

My heartbeat shifted instantly into overdrive.

"You're in?"

"I'm flattered you considered me for the role. I'm with you. I'll do it."

. . .

EDWARD CHARLES O'BANNON JR. PROVED to be a textbook lead plaintiff. He had personally suffered from the NCAA's onerous business practices. He was a renowned collegiate basketball player. He could express himself confidently and articulately. He wasn't doing it for the spotlight or ego gratification. He was likable, sincere, and genuinely credible. He clearly understood the issues at hand, the racial components, the farcical fraudulence of the NCAA's "student-athlete" sham.

Eddie *had been there.*

He'd put in fifty hours a week as an athlete. He knew the demands that a major program imposes. He'd achieved the highest honors in college sports. And he believed with all the soul and fiber of his being that college athletes—past and present—were being screwed by the biggest swindle in the history of big-time sports.

He took the step others *just couldn't.*

"You're sure?" I asked. "Rosa's comfortable with everything?"

"I know I'm in for a fight," Ed said, his voice tapering off. "But this has to stop. If it doesn't end now, they'll get away with it forever."

And with that, *O'Bannon v. NCAA* began its whipsaw, torturous, decade-long journey through discovery, depositions, trial, and appeals process.

I chose the words *whipsaw* and *torturous* with purpose. The NCAA had litigated and relitigated their "amateurism" mantra over decades. By now, they had long since perfected the art of delay and denial, the art of Kabuki theater.

Hausfeld, meanwhile, was thrilled, as elated as I'd ever witnessed. He viewed Ed as the perfect face and voice at the top of our legal filing. And, as Ed made clear over and over as the case ground forward in fits and starts, it was not about him: "It's not just for the past, not just for the present, but for the future."

Now all we had to do was get before a federal judge.

．．．

EDWARD C. O'BANNON, JR., ON *Behalf of Himself and All Others Similarly Situated v. National Collegiate Athletic Association, aka, the NCAA, and Electronic Arts, Inc.; Collegiate Licensing Company, aka, CLC,* an antitrust class action lawsuit, was filed in the United States District Court for the Northern District of California on July 21, 2009. As the Associated Press reported the news:

> In a federal lawsuit filed Tuesday, Ed O'Bannon says the NCAA
> illegally has athletes sign away their rights to the commercial use of
> their images and does not share any of the proceeds from their use
> with former athletes. "While the NCAA, its member conferences and
> schools, and its for-profit business partners reap millions of dollars
> from revenue streams . . . former student athletes whose likenesses

are utilized to generate those profit centers receive no compensation
whatsoever," the lawsuit claims. . . . It also seeks an injunction on
behalf of current student athletes barring the NCAA from licensing
the rights to their images.

With so much at stake, the NCAA's legal defense team immediately swung into what I can only describe as molasses mode, reverting to their now-familiar tactics of obstruction and delay. Filing motions to have the case dismissed—nine different times—reassigned, downgraded, pared down, silenced. The original judge, Vaughn Walker, from the Ninth Circuit in San Francisco, retired before hearing anything more than motions. Discovery and depositions alone took more than two years.

. . .

THE TRIAL WAS FINALLY SET for June 9, 2014. It had been 1,784 days—nearly five years—since the case was first filed on July 21, 2009.

As *Sports Illustrated* accurately portrayed, the NCAA was staring down the barrel of a loaded gun—at least as far as Walter Byers had constructed it. If successful, the lawsuit could upend the NCAA's current model built upon the concept that college athletes are amateurs and shouldn't be compensated beyond tuition and basic room and board.

The Ronald V. Dellums Federal Building and United States Courthouse in Oakland, where the trial was finally held, is an understated seventy's modernist structure—a far cry from the ornate, architectural grandeur of Judge Walker's courtroom in San Francisco where the initial filings were introduced.

Every day for three solid weeks, Pam and I walked the two blocks up Oakland's busy Eleventh Street, then three blocks up Jefferson to take our place in line before the court's doors opened at 8:30 a.m. Sometimes we'd be joined by Eddie, sometimes Michael Hausfeld.

With five decades of frustration and disgust pent up inside, I wasn't about to miss a single minute of the trial.

As I knew from the outset, Michael Hausfeld was the heart and soul of our case. Though reserved, humble, and understated, he was the clear, resolute leader on our side of the bench. Driven by principle, he possessed a laser focus and assassin's will to pursue this cause to its ultimate resolution, whatever the demands. It was inspiring to watch him guide the strategy and tactics of our consortium of high-powered law firms—each performing like a skilled team of neurosurgeons probing the NCAA's convoluted arguments and smoke-and-mirrors defense. Nearly every night after court adjourned, we would meet with Michael and DC attorney Bill Isaacson, his right-hand man and a preeminent litigator from the powerhouse law firm of Boies Schiller Flexner.

In a Marriott restaurant for dinner and our daily debriefing, Michael rarely ate. He'd have a soft drink—never alcohol—and reflect on the day's events, further elaborating on the NCAA's strategies and gambits. His nightly analysis and insights proved fascinating to Pam and me. Then he would politely excuse himself and retreat to the suite to work with the other trial lawyers and advisors late into the night, preparing for the next day's witnesses.

Isaacson and Hausfeld had worked together in a previous antitrust case. An avid basketball fan, Bill was Michael's "sports translator," and a godsend on the case, especially in key strategy sessions and during critical cross-examinations at trial.

The thrust of our case was to debunk the mystery surrounding a single word—*amateurism*—and the aura of immunity the NCAA had always leaned on to deflect the fact they were abusing a system and the people in it. *Amateurism*, we argued, was nothing more than a ruse—what they contrived it to mean. A classic example: When one NCAA president was asked why amateurs aren't paid, his answer was "Because they're amateurs." And why are they amateurs? His answer: "Because they're not paid." Reductive circular logic at its finest.

As one might expect, the trial was chock-full of strident inter-actions, bickering, indignant posturing, eloquent elocution, verbal flare-ups, and (seemingly) forty thousand objections. All day every day, Eddie, our lead plaintiff, was the picture of calm and composure, sitting at the lawyers' table throughout, fully engaged and alert.

For me, it was worth the price of admission to watch Bill Isaacson dismantle NCAA president Mark Emmert. With his boyish-angelic face and impeccably coiffed silver hair, Emmert, the former president at both LSU and the University of Washington, was no stranger to the spotlight. Yet he struggled to maintain his composure as Isaacson, in his matter-of-fact tone, using little more than Emmert's own pub-lic comments, elegantly and methodically tore apart the hypocrisy of the NCAA's long-standing commercial business model. As *The Wall Street Journal* later reported, Isaacson's cross-examination of Emmert "laid out, one by one," the "deeply embedded contradictions and occa-sional bits of absurdity" of the NCAA's positions.

One of the more absurd moments came after Isaacson had Emmert detail his reform agenda before asking what he had done with that agenda regarding the commercial exploitation of athletes. Emmert was forced to admit nothing had been done in that regard before add-ing, almost as an aside, "Maybe we can get together sometime and talk about it." At which point, the courtroom erupted in laughter as a "What are you talking about?" look appeared on Judge Claudia Wilk-en's face as she gaveled the courtroom back to order.

· · ·

FROM THE START JUDGE WILKEN proved a commanding presence fully in control. In her opening remarks she presented herself as com-posed, civil, well reasoned—and where appropriate, stern. She alone would issue the final judgment. There were no jurors to be confused, charmed, or cajoled by the lawyers and their fluent legalese on either side. As I watched her preside over the proceedings, it occurred to me that she was brilliantly up to the task.

As the trial progressed, Judge Wilken's relative naivete in the intricacies of big-time college athletics led her to inquire about the machinations and maneuvers behind various NCAA practices and revenue-sharing arrangements. We introduced evidence by economists showing the six-figure return-on-investment value each D1 football and basketball player represented to universities. Her ability to absorb and distill issues with clarity, then apply the actual intent of the Sherman Antitrust Act of 1890 to those matters—which prohibits activities that restrict interstate commerce and fair competition in the marketplace—was something to behold.

Watching the NCAA's economic and antitrust experts testify was enlightening. Having been a gambler for four decades, the "tells" you could intuit from a succession of experts made it easy to decipher the degree of belief they had in their own words. I couldn't help but wonder whether Judge Wilken perceived the relative honesty, credibility, and integrity of the witnesses with the clarity I did. It was apparent to me that several "experts" testifying for the defense didn't seem to believe their own words. Like the NYU professor who was forced by Isaacson to admit that he'd written a textbook that included a case study entitled "The NCAA Cartel." Or the Stanford athletic director who told the court how special and unique and caring his university was to student-athletes before watching live as Isaacson's paralegal stood in the campus bookstore and held up photos of those same student-athletes being sold at different price points.

In Hausfeld's mind, the turning point came when we exposed what he later called "decades of camouflage" by the NCAA, the mirage of playing a sport in exchange for an education. The beauty was the bombshells that arrived in the form of two people who weren't there to testify—former NCAA president Walter Byers and Wally Renfro, the association's longtime public relations czar and chief policy advisor, in many ways the power behind the throne for nearly forty years. As our legal team pointed out, in his 1995 memoir *Unsportsmanlike Conduct: Exploiting College Athletes*, Byers had railed against the very kingdom he had created. He described the NCAA as a "cartel," and called amateurism a "modern day misnomer of economic tyranny" and mocked its exalted mission of protecting athletes from commercial exploitation. "This is not about amateurism," he wrote. "This has to do with who controls the negotiations and gets the money."

Renfro's own words in emails and meeting minutes, introduced in court, proved the final nail in the association's legal coffin.

When Hausfeld and Isaacson were finished, it was clear the NCAA was running a business and that "amateurism" was nothing less than a facade to cover the fact that the association had almost from the beginning exploited its labor force.

In the end, I'll let Judge Wilken's ruling on August 8, 2014, speak for itself. Its impact in the years to come was nothing less than the fuse that lit the bomb destined to blow up the NCAA and its phony amateurism/NIL argument.

> *The Court finds that this [NCAA] restraint does violate antitrust law. . . .*
>
> *Accordingly, under a rule of reason analysis, O'Bannon pleads facts to make out a prima facie case that Defendants' [NCAA's] conduct constitutes an unreasonable restraint of trade. . . .*
>
> *The Court will enjoin the NCAA from enforcing any rules or by-laws that would prohibit its member schools and conferences from offering their FBS football or Division I basketball recruits a limited share of the revenues generated from the use of their names, images, and likenesses in addition to a full grant-in-aid. . . .*
>
> *The Court will enter an injunction, in a separate order, to cure the specific violations found in this case.*

After decades of stops and starts and plaintiff lawyers putting fees in front of principle, if ever a case opened the door for athlete empowerment and compensation it was *O'Bannon*. In the face of the NCAA's predictable appeal, the critical elements of Wilken's antitrust ruling held up, allowing Power 5 schools to pay what's now known as "full cost of attendance"—up to $6,000 more per athlete per year. Other key antitrust cases, like *Alston* and *House*, eventually threw the legal door wide open to a historic 9–0 Supreme Court ruling on July 1, 2021, and these eviscerating words:

> *The NCAA couches its arguments for not paying student athletes in innocuous labels. But the labels cannot disguise the reality: The NCAA's business model would be flatly illegal in almost any other industry in America. . . . Price-fixing labor is price-fixing labor. And price-fixing labor is ordinarily a textbook antitrust problem because it extinguishes the free market in which individuals can otherwise obtain fair compensation for their work. . . . Nowhere else in America can businesses get away with agreeing not to pay their workers a fair market rate on the theory that their product is defined by not paying their workers a fair market rate. And under ordinary principles of antitrust law, it is not evident why college sports should be any different. The NCAA is not above the law. . . .*
>
> *The NCAA and its member colleges are suppressing the pay of student athletes who collectively generate billions of dollars in revenue for colleges each year. . . . But the student athletes who generate the revenues, many of whom are African American and from lower-income backgrounds, end up with little or nothing.*

That ruling by the highest court in the land made NIL the law of the land, a new fact of athletic life, the forerunner of the landmark settlement in *House* and two other critical cases in May 2024 in which the NCAA and major conferences agreed to pay $2.8 billion and allow individual D1 schools to share some $20 million a year with their athletes.

The day news of the settlement broke on literally every media outlet in America, I fielded one congratulatory call after another from the likes of Michael Hausfeld, Kenneth Feinberg, Bill Isaacson, Joe Nocera (coauthor of the brilliant NCAA-based book *Indentured*), Lowell Bergman, and most important, Ed and Rosa O'Bannon.

The only voice I so longed to hear that day but couldn't belonged to Rob Ades. Eleven years earlier, on September 1, 2013, Rob had passed away after a brief battle with leukemia. The man who'd orchestrated my meeting with Ken Feinberg never lived to celebrate the victory with us.

After the trial, our relationship with the O'Bannons deepened. I now have even greater admiration for the selfless courage Ed showed in our pursuit of justice for a future generation of kids neither of us will ever meet and who likely won't know the dimensions of what we had managed to pull off.

In my mind, Ed will forever be remembered as *The One*: the one who looked at all the reasons he could have said "no" and instead raised his right hand and said, "I'll do it"—a resolute act of courage and commitment that helped open vast new avenues of economic opportunity for present and future generations of college athletes and their families.

Postscript

Interestingly, much of the current conversation and confusion relative to NIL and revenue sharing could have been resolved years ago and be operational by now.

Little did the public know, but in the aftermath of Judge Wilken's initial ruling we set up the Former College Athletes Association

(FCAA), a nonprofit designed to help determine the methods and manner in which D1 athletes would be compensated. The foundation was initially funded by a $50,000 donation from SESAC, a well-regarded performance rights organization that today licenses more than 1.5 million songs on behalf of thousands of songwriters, composers, music publishers, and television shows. SESAC could have easily overseen the nonprofit and an equitable pay formula. Kenneth Feinberg would have been the chairman.

At Mr. Feinberg's behest, a letter was sent to every (then) Power 5 conference commissioner, as well as Notre Dame's influential athletic director, Jack Swarbrick. In it, Ken requested a private meeting among the parties to begin the conversation—"in confidence and without public fanfare"—to discuss how collegiate athletic stakeholders might begin to develop a set of rules that would govern the relationship (educational, financial, health, and safety) between the NCAA, major conferences, and current and former athletes.

In a sign of the times, just one individual responded, the other recipients not even bothering to dignify Feinberg's letter with a professional reply. The lone reaction from University of South Carolina president Harris Pastides seemed to sum up a collective thought: "I do not think that it is necessary to meet at this time."

I thought of that quote and the FCAA as I watched the SEC and Big Ten annual grant of rights (GOR) media payments push past $60 million per year per school.

28

A Contentious Un–Raveling

I thought long and hard before bringing up the name George Raveling again into these pages. I had briefly mentioned him earlier as the person who sat silently during my initial meeting with Michael Jordan in Santa Monica, the former head basketball coach at Washington State, Iowa, and USC, and the best man at my wedding to Pam at Caesars Palace.

Basketball's ruling class has long been acutely aware that George and I have not spoken a word to each other, cordial or otherwise, in twenty-plus years now. Our twenty-five-year near-brotherly relationship replaced by a visceral hostility (on my part) mistakenly attributed to our Shoe Wars rivalry—George at Nike, me at Adidas—and our antipathy such that it occupied an entire chapter in Dan Wetzel and Don Yaeger's 2000 bestselling book, *Sole Influence*. As they wrote, "It's the nastiest feud in all of basketball and your average fan's never heard of it."

That chapter of my life was permanently shuttered long ago, never to be revisited (again, on my part).

I never even considered including any mention of George in these pages until I was blindsided by a September 30, 2015, article in *USA Today Sports* written by Josh Peter, headlined, "Error Jordan: Key Figures Still Argue over Who Was Responsible for Nike Deal." In it, Phil Knight and Michael Jordan, along with their co-conspirator Raveling, engaged in a fully fabricated rewrite of arguably *the* seminal moment in

Nike history—one I, perhaps naively, believed had gone unquestioned for the better part of three decades. In the article, rife with outrageous distortions, outright lies, and revisionist history, Knight, Jordan, and Raveling portrayed me as inconsequential in Jordan's groundbreaking decision to sign with Nike in 1984. It implied that I had been altering factual events to enhance my influence in the most important single endorsement deal in Nike's history.

They have their recollection. I certainly have mine.

Through their efforts to render me "null and void," the contributions of both myself and others in Nike's emergence from relative obscurity in Beaverton, Oregon, to become the most dominant sports brand in the world were suddenly thrown into question.

Not three paragraphs into the *USA Today* article that Wednesday morning as I sat down to breakfast, my blood was already boiling.

"The signing of Michael Jordan, yeah, success has a thousand fathers and failure is an orphan," Knight told Peter in a rare interview. "A lot of people want to take credit for signing Michael Jordan, most obviously, Sonny Vaccaro."

In turn, Jordan told the newspaper, "It was actually George Raveling" who was the person responsible for him signing with Nike.

"I've always felt that Michael's and my version about how he got to Nike was totally different than what was being perceived out there or people were saying," added Raveling.

So as *that story* goes, I was just a guy, an inconsequential *intermediary*. They portrayed me as a mere asterisk in the proceedings, barely worth a mention. The assignment: Delete me from the sequence of events that lead to the signing of the most iconic athlete among all athletes who have ever endorsed Nike.

Conveniently forgetting that nobody at Nike knew Michael was considering turning pro that summer after his junior year or cared one whit about signing him until I championed his singular talent and gigantic upside potential and *put my job*—and Nike's entire

$500,000 sponsorship budget—on the line to bring that possibility about.

Never once had I suggested or even intimated that there wasn't a spectacular assemblage of people who had brought Jordan to Nike— Knight, Strasser, Peter Moore, along with Michael's dear parents. The role I played at the time had long been regarded as common knowledge—an undisputed fact verified and repeated ad infinitum in interviews and news stories, on television, and in books and documentaries.

In my mind, Phil and his "Revenge Tour" cohorts had an insidious reason for suddenly speaking out. It was obviously intended to embarrass and discredit me. In a clever way their rendition put me in a lose-lose situation from an *optics point of view*: By refuting them I became, de facto, a self-aggrandizing publicity hound, made to appear as someone trying to *unjustifiably interject* himself into the paradigm-shifting Jordan/Nike union.

They were attempting to invalidate a story that was, to those in the loop at the time, *incontrovertible*. If I do nothing, then their widely reported neo-revisionist version of history might put the objective facts in doubt.

When there's a very public attack on my integrity by people who were at one time compatriots and friends, a *nonresponse* from me would seem a bit too much to hope for. In fact, *impossible*.

So, I found myself in an unenviable position: having to defensively debate the facts with two sports-industry giants—the odds of anyone believing my account against a sports icon and one of the greatest entrepreneurs of all time were long at best.

I have a good idea of Phil's motives—but why would Michael concoct a fairy-tale version of his decision to sign with Nike? The story contained not lies from third parties but *lies by people who know the truth*. Even Jordan's mother and father knew the truth.

I completely understood with crystal clarity that Knight couldn't rationally bring himself to weave a breakaway group into the scriptures of Nike's glorious history. But that fallacious version leaves a void from a historical standpoint. In his mind Rob Strasser, Peter Moore, and Sonny Vaccaro, all of whom ended up at Adidas, *needed to be portrayed* as bit players turned traitors. Especially me.

Thankfully, Peter spoke up.

"The truth lies very close to Sonny," Moore told Josh Peter for his story. "This whole episode is very typical of Nike history. You get a slightly different story from everyone you talk to."

When asked by Josh Peter to respond to the "Who deserves credit?" imbroglio (and angry as hell), I wasn't inclined to mince any words: "Phil Knight's lying, Michael's lying more than Phil, and Raveling is insane," I said. "All three of them need to destroy me to live happily ever after. Everyone's trying to rewrite history."

Though nowhere near as important, the true unfiltered story behind the dissolution of my relationship with George needs to be put on the record as well, to provide a broader context of that moment in time. The one that fills in the blanks.

. . .

AT THE HEIGHT OF HIS influence George Raveling was a beloved figure in the coaching profession. In person, he came across as warm, sincere, and genuine. Sometimes called "The Great Communicator," he had an engaging personality many found charming, including myself.

After college at Villanova, where George had become its all-time leading rebounder, he went to work for the Sun Oil Company, soon discovering he wasn't ready to leave the game he had grown up in. Realizing he had an affinity for scouting, he joined the Villanova basketball staff as an assistant with dreams of someday becoming a head coach. After six years at 'Nova, he went on to become an assistant on

Lefty Driesell's staff at Maryland in 1969. His ability to spot talent proved beneficial to me as well, suggesting and helping recruit top kids from the Philly and South Jersey area for the Roundball.

As a scout and recruiter, George was meticulous, compulsive in his note taking. He kept index cards, stacks of them, filled with details, not just chronicling young athletes and their strengths but everything pertinent to his life; restaurants, jazz clubs, men's clothing stores, X's and O's, even good jokes and stories were indexed as well. He'd once slept in my bed at my parents' house in Trafford while recruiting in the Pittsburgh area. We had broken bread many times, often with some of the top coaches in the nation.

I brought George on board the exclusive Nike Coaches Council, though his teams weren't nearly as successful in the tournament as the other premier coaches I'd invited (John Thompson, Jim Boeheim, Abe Lemons, Eddie Sutton, Lute Olson, Jim Valvano). I took George on as an accommodation of sorts. He'd had a few twenty-win seasons to justify my decision when Strasser questioned, "Raveling? Really?"

I have to concede also that our friendship blinded me to certain odd quirks and aberrations that had cropped up here and there over time. Like the first and only time I was ever called on the carpet by Strasser, as upset as I'd ever seen him.

"Are you aware of what your buddy Raveling has been doing at Iowa?" Rob screamed into the phone.

"Hold on, Rob. What are you talking about?"

"Retailers are calling our people in Iowa. Raveling is wearing someone else's sweat suits at home games!"

"What?!" The skin on my face burned beet red.

George, despite a very generous Nike contract complete with stock options, wasn't wearing our apparel at games. He'd somehow struck up a side deal with a small entrepreneurial start-up called Hang Perfect that was in direct competition with Nike. Not only was George stalking the sidelines in their warm-ups at Iowa games, he was out promoting the other company. In addition, George was dropping quotes to the media, calling Hang Perfect's products "the Calvin Klein of athletic leisure wear." He was also actively trying to get Nike coaches and others to wear a competitor's brand. Some show of loyalty, right?

"You call that good judgment, George? Are you trying to get both of us fired?" I yelled.

I never did get a straight answer about why George had pulled a stunt like that. To this day I remain mystified by his poor judgment and my own serious misjudgment in that episode. I never assumed he lacked the common decency to support the company that had essentially doubled his salary. I never in a million years imagined he'd disregard and disrespect both me and the brand that had banners hanging everywhere in Carver-Hawkeye Arena.

Which brings us, in a roundabout way, to the crux of our contentious feud—the inciting incident, as they say in the movie business.

After twenty-five years of friendship, Raveling knew me well enough to know I had never—*would never*—steer players to any school. Because of my close relationship with John Thompson, one sportswriter intimated that I had steered Alonzo Mourning to Georgetown—as if Alonzo needed my input to make up his mind for him.

The topic still infuriates me.

What Wetzel and Yaeger wrote in *Sole Influence* was absolutely spot on: "If Vaccaro was regularly steering players to certain schools, he would have been run out of the business long ago."

Maintaining strict neutrality with the players' choice of colleges was an unbreakable personal guardrail. Many were Nike schools. If I favored one over another, I'd compromise not only long-standing relationships, but the integrity of the events I put on. It not only went against my belief system, but doing so would have destroyed my relationships with the entire coaching fraternity.

Still, in 1990, George assumed that I'd somehow temporarily waive my moral code to help him recruit players at USC, where five years earlier he had been named head coach.

In this case, one very *specific* player.

Ed O'Bannon.

I vividly recall the first time George asked me to intercede on his behalf with Eddie. I was in Las Vegas. One way or another George had tracked me down at the Barbary Coast.

With slot machines *ding-ding-dinging* and the whirl of roulette wheels in the background, the operator patched him in.

"Yeah, George, what's up?"

"I need your help with Ed O'Bannon."

"What kind of help? He's—"

"Sonny, he's been released by Tark, he's not going to UNLV now."

Two months after losing in the semifinals against Duke, the Runnin' Rebels had been put on probation by the NCAA for recruiting infractions dating back to Tark's time at Long Beach State. The penalty had been withheld for years while Tark, UNLV, and the NCAA battled their way through the court system. Because of the forthcoming sanctions, both Tark and his top assistant, Tim Grgurich, had urged O'Bannon, the star of their '90 recruiting class, to do what was best for himself, releasing him from his signed Letter of Intent.

My jaw hit the ground.

"Look, George, I've got to find out what happened. I gotta get hold of Tark. I'll get back to you."

"Okay, my friend," Raveling replied. "Get back to me. It's important."

I immediately called Grgurich. We talked for a long time. He told me, at first, Eddie resisted. He loved Tark and the Runnin' Rebels, and wanted to honor his commitment, but finally took their counsel and decided to switch schools. Eddie wanted to stay in Southern California. It was between UCLA and USC.

I didn't call George back.

You never forget that sickening feeling in your stomach when a close friend asks you to cross a moral precipice *he already knows you cannot cross.*

George asked anyway.

He called again, this time in tears, pleading. Never had I seen George, normally urbane and good-humored, this desperate and distraught. He said he needed Eddie to compete against Jim Harrick at UCLA. Raveling could live with O'Bannon going to UNLV—but not his crosstown rival.

"You know what it's like in this town, Sonny," he said. "Outside the tournament, that's the only game that matters in LA."

"George," I said evenly, "Eddie and his family are going to make that decision. I'm not part of it."

The third time George brought O'Bannon up was in a car on our way to one of the many prep tournaments spread across Los Angeles that summer. John Thompson was in town and in the car with us. Both of them were scouting prospects. George would not let the O'Bannon thing go.

"So did you talk to Eddie, Son?"

"No, George. I didn't. And you know I'm not going to."

That's when John interjected.

"Stop asking him, George," he said. "Didn't you hear him?"

Leaving the rest of our trip silent.

George knew Ed's parents. He'd already been in contact with them. He knew they were by far the most critical influence in their son's decision.

The fourth instance when O'Bannon came up—and the final straw—was a telegram sent via Western Union to our home in Pacific Palisades.

The messaging remains vividly implanted in my mind. He desperately needed my help and pleaded for me not to let him down. Artfully nondescript, plausible deniability implicit in its phrasing. And shamefully scheduled to arrive at our front door at the very moment Pam and I were hosting a lunch with the O'Bannons.

Pam answered the door, opened the telegram, read it to herself, and placed it on the counter, never mentioning a word until the O'Bannons left.

George knew hundreds of people in LA so I have no idea who tipped him off. The O'Bannons had chosen the occasion to tell us in person that Eddie had decided to go to UCLA. We hugged and celebrated Ed's choice. I never mentioned George's repeated requests to Ed or his parents until over twenty years later, following the conclusion of our NCAA antitrust trial.

George never forgave me for *not making an exception* for him. He also knew that O'Bannon at UCLA would practically guarantee four years of dominance for his crosstown archrival.

In half a century, no kid has ever accused me of influencing them to make a choice of one college over another—nor has a single coach.

In the aftermath, it wasn't enough for George to simply stop talking to me—or vice versa.

He shifted into overdrive to exact revenge. In the aftermath of O'Bannon's decision, George abruptly left Nike and signed with the long-since departed fashion upstart LA Gear—at $175,000 a year.

By the fall of 1990, George had piggybacked his coaching celebrity into the realm of basketball politics, escalating our acrimony to the point of no return. Never once mentioning my name directly, he led a full-frontal assault against the world of basketball camps I was synonymous with at the time, his intent unequivocal and transparent.

Preaching straight from the NCAA's playbook, he decided to use me as the scapegoat for all the ills associated with summer basketball, making it his mission to vilify me in a very clever way. Without referencing me directly, Raveling became the summer league's most vocal critic, seizing on well-worn themes the NCAA and others had been grousing about for decades. At venues and events across the country, he made speeches attacking the entire grassroots community—with one individual ever-present in the subtext. His sincerity and authority made you believe he was *very, very concerned* as he vocally denounced high school camps and all-star games, positioning himself as the erstwhile "sheriff" of summer league basketball, but to what end? Securing a job as the NCAA's out-front hit man? In doing so, he artfully cherry-picked inflammatory little gems like "unsavory elements," "middlemen," "street agents," "hustlers," "intermediaries," "the cancer of summer basketball," and "increasing levels of abuse taking place." His favorite allusion was the "culture of summer basketball."

By implication, George placed himself above reproach, interested only in cleaning up what he termed "the fetid murky swamp of summer basketball."

Amid all this withering cascade of criticism, there was nary a word about the NCAA's repression and needlessly cruel punishment of the young athletes—athletes George had coached for decades—many of whom were Black.

While a small proportion of "bad actors" were certainly ever-present and angling to influence players for their own self-interest, Raveling's campaign ignored a legion of caring head coaches, assistants, parents, and supporters who adhered to the mission of the summer grassroots world. Thousands of kids who participated would never end up at elite programs but still had their dream to attend college on scholarship fulfilled.

If that wasn't enough, out of nowhere during the 1991 men's Final Four weekend in Indianapolis, Raveling's crusade reached a crescendo. He announced that he was introducing legislation to the National Association of Basketball Coaches (NABC) in which they would become the entity in charge of oversight of all summer camps. "Division I, II, and III coaches would be permitted to evaluate talent at these camps only. They would be banned from events like the Nike, Five-Star, and B/C All-Star camps," he intoned.

That was it—just an announcement. Pure theater. No white paper on "summer corruption," no manifesto, nothing based on actual facts. Still, he was successful. His efforts were influential in convincing the

NCAA, in cooperation with the NABC, to place limits on the number of events players could attend at the summer camps and all-star games—a self-defeating move that limited the range of options open to kids to audition for college scholarships. Instead of greater opportunities, he lobbied to impose limits. His motives—as I saw it—were cynical, self-aggrandizing, and hollow. A dog and pony show to enhance nothing more than his own what? Virtue? His grandstanding sickened me.

My lack of respect for him morphed into an intense loathing and disgust.

Someone I thought I knew very, very well had become unrecognizable—the single biggest example of misplaced judgment in my life. That remains true to this day.

* * *

IN SEPTEMBER 1994, GEORGE WAS commuting in his Jeep in LA when he was blindsided in a two-car collision in which he suffered terrible, potentially life-threatening injuries. The long recovery period led him to retire from USC at the age of fifty-seven (though back-to-back 9–9 Pac-10 seasons may also have been a factor; the alums were getting restless and losing patience).

When George was finally healthy enough to work, Coach John Thompson suggested to Knight that Raveling take over *my former role* at Nike. Knight needed to fill a vacuum in their grassroots program and George needed a job.

You can imagine my surprise when Phil, with Nike no longer a player in the summer game, hired George. A man previously so utterly offended and disgusted at the AAU scene that he had been denigrating for years again swallowed his principles and jumped at the first paid opportunity to join Nike. The same person who had unceremoniously abandoned the Swoosh four years earlier at USC returned to the fold. I'd never seen Phil take *anyone* back who had voluntarily—or involuntarily, for that matter—left Nike, not a single person.

Still Nike had an undeniable void in grassroots basketball, and to fill it, he needed someone of stature to go against me in the summer fray.

The person who railed against the summer scene was now back in this so-called "quagmire of malfeasance" up to his neck.

Freshly funded with a budget 350 percent larger than the one I had at Adidas—millions more—the suddenly summer-basketball-loving Raveling was making amends by outspending everyone else in the category he had roundly condemned. With more than double the staff and triple the budget, Raveling still failed to outflank me and my team. Knight's sadly misplaced confidence ended up costing him millions of dollars. Still, I was happy to see the infusion of money into the summer leagues. Nothing could have been better for the kids.

To this day, College Basketball Hall of Famer or not, it nauseates me to hear George's name bandied about in the same conversation as coaching legends like John Thompson, John Chaney, Nolan Richardson, Clarence "Big House" Gaines, Ed Martin, or Fred Snowden.

I have no sense of bitterness or remorse that George and I were once friends—only disappointment that it took me so long to accurately unravel the man.

Most people have a friendship or two they regret losing in their life. I don't count George Raveling among those in mine.

29

Air: A Hollywood Nanosecond

We were in the middle of working on this book when in November 2021 a friend named Jon Weinbach, a writer / producer / director / film executive whom I had known since his days at *The Wall Street Journal*, unexpectedly called.

"I've got some pretty exciting news for you . . ." Weinbach said.

"Who doesn't like good news?" I responded.

"We're going to bid on a movie focused on the story about how Michael Jordan ended up at Nike."

Rarely speechless, I paused. "Wait . . . what?"

"Yeah. We've read the script, not finished yet. You're in it, of course, Jordan, Phil Knight, Peter Moore, Rob Strasser."

A mid-forty-ish dark-haired Yale grad ('98) and ex-high school athlete (Beverly Hills High) with smiling eyes and an easy way about him, Jon had just become the president of Skydance Sports, a Hollywood film production company.

His first notable splash in the sports content business was his script for the ESPN 30 for 30 documentary *Straight Outta L.A.* Jon's directorial debut came on *Sole Man*, the documentary that detailed my career in grassroots basketball and my Nike and Adidas days. We crossed paths again a few years later when Jon was a producer on ESPN's critically acclaimed docuseries *The Last Dance*, about Michael Jordan, Nike, and Jordan's championship Chicago Bulls days.

I had done about half a day of filming in Palm Springs for *The Last*

Dance. When it was released, to my surprise, in the entire ten episodes of the series, I ended up appearing for a grand total of less than three seconds—a still photo showing the back of my head. Hours and hours of interviews, and someone made the editorial decision that Sonny Vaccaro would only appear in a flash shot. Hmmm, let's see . . . ?

As I slowly came to my senses I said, "A *movie* movie, not another documentary?"

"Yes. A *movie* movie," Jon said. "A newcomer named Alex Convery wrote the script titled *Air Jordan*. We're going to try to lock it up."

Convery's personal story could well have been a movie within the movie. He'd been an intern on *Sole Man* and managed to see an early cut. Hunkered down during the COVID-19 pandemic, he decided to write a spec screenplay about Sonny Vaccaro and the beginning of the Michael Jordan era at Nike, exploring that signing's impact on the company. Written as a "dramedy," it covered a finite four-month period of my long career at Nike, the weeks leading up to Jordan's signing and what happened next. Several production companies were interested in acquiring the rights to the script, which had made its way onto the prestigious Hollywood "Black List" of the most promising screenplays yet to be produced.

In November 2021, Convery had decided to put his script in the hands of Weinbach at Skydance and Peter Guber, the chairman and CEO of Mandalay Entertainment, whose previous movies had garnered more than fifty Academy Award nominations. If a script ever needed the endorsement of a player to get made into a movie, you'd be hard-pressed to find a person with more stature than Peter Guber.

"Can you meet with the writer in Palm Springs if I can set it up?" Jon asked.

I knew no script would have the story exactly as it happened, and I could accept Hollywood taking some literary license to add drama and tension—but I hoped the narrative wouldn't drift too far afield from the actual story.

In early January 2022, Alex drove to Palm Springs to discuss the remaining details of the story and fill in certain blanks in the narrative. An amiable, earnest young writer, he honestly had the appearance of a college freshman—though he must have been approaching thirty by then. We met for breakfast in the dining room of the Westin in Rancho Mirage. He was still fine-tuning his latest version of *Air Jordan*. Pam and I spent over two hours with Alex, offering him full access to my recollections and clarifications. To his credit, Alex was both respectful and attentive, feverishly jotting notes in a spiral notepad, flipping pages as each filled up. I took an immediate liking to him. He was young and unafraid, and had the courage to tell the story that filled in a glaring omission from the entire ten hours of *The Last Dance*.

The following month we were invited to meet with Guber, Weinbach, Alex, and a group of key production executives at Guber's home in Bel Air, just north of the UCLA campus in West LA. Peter viewed the meeting as an opportunity for his production team to spend some time with one of the main characters in the script. I was equally interested in meeting the people who'd be bringing the story to life.

It was about 1:30 p.m. on a balmy winter afternoon when we arrived at Peter's home. As you entered the gates, off to the right was a separate wing of the estate that served as his office. As Pam and I passed through the glass entry doors we found Peter and Jon waiting in the foyer. More than a dozen beautifully framed, perfectly aligned movie posters were hung on the walls, each with its own lighting. Film classics like *Rain Man*, *Midnight Express*, *The Color Purple*, *Flashdance*, and *Batman*.

"Sonny, I presume," Peter said as he approached to greet us. We shook hands. We both hugged hello with Jon. Casually dressed, their welcome was as gracious as if we were old friends.

The conference room was a grand paneled space, something you could imagine Jack Warner or Samuel Goldwyn inhabiting in the heyday of Hollywood. The chatter settled as we all took our seats. Peter was first to speak. He introduced Pam and me to the executives and producers' group gathered around the imposing, oversize dark wood conference table. Eight of us in all, including Alex.

"This is a project we're very excited about, as you all know," Peter said, his gaze moving around the table. "Alex has written a really wonderful script, and I thought it was time to meet the guy at the center of it all," nodding toward me.

"I'm going to be hearing from Nike," Peter continued. "And from Michael Jordan's assistant—they're going to be calling. I'm going to listen to them, and I'll listen respectfully. But we are going to make the movie we all want to make. We're not going to make a Nike commercial."

I was in no way involved in the overall direction of the movie, only as a character in the main storyline. I had no veto power in the process. I had been warned that the final story could be drastically different from the original given "that's just how things work in Hollywood."

That convivial meeting wrapped after about an hour, with Peter assuring me, "Sonny, we're going to make a movie we're all going to be proud of."

In the end, a movie deal came together with Artists Equity, Ben Affleck and Matt Damon's new film production company. Affleck had expressed an interest in directing. He also thought Damon would be good as me.

Given the fact that both Affleck and Damon were award-winning screenwriters themselves, there was no doubt the script would soon undergo further revisions, especially after Affleck took a trip to Florida to meet with Jordan. Ben had gone there to personally deliver the news to Michael that he was proceeding with development of the script. Jordan was well aware it was about his surprising signing with Nike—and that I was going to play a prominent role in the movie.

While puffing on a cigar, Jordan didn't exactly endorse the project, but he didn't try to quash it, either. He did, however, make some specific requests he hoped Ben could accommodate. He wanted his mother, Deloris, to have a prominent role, and he hoped Ben could get Academy Award–winner Viola Davis to play his mom. He also wanted his father, James, represented in the movie, along with George Raveling and Howard White.

Affleck agreed to all those requests. Later, I got word that Michael also said, "I don't have a problem with Sonny."

In the aftermath of the Florida meeting, Alex went back to rework the script with Damon. Something close to a final version was completed in May 2022, with production set to begin in June. By then, Amazon Studios had come on board. The movie was originally set to be released for streaming on Amazon Prime as a feature presentation, but later, after seeing the dailies, Amazon saw a bigger opportunity. They chose *Air* to be their first-ever theatrical release, opening exclusively in theaters around the world before streaming on Prime.

The day before shooting was to begin, June 5, Weinbach arranged a Zoom call between me and Damon, the first time Matt and I had ever spoken. He wanted to know details about my time with Michael, just random recollections about our rapport and some of the feelings I recalled. He was curious about why Jordan's final shot against Georgetown in the NCAA final had stuck in my mind.

Three weeks later, Pam and I were able to visit the set and watch a scene being filmed. We arrived at a vintage seventies building located at an aging office park off Ocean Avenue in Santa Monica. We knew the area well—our first apartment in California wasn't more than two miles from that location, just off Lincoln Boulevard farther west. We were expecting to be on set for only a couple of hours at most. Jon met us outside the building, and we exchanged greetings and talked while our required COVID tests took place. Movie production trucks filled the parking lot. After we tested negative, Jon showed us inside. The set designer, François Audouy, had decorated the lobby entrance of the building to look like Nike's first office building, and it could have fooled me.

Before shooting began, I literally took a stroll down memory lane. We were given a tour of the various Nike-of-the-eighties sets built on-site inside the building. The conference room, the kitchen inside Michael's childhood home, Rob's office, Peter Moore's design studio, my borrowed cubical (in my entire time at Nike I never had an actual office), it was all there and remarkably authentic. I felt as if I'd been transported back in time, remembering the prosaic "ordinariness" of Nike's early days.

That particular day they were shooting a scene with Matt (as me) speaking on the phone to Chris Messina, playing Jordan's high-powered agent David Falk. We watched on monitors near the set as Affleck directed and shot several takes of the conversation.

Peter Guber, whom we hadn't seen since February, stopped by a little later on, and was just as genial and warm as he'd been the first time we met. This time we hugged hello. As ego gratification goes, I can't remember a much better day in my life.

A minute or two after Affleck yelled, "Cut! Wrap for lunch," he came around to the area where we were seated. Like Peter, Ben couldn't have been more congenial. A moment later, Matt showed up. More warm hugs.

Both asked (with genuine interest) how we liked what we saw. I told them (and meant it) they had nailed it. There were smiles and I believe they appreciated the confirmation that their portrayals rang so true.

"Exactly like the conversations Falk and I used to have!" I exclaimed.

Moments later, Chris Messina appeared. Before he said anything, I repeated what I'd just said: "You absolutely nailed it, young man—you were great—right down to Falk's swearing." Everyone laughed, including the crew members.

The day ended with late-afternoon goodbyes, and I'm not sure my adrenaline level returned to normal on the entire crawl back home. I was thrilled with how our Hollywood afternoon on set had gone.

By mid-July 2022, filming was complete and the footage in Affleck's hands. About six months later, Affleck had his movie completed and an official title: *Air: Courting a Legend*.

Later, as I watched *Air* for the first time, I quickly realized whatever Damon had gleaned from our ninety-minute Zoom call had resulted in an absolutely spectacular performance. I even detected a hint or two of actual words from our conversation. Of course, Matt looked nothing like I did in the eighties, but his portrayal captured my fast-talking style and frenetic energy in a way I found totally believable.

The following month Pam and I went to the NBA All-Star weekend. It was a Friday night and Ben was there with his son, Sam, to watch the annual celebrity game. Ben had flown in for the launch of the *Air* marketing and publicity campaign, which debuted that night at the game. As the crowd suffered through the usual antics of celebrities cavorting in a pretend basketball game, *Air* commercials ran on the jumbotron and on television during the game's broadcast. Around Salt Lake City's Huntsman Center, *Air* promo materials were prominently displayed everywhere. Ben and I only spoke for a few minutes, but one thing he said stuck. As we hugged goodbye he leaned into my right ear and said, "You've led a fascinating life." His movie was certainly going to make it even more so.

When the *Air* public relations and promotional blitz started hitting the airwaves and mainstream media, I imagine it caused quite a stir in one particular precinct in Oregon. As Peter Guber had predicted, Nike's lawyers repeatedly requested access to review the script and footage throughout the production process, their inquiries rebuffed out of hand. Affleck had never sought their permission or guidance on a single frame of his movie.

• • •

AIR FINALLY PREMIERED AT THE South by Southwest (SXSW) festival in Austin in March 2023, a surprise screening on the closing

Sunday night, March 19. This was the hippest of hip cultural festivals, and an auspicious first public viewing.

This was the moment when the first real feedback would begin its viral growth cycle. As Weinbach later called to report—with a mix of great relief and barely contained excitement—*Air* had received a hoot-filled, extended-applause standing ovation at the sneak. It seemed modern popular culture somehow connected with a sports / pop culture story from nearly forty years earlier. Jon, Ben, and Peter Guber each had to have been thrilled as the news of the cheers were confirmed by overwhelmingly positive reviews. Jon sounded on the verge of joyful tears when we touched base the following morning.

Across the country, free screenings—something like ninety or so—were taking place on military bases, college campuses, and other non-theater settings to get "word of mouth" building before the movie opened in theaters. We even arranged for a screening at my alma mater, Youngstown State. That's when I began getting calls from both current and long-lost friends expressing happiness that I was "getting the credit I deserved."

While Ben and Matt appeared on the morning shows, with short movie trailers over a carefully planned schedule of appearances, the marketing team thought I might be useful in the rollout as well. Jeff Freedman, a motion picture PR master out of LA, was in charge of my slate of interviews, appearances, and Zooms, with sports television, radio, newspapers, websites, and podcasts. In all, I spoke to something like seventy-five different media and broadcast outlets here in the States, Australia, and other foreign countries. All of the big sports talk shows—from Dan Patrick to Colin Cowherd—could not have been more receptive. Suddenly, my relatively predictable daily routine went from going to Costco a couple of times a week and working on this project to a life filled with interviews scheduled weeks into the future.

Interviews dominated my days until the movie's official Hollywood premiere on Monday, March 27—at the Fox Theater in West-wood Village, an iconic theater built in the thirties distinguished by a 170-foot-tall tower adorned with a blue vertically stacked neon Fox sign glowing against the white stucco.

Pam and I had received an invitation from Jeff Freedman, the PR lead. We had hotel reservations at the Four Seasons Hotel in Beverly Hills and Jeff sent a car to pick us up for the grandest opening of my life. I hadn't been this nervous since the night of the first Dapper Dan half a century earlier.

Pam and I found ourselves seated directly behind Peter Guber. When Ben Affleck stepped onstage to make remarks before the screening, an enthusiastic round of applause greeted him. Ben was modest and low-key, but possessed a powerful, laid-back presence. He thanked everyone for being there, thanked the people who had made his movie happen, praised the writer, and—I'm sure, full of trepidation—hoped his vision and story would be well received by a tough and influential Hollywood-centric crowd.

How can I describe how I felt as the credits rolled 112 minutes later? As it had at SXSW, the movie received a prolonged standing ovation, cheers echoing across the ornate ceilings of the theater. The audience wasn't clapping for me, of course, but I couldn't have been more euphoric if they had been. How could seeing Sonny Vaccaro portrayed by Matt Damon—in a movie about the Jordan days at Nike with *that* cast and *that* script and *that* director—on a two-story silver screen NOT affect me.

Amid the applause and chatter, and a tear or two, with the house lights still dimmed, Peter stood, turned, and leaned toward Pam and me and said, "I told you we were going to make a great movie, didn't I?"

I squeezed his arm and over the applause shouted back, *"You absolutely did—and you absolutely did!"*

A few weeks after the movie opened, Amazon began hyping the

release of *Air* on Prime. Given the kind of global dominance Amazon wields, the movie got intense play all over the world, with trailers, interviews, YouTube videos, and talk shows. Once it played on Prime, I heard from even more friends. People who told me they'd watched it three or four times. As congratulatory calls came in, I was having a sort of high school or college reunion over the phone and in texts.

Most of my contemporaries in the sports world knew the truth behind the Jordan story and Nike's resurgence from that point on. But a couple of generations later, many people still didn't. I will be eternally grateful that an intern named Alex Convery with an idea for a movie somehow got that story in front of four powerful men with a passion for great storytelling—Jon Weinbach, Peter Guber, Ben Affleck, and Matt Damon—even if that story took some creative license. And Affleck did get the incomparable Viola Davis as Michael's mom, Deloris.

The brilliance of their effort had, at long last, settled a decades-old debate about whether Michael and Nike would have ever had their First Dance let alone their Last had I not been in the mix. Thanks to *Air*, any revisionist myths regarding what unfolded at that pivotal moment back in 1984 had finally, gratefully, been laid to rest.

ENCORE

It felt good to be back in the game, in front of cameras, on podcasts. For a three-week stretch between Memorial Day weekend 2024 when the NCAA settlement was announced and June 11 when *Air* was shown on network television as part of ABC Sports' coverage of the NBA playoffs—a first on linear TV for Amazon Prime—my cell phone never stopped ringing. One coach or friend or media person after another checking in with congratulations, each conversation ending with a simple, straightforward question I struggled to find an answer to:

So what are you going to do next?

I didn't have time to conjure a good answer. In the midst of that flurry of calls, Pam and I were in the middle of our final move. Putting the Southern California desert community of Rancho Mirage in our rearview mirror in favor of a return to Northern California to be closer to family, under the spell of Pebble Beach's chilly nights, rustling pines, and crashing waves. Coming along for the ride (and destined for the Sonny Vaccaro Archive at a university) was my treasure trove of collected memories—thirty-five boxes in all that I've been amassing for a half century or more. Videos, CDs, newspaper clippings and magazine articles, treasured photos, contracts, thank-you cards, court and legal documents, minutiae and memorabilia—in many ways, the paper trail of my now octogenarian life.

When the final buzzer sounds, my fervent wish is that there will be little or no debate about whatever footprints I may have left in the sand over a career that spanned more years and provided more rewards than I could ever have anticipated. Not as a spectator, but a participant, engaged and energized, seeking new opportunities to accomplish things that in some way made a difference: having a part in innovations that changed the way a game was marketed and played; smiling and proud that revenue-producing athletes finally received, if not their fair share, at least a substantial share of the billions in revenue they helped generate—and are at last free to negotiate for themselves. For any of us, there is enormous satisfaction in believing that you accomplished meaningful things, made positive contributions, watched your innovations change lives and build businesses. What more could a middle-class Italian kid from a single-stoplight town in Western Pennsylvania, who harbored a dream of one day following in the tracks of some of Pittsburgh's all-time baseball greats, ask for?

As those who know me can confirm, none of what I accomplished at Nike and beyond would have been possible without my wife, Pam. I marvel at the woman who some forty years ago, in the early eighties, proposed that we partner up and pursue the unchartered journey forward together.

So . . . what's next?

I can't answer that definitively but the word "encore" somehow seemed fitting for what certainly will be one final turn onstage. As these pages have demonstrated, pure, random happenstance—*improbability*—may be the most prominent recurring theme throughout, and given that, I can't help but believe that, yet again, fate may spring one more complete surprise on me before it's all over.

My plan now is to use whatever platform these pages provide to continue to speak out about issues and cross currents still roiling the summer game and college sports and the athletes who play them. Much is yet to be resolved (NIL will take years before the dust settles) in an arena that continues to attract billions and billions of dollars, thousands and thousands of athletes, and millions and millions of fans. As far as we've come, myriad issues still continue to confront and challenge those of us who understand how much sports influences our culture, our institutions of higher learning, our way of life. That's not going to change now or ever.

Forgive me if I wax a bit too poetically but that's how immeasurably important sports has been in my life—and the lives of almost anyone else I've known.

I still keep in contact with a good number of the kids who touched my life, a few of whom I have gone from watching as shy, gangly teenagers playing at one of my camps to being in the audience as they deliver heartfelt acceptance speeches at Hall of Fame ceremonies.

So back to that recurring question—*What's next?*

My phone rings. A familiar voice from the distant past, a former coach now interested in a second life scouting high school talent, asking what I've heard, which places to visit, who to contact. Then Jermaine O'Neal, who went straight from a South Carolina high school to a successful sixteen-year career in the NBA, checks in with a thank-you for my part in the NIL settlement; he's now a father with a son who's an already-being-scouted high school athlete harboring aspirations of his own. Not long after, Chicago Bulls head coach Billy Donovan calls with an inspiring story a preacher related about my movie character after seeing *Air.*

And that's when it hit me: Maybe what I'm doing now is the last and least *improbable* act of all.

Traveling a lot less but continuing to do what I've always done— open doors, share unfiltered advice, and offer what counsel I can when asked. Vicariously sharing the happiness of the friends and athletes I've encountered, enjoying their successes as if they were my own.

As happens with everyone in the sports world, I too will pass the torch to the next wave of participants in this marvelous, exhilarating, inspiring, captivating, sports-centric cornerstone of modern life, thanking God (*Thank you, God! Thank you! Thank you!*) for the opportunities I can never hope to reciprocate or repay. In the end, I can only wish to be thought of as a person whose heart was in the right place, doing whatever I could to give back all the blessings that found their way to my doorstep.

Considering the past six decades, in the end, that's not a bad way to be remembered.

ACKNOWLEDGMENTS

If I had to estimate, I would guess that I have possibly two to three thousand people to thank for their meaningful contributions—both big and small—to the life story, now in its eighth decade, that comprises this book. For the past six months or so, I've racked my brain to recall a great number of the people who deserve to be acknowledged. When we reached the eighth single-spaced page of the list—friends, players, and parents of players; high school, collegiate, and professional coaches; basketball legends, All-Stars, and Hall of Famers; Hollywood writers and actors; all the management and associates and creative people I've worked with while at the three largest shoe companies in the world; all the media personalities, truly world-class lawyers, beat writers, and authors; the vast network of basketball personalities and talent scouts; event coordinators, uniform designers, camp staff, player agents, supporters, and on and on—Pam and I realized the futility of such an enterprise. It would amount to a phone book full of names and still not do justice to so many wonderful friends, cohorts, and associates—many of whom I'm sure I'll be in touch with after this book is in print.

But know that this story couldn't have happened the way it unfolded without the joy, friendship, partnership, and invaluable input your participation and presence in my life represented over the years. I hope before the last sunset, I can personally thank many of you and share my deep appreciation for what you've added to this journey.

And, of course, to our families, both Pam's and mine. Each of you has our deepest love and gratitude for the lifetime of unfading memories you've blessed us with.

Finally, in writing this book, I made the conscious decision to keep the focus exclusively on my professional life—and areas of my younger days that influenced so much of my life in basketball and the business of sports.

So, with that proviso and apologies for not naming you individually, let me instead focus on the manageable: expressing my thanks to the small circle of special people who after more than a decade of effort brought Sonny Vaccaro's last and final testament to realization.

To Angela Guzman and the HarperOne team, for your professionalism, creativity, buoyant spirit, and willingness to bring a story to light that so many mistakenly thought they already knew.

To Simon Green, for your guidance, constant patience, and steadfast belief in the manuscript. You have been an invaluable guide in shaping the narrative and negotiating the many challenges inherent in the publishing process. Thank you for getting us to the finish line.

And to my extraordinarily gifted collaborators, without whom this book would not exist:

To Armen Keteyian—who knew forty years ago when we first met that we might end up doing something like this project together. You jumped in and helped bring these pages to life with masterful prose, suggestions, and edits. Thank you for being a friend and for so selflessly sharing your time, talent, and intellect to move this forward to completion. Your willingness (and Dede's) to join me on this venture will never be forgotten.

To Max M—whose vivid writing channeled my transient thoughts and stories after decades of listening and brought them to these pages with accuracy and authenticity. Thank you for the voluminous research, the interviews, the chapter and verse, and the ten thousand details that, after twenty-five years in the making, coalesced into a book we are all very proud of. I'm forever grateful.

SONNY VACCARO's visionary innovations continue to influence modern sports marketing. He is widely known for the signing of college coaches and later both Michael Jordan and Kobe Bryant to deals with Nike. Vaccaro has had an unmistakable impact on sports and the cause of athletes' rights and empowerment at every level. He continues to be a voice in contemporary sports issues from his home in California.

ARMEN KETEYIAN is an eleven-time Emmy Award–winning journalist and the author or coauthor of six *New York Times* bestsellers, including *The System* and *Tiger Woods*. He lives in Connecticut.